ALBERT'S WAY

ALBERT'S WAY

The First North American Congress on the Carmelite Rule

Edited by

Michael Mulhall, O. Carm.

Carmelite Monastery
89 Hiddenbrooke Drive
Beacon, NY 12508-2230

Institutum Carmelitanum
Rome

The Province of the Most Pure Heart of Mary
Barrington, Illinois

1989

Copyrught © 1989 by The Province of the Most Pure Heart of Mary and the Intitutum Carmelitanum. All rights reserved. No part of this publication may be reproduced, stored in a retrieval system, or transmitted, in any form or by any means, electronic, mechanical, photocopyng, recording, or otherwise, without the prior written permissions of the publisher.

Cover design and photographs by Riccardo Palazzi, O. Carm.

ISBN: 88-7288-010-6

The Province of the Most Pure Heart of Mary
Box 370
Barrington, Illinois 60011

Institutum Carmelitanum
Via Sforza Pallavicini 10
00193 Roma

DEDICATION

To the men and women
who have made this
Congress on the Rule
a sign of our way of life
in the one Family of Carmel

I am listening to the roar and seething of Niagara Falls, ... to the water pouring past me ... I see not only the richness of the nature of water, its measureless potentiality; I see God operating through the work of his hands and the revelation of his love.

— Blessed Titus Brandsma

CONTENTS

Carmelite Monastery
89 Hiddenbrooke Drive
Beacon, NY 12508-2230

ACKNOWLEDGEMENTS

In putting together this Congress on the Rule I would like to thank the many people who helped bring the various strands together. First of all there is Patrick McMahon who was with me at Nocera Umbra, outside of Assisi, when the idea first came into being. He has been a constant source of encouragement from its very beginning. Then there are the members of the Carmelite Forum who responded warmly to the plan and made valuable suggestions and contributions. The Province of the Most Pure Heart of Mary in connection with the Province of St. Elias put together a wonderful support committee headed by Ashley Harrington along with John Welch, Robert Colaresi, David Simpson and John Weber. David Simpson opened his house in Scipio, Kansas, for our first meeting.

Others helped prepare the excellent liturgies, particularly Raymond Bonin and Michael Kwiecien who graciously responded to the challenge. During the Congress some wonderfully talented people stepped forward such as Kees Waijmaan with his unforgettable solo guitar playing, and the presiders at the Eucharist and the Morning and Evening Prayer celebrations.

We cannot forget the invaluable service rendered us by Riccardo Palazzi of the Roman Province who kept two videocameras running to record all the sessions of the Congress, as well as took a great number of wonderful pictures of the Congress.

Paul Chandler of our Australian Province took time out to proofread the original script that was submitted to the Carmelite Institute in Rome for publication. His comments and suggestions have been most helpful. He also prepared the selected bibliography for further reading. Louis Rogge has taken upon himself the task of seeing the book through the long process of publication in Rome while Joachim Smet has graciously volunteered to do the proofreading of the final text. Such services cannot be underestimated.

Finally, I wish to thank the speakers themselves for their great willingness to take on so great a responsibility, when this stranger showed up suddenly, often unannounced, on their doorstep, whether in Edinburgh, Nijmegen or at the in-naugural festival for the Nada Hermitage in Crestone, Colorado. Their trust that such a Congress would ever take place produced what all agree was an outstanding contribution.

Many unthanked people filled in all the gaps that inevitably seem to threaten to bring down the most carefully planned event of this kind. Only the Lord can thank the various participants for what they brought in a spirit of friendliness and openness to this Congress. May the bonds that were forged or strengthened here grow deeper, richer and more extensive as time passes and the Carmelite Family claims its full inheritance as brothers and sisters.

PREFACE

The medieval church existed at a period of time, from about 1100 until 1500, which saw numerous creative, spiritual movements take shape. Among these was the establishment of the Latin Kingdom of Jerusalem in the Holy Land, a joint venture of a number of European countries which lasted from 1099 until 1291, approximately two hundred years. Somewhere in the mid-point of that Crusader Kingdom conditions allowed a small group to settle in a newly liberated area just south of the military capital at Acre. There, in a spring fed wadi of the Carmel mountain range overlooking the Mediterranean Sea, an anonymous band of Latin pilgrims, intent on following in the footsteps of Jesus in his native area, insinuated themselves into the blood soaked landscape that echoed with conflict back to the time of the revered prophets Elijah and Elisha. Even so, their devotion to these two ideal figures may stem less from contact with the Holy Land than from the medieval culture which saw in them the soon-to-come biblical figures heralding the end of the ages.[1]

The Carmelites, then, represent one offshoot of that rich, fervent and creative society that formed Europe's medieval, and particularly Norman, society. The Rule which confirmed them in their "way of life" exists today, not only as an histori-

---

[1] Frequent artistic representations of one or both these prophets abound in the medieval cathedrals, although the two biblical figures are not, in fact, named in Rv 11:3-12 and are subject to various identifications. Cf. John M. Court, *Myth and History in the Book of Revelation* (Atlanta: John Knox Press, 1979), pp. 82-105.

cal artifact, but in a way that continues to generate interest and activity. From the earliest times we find tension and conflict associated with those who put themselves under this Rule. Within the first century of receiving it we see a Prior General angrily resigning from office and retiring to a hermitage to protest the direction his fellow hermits-becoming-friars were beginning to take. Over the centuries reform movements would continue to address a perhaps indefinable, but no less real, call from deep within the tradition itself. Many, in all branches of the Carmelite Family, have struggled to make the Rule's inner vision speak more loudly to their contemporaries in the wider church.

The present state of the Carmelite family with all its divisions and sub-divisions reminds us of those creative tensions alive within the Rule. Why should we be surprised or saddened at this? The original group produced a text that linked together in a highly suggestive way many insights from Scripture and from the earlier traditions of the Desert Fathers and later cenobitic communities, as they were then understood. Even to this day, as the papers presented here testify, we find ourselves struggling to comprehend the balances and meanings which this text has released in history and is still releasing today.

A dramatic instance of the change in perspective since the giving of the Rule is the active presence of women within the tradition of Carmel. While the Carmelites delayed establishing official enclosures for nuns within the Order for 250 years,[2] today the Order is widely regarded in the popular mind as "feminine." Even the saints which nourish the ideals of Carmelites of every age within the Order today are mostly women. While young men coming into the Order are given models such as Elijah or John of the Cross to emulate, the male

---

2 Joachim Smet, *Cloistered Carmel* (Rome: Institutum Carmelitanum, 1986), p. 10. He notes that while all the other Mendicant Orders set up such institutions immediately, the Carmelites only obtained this privilege from Pope Nicholas V with the decree *Cum nulla* of October 7, 1452. Cf. p. 26.

saints seem to be either historically remote or somewhat "unreal." Elijah did the stupendous and then flew off to heaven. John of the Cross wrote mysterious and alluring poetry, but comes across as a complex and difficult person. Even Titus Brandsma, who helped establish the University of Nijmegen, is more remembered because he died a martyr's death in the concentration camp at Dachau.

By contrast, Teresa of Jesus seems immediately accessible, even from a distance of 400 years. Her common sense insights into prayer in her *Way of Perfection* still speak to us today. The pithy observations in her *Life,* as well as in the *Book of the Foundations,* give her a contemporary vividness that is amazing. Thérèse of the Child Jesus, whose autobiography has been familiar to more than one generation of "ordinary" Catholics, has just become the subject of a very successful movie.[3] The journey of Edith Stein from being an associate and student of one of the founders of phenomenology, Edmund Husserl; her entrance into the Church, then into the Carmel of Cologne; her flight to The Netherlands in the middle of the night; to her death at Auschwitz in Poland on August 9,1942, reads like a modern novel while making a moving witness to contemporary Carmelites, men and women alike.[4]

While it is the women of the Order who seem to have captured the "essence" of what being Carmelite may mean, this may be partially an illusion. The suppression of religious orders in Europe during the *Kulturkampf* of the nineteenth century[5], along with the emphasis on external discipline advocated for American clerics and religious after the Second and

---

3 The movie *Thérèse* won 7 César's at the 1986 Cannes film festival.

4 Cf. her uncompleted autobiography, *Edith Stein: Life in a Jewish Family 1891-1916,* Vol. I of *The Collected Works of Edith Stein,* ed. by L. Gelber and Romaeus Leuven, OCD. (Washington, D.C. : ICS Publications, 1985).

5 Joachim Smet says that the suppressions of the 19th Century were in many ways more severe and more destructive to religious life than the Reformation itself. Cf. his work *The Carmelites: A History of the Brothers of Our Lady of Mount Carmel* (Darien: Carmelite Spiritual Center, 1985), IV: 1-18.

Third Plenary Councils of Baltimore,[6] served to place the devotional life, common recitation or chanting of Divine Office and penitential practices in high relief. Such external emphases obscured the necessity of dialoguing with the traditions at a time when the Order found itself virtually incapable of realizing any deeper rapprochement with its own treasures. Coming out of such an externalized sense of religious discipline communities of women, as well as of men, find themselves living in an unfortunately deprived state of religious consciousness today. Unable to find entrance into the world of meaning that the Rule is designed to mediate, people have been obliged to turn to forms of devotional and ecclesial piety to fill the void.

Perhaps because the external discipline of the Order, especially as captured in the familiar picture of high walled cloisters with grills and turns keeping the secular world at bay, has proved such a vivid cultural symbol, we have failed to appreciate the classic nature of the Rule which gave rise to such images. Although the rules of Benedict and Francis, and perhaps even *The Ancrene Riwle*,[7] are more well known to contemporary scholars, nonetheless the Carmelite Rule certainly ranks among the classics of Western religious culture, no matter how few people are aware of it.[8] The Rule is a classic, not

---

6 Peter K. Guilday, *A History of the Councils of Baltimore (1791-1884)* (NY: The Macmillan Company, 1932), pp. 207-249. The Third Council (1884) repeated many of the disciplines of the Second Council (1866) which set down norms of clerical and religious decorum, forbade such things as attending the theater, practicing medicine or card playing, and mandated the use of the Roman collar in the streets and the cassock in the rectory.

7 A thirteenth century English rule written for women hermits attatched to local parish churches; cf. Michael Cox, *Handbook of Christian Spirituality* (San Francisco: Harper & Row, 1983), p. 131.

8 A selection of the Book-of-the-Month Club a few years ago was Robert Payne's book *The Dream and the Tomb: A History of the Crusades* (NY: Stein & Day, 1984). Payne was praised for his command of scholarship and his attention to history in tracing the history of the crusaders from the beginning of the First Crusade up to the fall of Acre on May 18, 1291. Yet not one word is devoted to the origins of the only Western order to be founded in the Holy Land at that very time.

because it is an artifact from the past, but because it is still operative and still has power to stimulate and guide the religious imagination of people eight centuries after it was given.

Yet the Carmelite Rule today is in danger of being under appreciated by the very people who profess their vows according to its authority. A classic on a bookshelf is not of very much use to anyone. After a certain amount of time it is possible to lose the key to the world of such classics. Much like pictures drawn millenia ago on cave walls and ceilings, it is possible to stand before the text of the Rule marveling and yet to have lost contact with the inner meanings it sought to enshrine. Like the cave paintings that were meant to express solidarity and communion with the mysteries of the earth that brought success in the hunt, so the Rule is a work of art that brings Carmelites into communion with the mystery of Jesus. The philosopher Hans-Georg Gadamer calls a work of art "the expression of a truth that cannot be reduced to what its creator actually thought in it."[9] Even though Carmelites must face a text without a clear author — a "work of art" with no definite artist there to claim it — its truth continues to demand our attention.

The Rule does not become a "work of art" just because it is well made, nor because it may be old, nor even because it is useful. An object becomes a "work of art" because it finds its place within a living community that values it through structuring itself and defining itself in the light of its terms. The art object expresses in a concrete symbol just what the community treasures within itself. In recognizing a "work of art" a society indicates its own inner openness towards the "objective" world, not in the sense of the here-and-now of what has already been accomplished, but in the sense of a world unfold-

---

[9] Hans-Georg Gadamer, *Philosophical Hermeneutics* (Berkeley: University of California Press, 1976), pp. 95-6.

ing itself in the direction of its true meaning.[10] That is, a society, a human community, moves towards the world and the truth of that world in a variety of ways. A society without "classics" is a community trapped in its own narrowness. A community that ignores its "classics" impoverishes itself and endangers its own future.

A "classic" is so named in terms of the culture that produced it and the wider world that recognizes it. This wider world is, first of all, that society itself as seen from the distance of later ages. A classic is a work that perdures and finds footings beyond the original designs of those who brought it forth. David Tracy calls its coming-to-be an "intensification" of the moment of experience joined to the moment of understanding.[11] In this moment the individual or community that has found itself a graced recipient of a particular aspect of reality finds the way to give shape and expression to it. What might have been only a fleeting experience of the divine can now be set down, meditated on and posed as a model to future generations.

If we take Tracy's insight seriously it becomes apparent that the Order was never set up to be simply a repository for the teachings of the past. It could receive ecclesial approbation only because it promised to foster a climate in which men and women could enter upon the very path towards communion with God which the original hermits followed so many centuries ago. The tapestry of the tradition demands only that certain themes and threads be employed from age to age. Above all, the Order is an opening for a "possibility." Heidegger talks about the struggle of Truth to find a place in the Open.[12] Truth looks for ways of breaking into a world that might content itself with a great deal of deadness. At the same time, he says,

---

10 Martin Heidegger, "The Origin of the Work of Art" in *Poetry, Language, Thought* (NY: Harper & Row, 1971), pp. 13-87.

11 David Tracy, *The Analogical Imagination* (NY: Crossroads Press, 1981), pp. 125-126.

12 *Op. cit.,* pp. 60-61.

"Truth is un-truth, insofar as there belongs to it the reservoir of the not-yet-uncovered, the un-covered, in the sense of concealment."[13] In this sense following the Rule slavishly and literally leads to the danger of falsification through unthinking obedience. Insofar as we presume that all the truth which the Rule has to tell has already been given and digested, we follow a spent beacon. At the same time, in presuming that everything has now been said, we claim for ourselves a "place" that is not really ours. Saints are canonized not because they have followed Christ as a mimic, but because they have understood the dynamism his Spirit has released in their own times through them. Orders contribute their charisms to the church only to the degree that they allow contemporary life stories to shape themselves around an ever-evolving truth.

If the truth has been totally spoken, then the Rule is essentially dead and following it would entail binding oneself to years of impersonal formalism. Yet what applies to uncovering the dynamics of Scripture also holds for the study of the Rule. Presumptions about its worn-out condition are premature. We find, instead, that we have hardly begun to explore the fertile ground of our own past. The Rule does not stop at the gates of medieval culture. In itself the Rule is both a mystical and mythical approach to living which has released enormous creative energy in ages past and keeps striving to do so. The Rule may be described as *mystical* in the sense that it describes a *way of life* that catches up the whole person in the disclosive life drama through which one wrestles with the very roots of revelation. The *mythical* dimension of the Rule refers to its inner directed communication of truth wherein the outermost layers of its language shield beginners from embarking too quickly on the truly radical nature of their calling. It is only after years of thinking one has been "observant" that one begins to suspect the real dimensions of reality to which one has pledged oneself, and which stay unsuspected until the

---

13 *Ibid.*

appropriate moment of inner transformation.

Centuries after the Rule was formulated, Carmelites find themselves in lands unknown and even unsuspected by their founders. The Rule by which they lived has gone beyond the confines and horizons of their own times into the religious imaginations of many ages and cultures. It calls out to men and women from every part of the globe. As we take up the difficult call to return to our own roots we liberate ourselves and future generations of Carmelites from turning anxiously in other directions in order to find authentic spiritual orientation.

We must take a very close look at our contemporary saints, and those whom we wish to bring forward in the church. Titus Brandsma was accepted for beatification under the title of "martyr" rather than "confessor." The debate that broke out in the Jewish community over the beatification of Edith Stein revolved around a similar point. They posed the question: Why is this woman being beatified? Was she not martyred only because she was Jewish? The logic here is arresting and calls for reflection. Both were Carmelites. Both have been put forward by the Order and have been accepted into the registers of the church. But are we sufficiently in touch with what it was that that made them both "Carmelite saints"? How much of their writings and reflections is available to us even today? It is only in the last few years that we have finally seen a substantive work in English presenting the early history of the Order.[14] Can we produce "Carmelite saints" or "Carmelite mystics" when we are forced to admit the terrible poverty of knowledge about our origins and traditions that afflicts the entire Carmelite family today?[15]

---

[14] Joachim Smet, *The Carmelites: A History of the Brothers of Our Lady of Mount Carmel* (Darien, IL: Carmelite Press, 1975-1987), 4 vols. Even here one sees the first 300 years compressed into one volume, covering the richest period in the Order's history.

[15] In addition to the problem of getting good histories of the Order in English is that of having access to the writings of other Carmelites. So far only Titus Brandsma's short series of lectures, published as *Carmelite Mysticism: Historical Sketches* (Darien, IL: The Carmelite Press, republished in 1986) has been available.

Today's Carmelite men and women find themselves trying to grasp an ideal that constantly illudes them. Our world seems to reach towards us with so many of its needs: prayer, hunger, disease, social reform, raising of consciousness, pre-Christianization, base communities, the dying, AIDS counsel - ing, parishes, listening to dreams and fears. In various ways we move in and out of this society. Some plunge in deeply to minister directly to society's wounds, others back away to ensure that places of stillness and refreshment will continue to be available. Some survive what they undertake, others disappear into that world unable to mediate its double and triple horizons. Some carve out eremitical niches whether in the deserts or in the cities, others band together in convents and monasteries — all trying to make sense of this "call," this "way" on which they have embarked.

Often we look back only to find ourselves with so few resources. Even Elijah had a raven supplying his needs before undertaking the journey to Horeb! Our roads seems less certain — or just as uncertain. We might well ask, Have we abandoned or lost our "way" a long time ago, now only keeping up the outmost affiliations? While communal celebrations of liturgy and prayer, coupled with meetings and get-togethers have often been taken for high-water marks of Carmelite living, has the true challenge to personal and communal inner renewal lain dormant in our self-understanding? Or might it not be truer to say that we really are deeply a part of the original mystery — like strands of starlight that have fallen on some planet in time zones far removed from where we first started, yet still one with their burning truth.

Against this backdrop of challenges and questions we present the work of this First North American Congress on the Rule. We see brought together a variety of Carmelites. For those not present at this congress, it is not just the presenters that speak to us, but the unseen audience: men and women from every part of the Carmelite family. We consider the *Sitz im Leben* of any work to be of great significance in evaluating it. For this congress we find gathered together the complete spectrum: hermits and friars, cloistered and apostolic men and women, the general of one branch, the former general of another, more than fifteen provincial superiors from as far away as Australia, Ireland, Great Britain, the Netherlands and all around North America. All these men and women in their various ways are attempting to live out the Carmelite charism in their own particular circumstances — and to listen more deeply to the call it makes to each of us today. Hopefully this will prove a sign to us for our future: that only by coming together, men and women of all branches of the Order, can we do justice to the task of understanding who we are.

In John's Gospel Jesus encountered a Samaritan woman at Jacob's well, but that water was no longer necessary for her. An eternally fresh source was springing up within her. So, too, this Rule need not be viewed as some stagnant cistern of brackish legislation that no longer enlivens the spirit, some dark reservoir of regulations, painstakingly scraped out by our ancestors of long ago, fenced around with hallowed memory, requiring the long rope of tradition, the pulley of ascetical strength and the bucket of submission before one can derive any benefit from its unseen depths. The papers that follow help to free us from the grasp of stereotyped visions of our origins. An attempt is made to rescue the language of the Rule from our over-familiarity with its phrases and our under-imagination of how it might be lived out, both on its historical level and in the hermeneutical horizons that it continues to encourage in us.

Michael Mulhall, O. Carm.
Niagara Falls, Ontario

The Bull *Quæ honorem Conditoris* of Innocent IV (October 1, 1247) that contains the most primitive text of the Rule of Saint Albert. It is considered the ‘official’ text.

— Archivio Segreto Vaticano, *Reg. Vat.* 21, ff. 465v-466r

tuisset dil. fil. magrm petrum archid. Sydonien in suu epm unanimit et concordit elegerunt. quo premissa in nra
pre referente nos attendentes qd h prouisio ab eodem patriarcha no potuit aliqs de iure committi qd de prefato Tybena
den epo fuit p eundem Ladden epm attemptatu de frm n. co. decreuim irritu et inane. electionem qua de predco ar
chid canonice celebrata inuenim confirmantes. Quocirca m. q. ipm ad eandem Sydonien eccam cu benedictionis
nre gra procedente affectu benigno recipiens et pertractans. e put ad te spectat. qui ei metropolitan existis mu
nus consecrationis impendas. et facias a subditis debita obediam ac reuerentia exhiberi. Contradictores etc. Dat
Lugd. iiij. Non Oct. Anno v. Uniuersis xi fidelib ad quos littere iste peruenerint. etc.

ccxxxvij.

Cum dil. fil. Prior et fres ordis heremitar de monte Carmeli secure nequeant sicut accepim ppt frequentes pa
ganor incursus in mansionib quas habent in transmarinis partib commorari. et ob hoc oporteat ex ipis aliquos se trans
ferre ad regiones uarias et remotas. Univ. u. to. et hor. att. man. q. ipos si ad uos eos uenire contigerit be
nigne recipientes ac tractantes honeste. eis de oportunis locis in qb secure possint famulari dno p diuina et
nra reuerentia liberalit et caritatiue puidere curetis. Dat Lugd. iiij. Non Oct. Anno v.. Priori et frib heremitis

.ccxxxviij.

Que honorem conditoris omnium et pfectu continet aiar roboris psidio sunt fulcienda pcipue set de monte Carmeli
illa precipue sup quib ap. se. auctas salubris prudentie studiu noscitur habuisse. Cum itaq nos ad nre supp insta
tia p dil. fil. n. H. tt sce Sabine pbrm card. et ve. f. n. G. Anteraden epm queda Regule nre dubia declarari
et corrigi ac etia queda ipi grauia misericordit fecerim mitigari. put in litteris inde confectis pleni continet. Nos
uris pijs desiderijs annuentes declarationem et correctionem ac mitigationem h auct ap. co. et pre. s. pa. co. Te
norem aut littar ipar de uerbo ad uerbum fecim presentib annotari. Qui tal est. Frat. H. miseratione
diuina tt sce Sabin pbr card. et frat. G. eadem miseratione Anteraden eps. Ca. in xo. fil. uiris Religiosis
Priori generali et diffinitorib capitli gnalis ordinis frm de Carmelo. salt in oium salutari. Accedentes
ad ap. se. fres dicti Reynald et petrus ordis uri ex parte ura a dno pp. humilit postularunt. ut queda que
in uro priuilegio et regula olim uob a. fe. me. Albto patriarch Jerlmitan tradita continet dubia declarare corri
gere ac queda grauia mitigare misericordit dignaretur. Cum g dno pp eor deuotis supplib annuendo nob
commisit ut declarationem correctionem et mitigationem h faceremus uice ipius scdm qd bono statui ordis et frm
saluti expediens uiderem. religioni nre qua fungimur auct m. q. regula a nob correcta declarata et mitigata
put expedire uidim deuote recipientes eam fir obseruetis et ad instar eidem alias uras regulas corrigatis
qua uob p eosdem fres sub sigillis nris mittim in hac forma. Albtus dei gra Jerlmitan ecce uocatus pa
triarcha. dil. in xo fil. B. et ceteris heremitis qui sub ei obedia iuxta fontem in monte Carmeli morant. in dno
salutem et sci spc benedconem. Multiphane multisq modis sci patres instituerunt. qualit quisq in quocumq ordi
ne fuit. ul quecumq modu religiose uite elegit in obsequio Jhu xi uiuere debeat. et eide fidelit de corde pu
ro et bona consca deseruire. Veru quia requiritis a nob ut iuxta ppositu urm tradam uob uite formula qua tene
re in posteru debeatis. illud in primis statuim. ut unu ex uob habeatis priorem. q ex unanimi oium assensu. ul ma
ioris et sanioris partis ad hoc offm eligat. cui obediam promittat quilibet alior et promissam studeat opibs ueri
tate suare cu castitate et abdicatione ppetatis. Loca aut hre poteritis in heremis. ul ubi uob donata fuerint ad nre
religionis obseruantia apta et comoda scdm qd priori et fratrib uidebit expedire. Preterea iuxta situ loci quem inha
bitare pposueritis singli urm singulas habeant cellulas separatas. sicut p dispositionem prioris ipius et de assensu alior
frm ul sanioris partis eedem cellule cuiq fuerint assignate. ita tamen ut in coi refectorio ea que uob eroga
ta fuerint comuniter aliqua lectionem sacre scripture audiendo. ubi comode poterit obseruari sumatis. Nec liceat alicui
frm nisi de licentia prioris qui p tpe fuerit deputatu e mutare locu. ul cu alio pmutare. Cellula prioris sit
iuxta introitu loci ut uenientib ad eunde locu primus occurrat. et de arbitrio et de dispositione ipius postmodum
que agenda sunt cuncta procedant. Maneant singuli in cellulis suis ul iuxta eas die ac nocte in lege dni
meditantes et in orationib uigilantes. nisi alijs iustis occasionib occupent. Hij qui horas canonicas cu
clericis dicere nouerint. eas dicant scdm constitutionem sacror patru et ecce approbata consuetudine. Qui eas no
nouerint. uigintiquinq uicib pater nr dicant in nocturnis uigilijs. exceptis dnicis et sollempnib dieb
in quor uigilijs predcm numm statuim duplicari. ut dicat pat nr uicib quinquaginta. Septies aut eade

dicatur oratio, in laudibus et matutinis. In aliis quoque horis septies similiter eadem singillatim dicatur oratio preter officia vespertina: in quibus ipsam quindecies dicere debeatis. Nullus fratrum aliquid esse proprium dicat, set sint vobis omnia communia et distribuatur unicuique per manum prioris idest per fratrem ab eodem ad idem officium deputatum, prout cuique opus erit, inspectis etatibus et necessitatibus singulorum. Asinos autem sive mulos prout vestra expostulaverit necessitas vobis habere liceat, et aliquod animalium sive volatilium nutrimentum. Oratorium prout commodius fieri poterit construatur in medio cellularum, ubi mane per singulos dies ad audienda missarum sollempnia convenire debeatis, ubi hoc commode fieri potest. Dominicis quoque diebus vel aliis ubi opus fuerit de custodia ordinis et animarum salute tractetis, ubi etiam excessus et culpe fratrum, si que in aliquo deprehense fuerint caritate media corrigantur. Ieiunium singulis diebus exceptis dominicis observetis a festo exaltationis sancte crucis, usque ad diem dominice resurrectionis, nisi infirmitas vel debilitas corporis aut alia iusta causa ieiunium solvi suadeat quia necessitas non habet legem. Ab esu carnium abstineatis, nisi pro infirmitatis vel debilitatis remedio sumantur. Et quia vos oportet frequentius mendicare, itinerantes ne sitis hospitibus onerosi extra domos vestras sumere poteritis pulmenta cocta cum carnibus. Sed et carnibus supra mare vesci licebit. Quia vero temptatio est vita hominis super terram, et omnes qui pie volunt vivere in Christo persecutionem patiuntur. Adversarius quoque vester diabolus tamquam leo rugiens circuit querens quem devoret, omni sollicitudine studeatis indui armatura dei ut possitis stare adversus insidias inimici. Accingendi sunt lumbi cingulo castitatis, muniendum est pectus cogitationibus sanctis, scriptum est enim: cogitatio sancta servabit te. Induenda est lorica iustitie ut dominum deum vestrum ex toto corde, et ex tota anima, et ex tota virtute diligatis, et proximum vestrum tamquam vos ipsos. Sumendum est in omnibus scutum fidei in quo possitis omnia tela nequissimi ignea extinguere. Sine fide enim impossibile est placere deo. Galea quoque salutis capiti imponenda est, ut de solo salvatore speretis salutem, qui salvum facit populum suum a peccatis eorum. Gladius autem spiritus quod est verbum dei habundanter habitet in ore et in cordibus vestris, et quecumque vobis agenda sunt, in verbo domini fiant. Faciendum iam est vobis aliquid operis, ut semper vos diabolus inveniat occupatos, ne ex ociositate vestra aliquem introitum aditum ad animas vestras valeat invenire. Habetis in hoc beati Pauli apostoli magisterium pariter et exemplum in cuius ore Christus loquebatur, qui positus est et datus a deo predicator et doctor gentium in fide et veritate, quem si secuti fueritis, non poteritis aberrare. In labore inquit et fatigatione fuimus inter vos nocte ac die operantes ne quem vestrum gravaremus non quasi nos non habeamus potestatem, sed ut nos metipsos formam daremus vobis ad imitandum nos. Nam cum essemus apud vos hoc denuntiabamus vobis quoniam si quis non vult operari non manducet. Audivimus enim inter vos quosdam ambulantes inquiete nichil operantes. Hiis autem qui eiusmodi sunt denuntiamus et obsecramus in domino Ihesu Christo ut cum silentio operantes, suum panem manducent. Hec via sancta est et bona, ambulate in ea. Commendat autem apostolus silentium, cum in eo precipit operandum. Et quemadmodum propheta testatur, cultus iustitie silentium est. Et rursus: In silentio et spe erit fortitudo vestra. Ideo statuimus, ut dicto completorio silentium teneatis usque ad primam dictam sequentis diei. Alio vero tempore licet silentii non habeatur observatio tanta, diligentius tamen a multiloquio caveatur. Quoniam sicut scriptum est, et non minus experientia docet, in multiloquio peccatum non deerit. Et qui inconsideratus est ad loquendum, sentiet mala. Item qui multis verbis utitur, ledit animam suam. Et dominus in evangelio: De omni verbo otioso quod locuti fuerint homines reddent rationem de eo in die iudicii. Faciat ergo unusquisque stateram verbis suis, et frenos rectos ori suo, ne forte labatur et cadat in lingua, et insanabilis sit casus eius ad mortem, custodiens cum propheta vias suas, ut non delinquat in lingua sua, et silentium in quo cultus iustitie est, diligenter et caute studeat observare. Tu autem frater B. et quicumque post te institutus fuerit prior, illud semper habeatis in mente et servetis in opere quod dominus ait in evangelio: Quicumque voluerit inter vos maior fieri erit minister vester, et quicumque voluerit inter vos primus esse, erit vester servus. Vos quoque ceteri fratres priorem vestrum honorate humiliter, Christum potius cogitantes quam ipsum qui posuit illum super capita vestra, et ecclesiarum prepositis ait: Qui vos audit me audit, qui vos spernit me spernit, ut non inveniamini in iudicium de contemptu, sed de obedientia mereamini eterne vite mercedem. Hec breviter scripsimus vobis conversationis vestre formulam statuentes, secundum quam vivere debeatis. Si quis autem supererogaverit, ipse dominus cum redierit reddet ei. Utatur tamen discretione que virtutum est moderatrix. Actum Lugduni. Anno domini M°CC°XLVII°. Domini pape Innocentii quarti. Anno quinto. kalendas septembris. Nulli ergo etc. nostre confirmationis etc. Si quis etc. Datum Lugduni kalendas octobris. Anno quinto. Filiis domus Theutonicorum de Starkemberch et de Gotenstein.

Presentium vobis auctoritate in virtute obedientie firmiter precipiendo mandamus quatinus de Starkemberch et de Gotenstein castra que castris tenentibus clare memorie. Dux Austrie tamquam inexpugnabilia ad tempora longa munivit, curetis cum omni diligentia et sollicitu-

REGULA SANCTI ALBERTI
THE RULE OF SAINT ALBERT

The Latin text of the Rule is that given by Bruno Secondin, *La Regola del Carmelo: Per una nuova interpretazione:* that of the 'Albertine' Rule is taken from the *Epistula Cyrilli* as found in the Bibliothèque de l'Arsenal, Paris, Ms 779, ff. 57v-59r; the text of Pope Innocent is from the Regestum Vaticanum ff. 465v-466r.

The English translation of both texts is found on facing pages.

Textus Albertinus

ALBERTUS, Dei gratia Hierosolymitanae Ecclesiae vocatus Patriarcha, dilectis in Christo filiis Brocardo et caeteris eremitis, qui sub eius obedientia iuxta Fontem in monte Carmeli morantur, in Domino salutem et Sancti Spiritus benedictionem.

Multifarie multisque modis sancti Patres instituerunt qualiter quisque, in quocumque ordine fuerit, vel quemcumque modum religiosae vitae elegerit, *in obsequio Jesu Christi* vivere debeat, et eidem fideliter *de corde puro et bona conscientia* deservire.

Verum, quia requiritis a nobis, ut iuxta propositum vestrum tradamus vobis vitae formulam, quam tenere in posterum debeatis:

Illud in primis statuimus ut unum ex vobis habeatis priorem, qui ex unanimi omnium

Textus Innocentianus

ALBERTUS, Dei gratia Hierosolymitanae Ecclesiae vocatus Patriarcha, dilectis in Christo filiis B. et caeteris eremitis, qui sub eius obedientia iuxta Fontem in monte Carmeli morantur, in Domino salutem et Sancti Spiritus benedictionem.

Multifarie multisque modis sancti Patres instituerunt qualiter quisque, in quocumque ordine fuerit, vel quemcumque modum religiosae vitae elegerit, *in obsequio Jesu Christi* vivere debeat, et eidem fideliter *de corde puro et bona conscientia* deservire.

Verum, quia requiritis a nobis, ut iuxta propositum vestrum tradamus vobis vitae formulam, quam tenere in posterum debeatis:

[1] Illud in primis statuimus ut unum ex vobis habeatis priorem, qui ex unanimi om-

Albert's Text

ALBERT, by the grace of God called to be Patriarch of the Church of Jerusalem, to his beloved sons in Christ, Brocard and the other hermits under obedience to him, who are living near the spring on Mount Carmel, health in the Lord and the blessing of the Holy Spirit.

In many and various ways our holy forefathers lay down how everyone, whatever his station or the kind of religious observance he had chosen, should live a life of *allegiance to Jesus Christ* and serve him faithfully *with a pure heart and a good conscience.*

However, because you have asked us, in accord with your proposal, to give you a way of life to which you will have to hold fast in the future:

The first thing we require is that one of you is to be the Prior, who is to be chosen for

Innocent's Text

ALBERT, by the grace of God called to be Patriarch of the Church of Jerusalem, to his beloved sons in Christ, B. and the other hermits under obedience to him, who are living near the spring on Mount Carmel, health in the Lord and the blessing of the Holy Spirit.

In many and various ways our holy forefathers lay down how everyone, whatever his station or the kind of religious observance he had chosen, should live a life of *allegiance to Jesus Christ* and serve him faithfully *with a pure heart and a good conscience.*

However, because you have asked us, in accord with your proposal, to give you a way of life to which you will have to hold fast in the future:

[1] The first thing we require is that one of you is to be the Prior, who is to be chosen for

assensu, vel maioris et sanioris partis, ad hoc officium eligatur; cui obedientiam promittat quilibet aliorum, et promissam studeat *operis veritate* servare.

nium assensu, vel maioris et sanioris partis, ad hoc officium eligatur; cui obedientiam promittat quilibet aliorum, et promissam studeat *operis veritate* servare, cum castitate et abdicatione proprietatis.

[2] Loca autem habere poteritis in eremis, vel ubi vobis donata fuerint, ad vestrae religionis observantiam apta et commoda, secundum quod priori et fratribus videbitur expedire.

[Praeterea, iuxta situm loci quem inhabitare proposueritis] singuli vestrum singulas habeant cellulas separatas, sicut per dispositionem prioris ipsius, et de assensu aliorum fratrum vel sanioris partis, eaedem cellulae cuique fuerint assignatae.

[3] Praeterea, iuxta situm loci quem inhabitare proposueritis, singuli vestrum singulas habeant cellulas separatas, sicut per dispositionem prioris ipsius, et de assensu aliorum fratrum vel sanioris partis, eaedem cellulae cuique fuerint assignatae.

[4] Ita tamen ut in communi refectorio ea, quae vobis donata fuerint, communiter aliquam lectionem sacrae Scripturae audiendo, ubi commode poterit observari, sumatis.

that office by the consent of all, or of the greater and maturer part of you. To him the others must promise obedience, and having done so try to fulfill it *in actual deeds.*

that office by the consent of all, or of the greater and maturer part of you. To him the others must promise obedience, and having done so try to fulfill it *in actual deeds,* along with chastity and the renunciation of ownership.

[2] If the Prior and brothers see fit, you may also have foundations in solitary places, or where you are given a site that is suitable and convenient for the observance of your Order.

[Next, in the vicinity of the place which you propose to inhabit,] each one of you is to have a separate cell, allotted by the disposition of the Prior himself, with the assent of the other brothers or of the more mature among them.

[3] Next, in the vicinity of the place which you propose to inhabit, each one of you is to have a separate cell, allotted by the disposition of the Prior himself, with the assent of the other brothers or of the more mature among them.

[4] However, you are to eat whatever may have been given you in a common refectory, listening in common to some reading from Sacred Scripture, where this can be done without difficulty.

Nec liceat alicui fratrum, nisi de licentia prioris, qui pro tempore fuerit, deputatum sibi mutare locum, vel cum alio permutare.

[5] Nec liceat alicui fratrum, nisi de licentia prioris, qui pro tempore fuerit, deputatum sibi mutare locum, vel cum alio permutare.

Cellula prioris sit iuxta introitum loci, ut venientibus ad eumdem locum primus occurrat; et de arbitrio ac dispositione ipsius postmodum, quae agenda sunt, cuncta procedant.

[6] Cellula prioris sit iuxta introitum loci, ut venientibus ad eumdem locum primus occurrat; et de arbitrio et de dispositione ipsius postmodum, quae agenda sunt, cuncta procedant.

Maneant singuli in cellulis suis, vel iuxta eas, *die ac nocte in lege Dei meditantes* et *in orationibus vigilantes,* nisi aliis iustis occationibus occupentur.

[7] Maneant singuli in cellulis suis, vel iuxta eas, *die ac nocte in lege Domini meditantes* et *in orationibus vigilantes,* nisi aliis iustis occasionibus occupentur.

Ii qui litteras norunt et legere psalmos, per singulas horas eos dicant qui ex institutione sanctorum Patrum et Ecclesiae approbata consuetudine ad horas singulas sunt deputati.

[8] Ii qui horas canonicas cum clericis norunt, eas dicant secundum constitutione sacrorum Patrum et Ecclesiae approbatam consuetudinem.

Qui, vero, litteras non norunt, viginti quinque vicibus *Pater noster* dicant in nocturnis vigiliis, exceptis Domini-

Qui eas non noverunt, viginti quinque vicibus *Pater noster* dicant in nocturnis vigiliis, exceptis Dominicis et sollem-

It is not allowed for any of the brothers to change his cell, nor to exchange it with another person's, except with the permission of whoever is Prior at the time.

The Prior's cell should be near the entrance of the place so that he might be the first to meet those who approach, and so that whatever has to be done subsequently may all be carried out as he decide and order.

Let each one remain in his cell, or near it, *meditating day and night on the law of the Lord* and *keeping vigil in prayer* unless occupied with other lawful duties.

Those who know their letters and how to read the Psalms should, for each of the hours, say those which have been set forth through the institution of the holy fathers and the approved usage of the Church for each of those hours.

Those who do not know their letters, however, are to say the *Our Father* twenty-five times for the night offices,

[5] It is not allowed for any of the brothers to change his cell, nor to exchange it with another person's, except with the permission of whoever is Prior at the time.

[6] The Prior's cell should be near the entrance of the place so that he might be the first to meet those who approach, and so that whatever has to be done subsequently may all be carried out as he decide and order.

[7] Let each one remain in his cell, or near it, *meditating day and night on the law of the Lord* and *keeping vigil in prayer* unless occupied with other lawful duties.

[8] Those who know how to say the canonical hours with the clerics should say them according to the practice of the holy fathers and the approved usage of the Church.

Those who do not know how are to say the *Our Father* twenty-five times for the night offices, except on Sun-

cis et sollemnibus diebus, in quorum vigiliis praedictum numerum statuimus duplicari, ut dicatur *Pater noster* vicibus quinquaginta. Septies eadem dicatur oratio in laudibus matutinis. In aliis quoque horis septies similiter eadem sigillatim dicatur oratio, praeter officia vespertina, in quibus ipsam quindecies dicere debeatis.

nibus diebus, in quorum vigiliis praedictum numerum statuimus duplicari, ut dicatur *Pater noster* vicibus quinquaginta. Septies eadem dicatur oratio in laudibus matutinis. In aliis quoque horis septies similiter eadem sigillatim dicatur oratio, praeter officia vespertina, in quibus ipsam quindecies dicere debeatis.

Nullus fratrum dicat sibi aliquid esse proprium, sed sint vobis communia, et ex iis quae Dominus vobis dederit, distribuatur unicuique per manum prioris, id est per hominem ab eo ad idem officium deputatum, prout cuique opus fuerit, inspectis aetatibus et necessitatibus singulorum. Ita tamen ut, sicut praemissum est, in deputatis cellulis singuli maneant, et ex iis quae sibi distributa fuerint, singulariter vivant.

[9] Nullus fratrum aliquid esse sibi proprium dicat, sed sint vobis omnia communia, et distribuatur unicuique per manum prioris, id est per fratrem ab eodem ad idem officium deputatum, prout cuique opus erit, inspectis aetatibus et necessitatibus singulorum.

Asinos autem, sive mulos, prout vestra expostulaverit necessitas, vobis habere liceat, et aliquod animalium sive volatilium nutrimentum.

except on Sundays and solemnities when we command that the stated number be doubled, so that the *Our Father* be said fifty times. The same prayer is to be said seven times for morning praise. Likewise for each of the other hours the same prayer is to be said, except for the office of vespers when you are to say it fifteen times.

days and solemnities when we command that the stated number be doubled, so that the *Our Father* be said fifty times. The same prayer is to be said seven times for morning praise. Likewise for each of the other hours the same prayer is to be said, except for the office of vespers when you are to say it fifteen times.

None of the brothers should call anything his own, but you shall hold all things in common; and from whatever the Lord gives you, each one shall receive from the Prior—that is from the one he deputizes to perform that office—so that his age and needs are attended to. However, as has already been stated, each one is to keep to the cell allotted him and live there alone on what is given him.

[9] None of the brothers should call anything his own, but you shall hold all things in common; and they shall be distributed to each by the Prior—that is by the one he deputizes to perform that office—according to his need, with concern for the age and needs of each.

You are permitted as many asses or mules as you need, as well as whatever livestock or poultry you require for nourishment.

Oratorium, prout commodius fieri poterit, construatur in medio cellularum, ubi *mane per singulas dies* ad audienda missarum sollemnia convenire debeatis, ubi hoc commode fieri poterit.

[10] Oratorium, prout commodius fieri poterit, construatur in medio cellularum, ubi *mane per singulos dies* ad audienda missarum sollemnia convenire debeatis, ubi hoc commode fieri poterit.

Dominicis quoque diebus, vel aliis ubi opus fuerit, de custodia ordinis et animarum salute tractetis; ubi etiam excessus et culpae fratrum, si quae in aliquo deprehensae fuerint, caritate media corrigantur.

[11] Dominicis quoque diebus, vel aliis ubi opus fuerit, de custodia ordinis et animarum salute tractetis; ubi etiam excessus et culpae fratrum, si quae in aliquo deprehensae fuerint, caritate media corrigantur.

Ieiunium singulis diebus, exceptis dominicis, observetis a festo Exaltationis sanctae Crucis usque ad diem Dominicae Resurrectionis, nisi infirmitas vel debilitas corporis, aut alia iusta causa, ieiunium solvi suadeat, quia necessitas non habet legem.

[12] Ieiunium singulis diebus, exceptis dominicis, observetis a festo Exaltationis sanctae Crucis usque ad diem Dominicae Resurrectionis, nisi infirmitas vel debilitas corporis, aut alia iusta causa, ieiunium solvi suadeat, quia necessitas non habet legem.

Ab esu carnium semper abstineatis, nisi infirmitatis aut nimiae debilitatis remedio sint sumendae.

[13] Ab esu carnium semper abstineatis, nisi pro infirmitatis vel debilitatis remedio sumantur.

Et quia vos oportet frequentius mendicare itinerantes, ne sitis hospitibus onerosi, extra

An oratory should be constructed in the midst of the cells as conveniently as possible, where you are to gather each day in the morning to hear Mass, where this can be done conveniently.

[10] An oratory should be constructed in the midst of the cells as conveniently as possible, where you are to gather each day in the morning to hear Mass, where this can be done conveniently.

On Sundays, and on other days if necessary, you should discuss your observance and spiritual welfare; at these times the excesses and faults of the brothers, if any are found, should be corrected in charity.

[11] On Sundays, and on other days if necessary, you should discuss your observance and spiritual welfare; at these times the excesses and faults of the brothers, if any are found, should be corrected in charity.

Every day except Sunday you are to observe a fast from the feast of the Exaltation of the holy Cross until Easter Sunday, unless sickness or physical weakness or some other good reason requires a dispensation from the fast, for necessity overrides the law.

[12] Every day except Sunday you are to observe a fast from the feast of the Exaltation of the Holy Cross until Easter Sunday, unless sickness or physical weakness or some other good reason requires a dispensation from the fast, for necessity overrides the law.

You are to abstain perpetually from eating meat, unless it be taken as a remedy for sickness or great weakness.

[13] You are to abstain perpetually from eating meat, unless it be taken as a remedy for sickness or great weakness.

And because those of you who travel may frequently have to beg, you may eat

domus vestras sumere poteritis pulmenta cocta cum carnibus.

Sed et carnibus supra mare vesci licebit.

Quia vero *tentatio est vita hominis super terram, et omnes qui pie volunt vivere in Christo persecutionem patiuntur; adversarius* quoque *vester, diabolus, tamquam leo rugiens circuit quaerens quem devoret:* omni sollicitudine studeatis *indui armatura Dei, ut possitis stare adversus insidias inimici.*

[14] Quia vero *tentatio est vita hominis super terram, et omnes qui pie volunt vivere in Christo persecutionem patiuntur; adversarius* quoque *vester, diabolus, tamquam leo rugiens circuit quaerens quem devoret:* omni sollicitudine studeatis *indui armatura Dei, ut possitis stare adversus insidias inimici.*

Accingendi sunt lumbi vestri cingulo castitatis, muniendum est pectus cogitationibus sanctis, scriptum est enim: *cogitatio sancta servabit te.*

Accingendi sunt lumbi cingulo castitatis; muniendum est pectus cogitationibus sanctis, scriptum est enim: *cogitatio sancta servabit te.*

Induenda est lorica iustitiae, ut *Dominum Deum vestrum ex toto corde et ex tota anima et ex tota virtute diligatis, et proximum vestrum tamquam vosmetipsos.*

Induenda est lorica iustitiae, ut *Dominum Deum vestrum ex toto corde et ex tota anima et ex tota virtute diligatis, et proximum vestrum tamquam vosmetipsos.*

Sumendum est in omnibus scutum fidei, in quo possitis omnia tela nequissimi ignea

Sumendum est in omnibus scutum fidei, in quo possitis omnia tela nequissimi ignea

food cooked with meat when you are outside your own houses, so as not to be a burden on your hosts.

Also at sea you may eat meat.

But because *life on earth is a time of trial, and all who seek to live devoutly in Christ suffer persecution*, and because *your adversary, the devil, as a roaring lion prowls about seeking someone to devour*, every *care must be taken to put on the armor of God, that you may stand firm against the cunning devices of the enemy.*

[14] But because *life on earth is a time of trial, and all who seek to live devoutly in Christ suffer persecution*, and because *your adversary, the devil, as a roaring lion prowls about seeking someone to devour*, every *care must be taken to put on the armor of God, that you may stand firm against the cunning devices of the enemy.*

Encircle your loins with the belt of chastity. Defend your breast with holy meditation, for Scripture says: *Holy meditation will save you.*

Encircle your loins with the belt of chastity. Defend your breast with holy meditation, for Scripture says: *Holy meditation will save you.*

Put on the breastplate of justice so that you *may love the Lord your God with your whole heart and your whole soul and your whole strength, and your neighbors as yourselves.*

Put on the breastplate of justice so that *you may love the Lord your God with you whole heart and your whole soul and your whole strength, and your neighbors as yourselves.*

In all thing take up the shield of faith by which you can extinguish every flaming dart

In all thing take up the shield of faith by which you can extinguish every flaming dart

extinguere: sine fide enim *est impossibile placere Deo. Et haec est victoria: fides vestra.*

extinguere: sine fide enim *impossibile est placere Deo.*

Galea quoque salutis capiti imponenda est, ut de solo Salvatore speretis salutem, *qui salvum facit populum suum a peccatis eorum. Gladius* autem *Spiritus, quod est verbum Dei, abundanter habitet in ore et in cordibus vestris.* Et *quaecumque a vobis agenda sunt, in* verbo *Domini fiant.*

Galea quoque salutis capiti imponenda est, ut de solo Salvatore speretis salutem, *qui salvum facit populum suum a peccatis eorum. Gladius autem Spiritus, quod est verbum Dei, abundanter habitet in ore et in cordibus vestris.* Et *quaecumque a vobis agenda sunt, in verbo Domini fiant.*

Faciendum est vobis aliquid operis, ut semper vos diabolus inveniat occupatos, ne ex ociositate vestra aliquem intrandi aditum ad animas vestras valeat invenire.

[15] Faciendum est vobis aliquid operis, ut semper vos diabolus inveniat occupatos, ne ex otiositate vestra aliquem intrandi aditum ad animas vestras valeat invenire.

Habetis in hoc beati Pauli Apostoli magisterium pariter et exemplum, in cuius ore *Christus loquebatur,* qui *positus* est et datus a Deo *praedicator et doctor gentium in fide et veritate;* quem si secuti fueritis, non poteritis aberrare.

Habetis in hoc beati Pauli Apostoli magisterium pariter et exemplum, in cuius ore *Christus loquebatur,* qui *positus* est et datus a Deo *praedicator et doctor gentium in fide et veritate;* quem si secuti fueritis, non poteritis aberrare.

In labore - inquit - *et fatigatio-*

In labore - inquit - *et fatigatio-*

from the evil one, for *without faith it is impossible to please God. Herein lies victory: your faith*

Then set the helmet of salvation on your head, that you place your hope of salvation only in the Savior, who *rescues his people from their sins.* Next *may you possess the sword of the spirit, which is God's word, abundantly in your mouth and in your hearts.* Just so *whatever you do, let it be done in the Lord's word.*

You must have something to work at, so that the devil may always find you occupied. No idleness of yours should allow him to find any entrance into your hearts.

In this regard you have the teaching and the example of blessed Paul the Apostle; from whose mouth *Christ spoke forth.* Him God *made* and set forth as *preacher and teacher of the Gentiles in faith and truth.* With him as your leader you will not go astray.

He once said: *We are among*

from the evil one, for *without faith it is impossible to please God.*

Then set the helmet of salvation on your head, that you place your hope of salvation only in the Savior, who *rescues his people from their sins.* Next *may you possess the sword of the spirit, which is God's word, abundantly in your mouth and in your hearts.* Just so *whatever you do, let it be done in the Lord's* word.

[15] You must have something to work at, so that the devil may always find you occupied. No idleness of yours should allow him to find any entrance into your hearts.

In this regard you have the teaching and the example of blessed Paul the Apostle; from whose mouth *Christ spoke forth.* Him God *made* and set forth as *preacher and teacher of the Gentiles in faith and truth.* With him as your leader you will not go astray.

He once said: *We are among*

ne fuimus inter vos nocte ac die operantes; ne quem vestrum gravaremus. Non quasi nos non haberemus potestatem, sed ut nosmetipsos formam daremus vobis ad imitandum nos. Nam, cum essemus apud vos, hoc denunciabamus vobis: quoniam si quis non vult operari non manducet. Audivimus enim inter vos quosdam ambulantes inquiete, nihil operantes. Hiis autem qui huiusmodi sunt, denunciamus et obsecramus in Domino Jesu Christo, ut cum silentio operantes suum panem manducent.

ne fuimus inter vos nocte ac die operantes, ne quem vestrum gravaremus. Non quasi nos non habeamus potestatem, sed ut nosmetipsos formam daremus vobis ad imitandum nos. Nam, cum essemus apud vos, hoc denuntiabamus vobis: quoniam si quis non vult operari non manducet. Audivimus enim inter vos quosdam ambulantes inquiete, nihil operantes. Hiis autem qui huiusmodi sunt, denuntiamus et obsecramus in Domino Jesu Christo, ut cum silentio operantes suum panem manducent.

Haec via sancta est et bona: *ambulate in ea.*

Commendat autem Apostolus silentium, cum in eo praecipit operandum, et quemadmodum propheta testatur: *cultus iustitiae silentium* est; et rursus: *in silentio et spe erit fortitudo vestra.*

[16] Commendat autem Apostolus silentium, cum in eo praecipit operandum, et quemadmodum propheta testatur: *cultus iustitiae silentium* est; et rursus: *in silentio et spe erit fortitudo vestra.*

Ideoque statuimus ut ab hora vespertina usque ad horam tertiam sequentis diei silentium teneatis, nisi forte necessitas vel causa rationabilis, aut licentia prioris, silentium interrumpat.

Ideoque statuimus ut dicto completorio silentium teneatis usque ad primam dictam sequentis diei.

you in labor and tiredness, working night and day, so as not to be a burden to anyone, not because we had no right, but that we ourselves might give you a model to imitate. For when we were with you we set down that anyone who did not wish to work should not eat. Yet we hear that among you there are such restless people circulating, who work at nothing. These types of people we charge and implore in the Lord Jesus Christ to earn the bread they eat in silent labor.

The Apostle recommends silence, for he specifies that one should work in it. In the same way the Prophet witnesses: *Silence fosters righteousness;* and again: *In silence and hope will lie your strength.*

Therefore we require that you keep silence from vespers until tierce of the following day, unless some necessity or good reason, or the Prior's permission, allows that you interrupt it.

you in labor and tiredness, working night and day, so as not to be a burden to anyone, not because we had no right, but that we ourselves might give you a model to imitate. For when we were with you we set down that anyone who did not wish to work should not eat. Yet we hear that among you there are such restless people circulating, who work at nothing. These types of people we charge and implore in the Lord Jesus Christ to earn the bread they eat in silent labor.

This way is holy and good: *walk in it.*

[16] The Apostle recommends silence, for he specifies that one should work in it. In the same way the Prophet witnesses: *Silence fosters righteousness;* and again: *In silence and hope will lie your strength.*

Therefore we require that you keep silence from after compline until after prime of the following day.

Alio vero tempore, licet silentii non habeatur observatio tanta, diligentius a multiloquio tamen caveatur, cum scriptum est, et non minus experientia docet, *in multiloquio non deerit peccatum,* et *qui inconsideratus est ad loquendum sentiet mala.* Item, *qui multis verbis utitur, laedit animam suam;* et Dominus in Evangelio: *De omni verbo ocioso quod locuti fuerint homines, reddent rationem de eo in die iudicii.*

Alio vero tempore, licet silentii non habeatur observatio tanta, diligentius tamen a multiloquio caveatur, quoniam sicut scriptum est, et non minus experientia docet, *in multiloquio non deerit peccatum,* et *qui inconsideratus est ad loquendum sentiet mala.* Item, *qui multis verbis utitur, laedit animam suam;* et Dominus in Evangelio: *De omni verbo otioso quod locuti fuerint homines, reddent rationem de eo in die iudicii.*

Faciat ergo unusquisque *stateram verbis suis; et frenos rectos ori suo; ne forte labatur et cadat in lingua sua, et insanabilis sit casus eius usque ad mortem, custodiens* cum propheta *vias* suas, *ut non delinquat in lingua sua;* et *silentium,* in quo *cultus iustitiae* est, diligenter et caute studeat observare.

Faciat ergo unusquisque *stateram verbis suis; et frenos rectos ori suo; ne forte labatur et cadat in lingua, et insanabilis sit casus eius ad mortem, custodiens* cum propheta *vias* suas, *ut non delinquat in lingua sua;* et *silentium,* in quo *cultus iustitiae* est, diligenter et caute studeat observare.

Tu autem, frater Brocarde et quicumque post te institutus fuerit prior; illud semper habeatis in mente; et servetis in opere, quod Dominus ait in Evangelio: *Quicumque voluerit inter vos maior fieri, erit*

[17] Tu autem, frater B. et quicumque post te institutus fuerit prior, illud semper habeatis in mente, et servetis in opere, quod Dominus ait in Evangelio: *Quicumque voluerit inter vos maior fieri, erit*

At other times, although you need not observe silence as strictly, be careful to avoid excessive talking, for as Scripture puts it, and experience teaches nothing less, *In much talking sin will not be far away*, and *The one who is careless in speech will come to harm.* Also, *Many words bring the soul to grief.* Again, the Lord says in the Gospel: *Forn every rash word uttered you will have to render an account on the day of judgement.*

So let each one *make a balance for his words and a careful rein for his mouth lest he stumble and fall in speech, and the fall be incurable, even mortal.* With the Prophet let him *be careful of* his *ways, that* his *tongue give no offense;* and let him carefully and studiously cultivate *silence, in which lies the fostering of righteousness.*

But you, Brother Brocard, and whoever may be constituted Prior after you, always keep in mind and put into practice what the Lord said in the Gospel: *Whoever wishes to be leader among you*

At other times, although you need not observe silence as strictly, be careful to avoid excessive talking, for as Scripture puts it, and experience teaches nothing less, *In much talking sin will not be far away*, and *The one who is careless in speech will come to harm.* Also, *Many words bring the soul to grief.* Again, the Lord says in the Gospel: *For every rash word uttered you will have to render an account on the day of judgement.*

So let each one *make a balance for his words and a careful rein for his mouth lest he stumble and fall in speech, and the fall be incurable, even mortal.* With the Prophet let him *be careful of* his *ways, that* his *tongue give no offense;* and let him carefully and studiously cultivate *silence,* in which lies *the fostering of righteousness.*

[17] But you, Brother B., and whoever may be constituted Prior after you, always keep in mind and put into practice what the Lord said in the Gospel: *Whoever wishes to be leader among you must mins-*

minister vester, et quicumque voluerit inter vos primus esse, erit vester servus.

Vos quoque, caeteri fratres priorem vestrum humiliter honorate, Christum potius cogitantes quam ipsum, qui *posuit* illum *super capita vestra;* et Ecclesiarum praepositis ait: *Qui vos audit, me audit, qui vos spernit, me spernit.* Ut non veniatis in iudicium de contemptu, sed de obedientia mereamini vitae aeternae mercedem.

Haec breviter scripsimus vobis, conversationis vestrae formulam statuentes, secundum quam vivere debeatis.

Si quis autem supererogaverit, ipse Deus, cum redierit, reddet ei.

Utatur tamem discretione, quae virtutum est moderatrix.

minister vester, et quicumque voluerit inter vos primus esse, erit vester servus.

[18] Vos quoque, caeteri fratres priorem vestrum humiliter honorate, Christum potius cogitantes quam ipsum, qui *posuit* illum *super capita vestra;* et Ecclesiarum praepositis ait: *Qui vos audit, me audit, qui vos spernit, me spernit.* Ut non veniatis in iudicium de contemptu, sed de obedientia mereamini aeternae vitae mercedem.

Haec breviter scripsimus vobis, conversationis vestrae formulam statuentes, secundum quam vivere debeatis.

Si quis autem supererogaverit, ipse Dominus, cum redierit, reddet ei.

Utatur tamen discretione, quae virtutum est moderatrix.

must minister to the others, and whoever wishes to be first among you will serve the others.

And you other brothers, reverence your Prior humbly, thinking of Christ rather than of the one He *has set up as your head,* and as He has said to the leaders of the Church: *Who hears you, hears me; who spurns you, spurns me;* so that you may not come to be found guilty of contempt, but may merit eternal life as a reward for your obedience.

We have written these things for you briefly, setting out a way of life you would do well to follow.

If, however, anyone goes beyond this, the Lord Himself at his return, will reward him.

However use discretion, which is the guide of the virtues.

ter to the others, and whoever wishes to be first among you will serve the others.

[18] And you other brothers, reverence your Prior humbly, thinking of Christ rather than of the one *He has set up as your head,* and as He has said to the leaders of the Church: *Who hears you, hears me; who spurns you, spurns me;* so that you may not come to be found guilty of contempt, but may merit eternal life as a reward for your obedience.

We have written these things for you briefly, setting out a way of life you would do well to follow.

If, however, anyone goes beyond this, the Lord Himself at his return, will reward him.

However use discretion, which is the guide of the virtues.

The Prior's cell should be near the entrance of the place ...

The Prior's Cell
Wadi 'ain es-Siah
Mount Carmel

I
THE HISTORY OF THE RULE

Carlo Cicconetti, O. Carm.

We know that the word "context" may mean "real facts" as well as very vague concepts. Generally speaking, the term includes a number of relevant factors which help us understand the meaning of a text. For example: context may mean a sentence (when related to a word we are explaining), a paragraph or a chapter; the author and his writings; the person to whom something is addressed. Context may refer to the actual, physical place, or to the psychological, historical or social environment in which the text or message was born, or where it can be in some way placed. The historical context is one of the relevant factors in interpreting a text. In fact, the meaning of a word or text is not established by the unchanging world of essentials. It is born of the changing mixture of situations which are subject to human, changeable situations.

The text of the Rule of Carmel makes reference to the situation in which the author, and those to whom it was addressed, lived; not just at the time when they received it, but also as they evolved and matured; as they submitted to the Rule and reacted to it; as they felt challenged and made decisions in the face of it. The Rule, therefore, reveals and communicates the experiences and the perspectives of the founding group on the situation or on the tangle of questions which the situation itself imposed upon them. It is a very precious perspective, because it is the result of a reading of faith, under the influence of the Spirit, of the situation which surrounded them. We are dealing here with the founding charism as lived in a particular circumstance.

The attempt to reconstruct the historical context of the Rule is limited to that situation and period in which the Rule was born, i.e., to its origins. What I am trying to do is to "bring the history back to that state of fluidity in which decisions had yet to be taken;" to "break up once again the contents, the results and the form of the finished work of action;" to appeal again, in a certain way, to "the living force of decision-making from which these works or these facts took their origin" (Hans Freyer).

When I use the term "origins," I do not want to limit myself to the time of the writing of the first draft of the Rule, which, besides other things, never reached us. By "origins" I mean the definitive, approved draft of 1247. I do not pretend to reconstruct the whole, overall context. I have to select between the various factors which, as I see it, serve to "introduce" the Rule and help us make our first acquaintance with it. In order to keep my selections within certain limits, I shall proceed along two distinct lines:

I. Dates and historical references: either found in the text of the Rule itself or in the writings of external witnesses.

II. The wider social and cultural context in which they can be placed.

I. Dates and Historical References

1. The Author

The first evident appearance of the Carmelites on the scene of history is documented by the prologue of the Form of life: *"a group of hermits who live near the Fountain, on Mount Carmel, under obedience to Brocard."* They ask Albert, the Patriarch of

Jerusalem, to give them a "Form of life" according to their proposal or project. Albert[1] is qualified in the text as Patriarch of Jerusalem, which helps us limit the time of the first drafting of the text, or better still, the time of its concession: i.e. between the year 1206 and 1214. In fact, Albert was elected Patriarch in 1205 and arrived in the Holy Land and fixed his See at Acre (a few kilometers away from Mount Carmel) during the first months of 1206.[2] He was murdered during the procession of the Feast of the Holy Cross (September 14) of 1214. Before being elected patriarch, he was Bishop of Bobbio in 1184, and of Vercelli from the year 1185 until 1205.

His formation as well as his experience are certainly useful elements in constructing the context, even from the point of view of its interpretation. I shall limit myself to reminding you of the following points in his life: his formation as canon regular of Mortara which entailed the constant reading of the sacred scriptures, the sharing of goods in common, a union of hearts, as well as a certain austerity of life. His juridical and literary preparation, his ability to solve conflicts and his knowledge of the phenomenon of his times known as "the mendicant movement," all were part of his previous experience. As a bishop he had, in fact, lived in a particularly lively area from the point of view of the existence of these movements: the Lombard Paupers, the Arnaldisti, the Chatari and the Humiliati. Equally important is the fact that he was delegated by Innocent III to give some sort of organization and a "Form of life" to the Humiliati, a group of workers who had

---

[1] Born into the Avogadro family about the year 1150, he was bishop of Vercelli from 1185 until 1205, when he was elected by the Canons of the Holy Sepulcher in Jerusalem to succeed Godfrey, who had resigned the patriarchate.

[2] For further information on Albert of Jerusalem (or, of Vercelli) cf. Joachim Smet, "St. Albert of Jerusalem," *Ascent* , (1965), 35-46. Vincenzo Mosca, *Profilo storico di Alberto patriarca di Gerusalemme,* a dissertation for the license in Canon Law, Rome (1983). Luigi Zanoni, *Gli Umiliati nei loro rapporti con l'eresia, l'industria della lana ed i comuni nei secoli XII e XIII sulla scorta di documenti inediti.* Milan (1911). Herbeert Grundmann. *Movimenti religiosi nel Medioevo.* Bologna: Il Mulino, 1974; pp. 65-74, especially p. 67, n. 10. For the historical dates of the hermits on Mt. Carmel cf. Joachim Smet, *The Carmelites: A History of the Brothers of Our Lady of Mount Carmel;* 4 vols. Darien, IL (1975-1985); cf. I:1-19.

had a few conflicts with the hierarchy. This movement comprised clerics, lay celibates, as well as some who had married. His qualification as "Patriarch of Jerusalem" and as "Papal Legate to the Holy Land" brought with it a special dedication to the "*obsequium* of the Cross" and laid on his shoulders the care of reintegrating the Holy Land.[3]

2. The Recipients of Albert's Form of Life

The newly constituted group had already left behind the initial stages of their coming together, and had already reached a definite point in their evolution. By now they were already constituted and, through their selection of a leader, were jointly bound to one another—all bearers of exactly the same charismatic imperatives. Their next step was to enumerate and codify their relationships as a group: within themselves, within the church and with their leader. They had to define unanimously their aims, their symbols, their means of livelihood, their mode of dress, their government, etc. This is what Albert did for them. His intervention, using technical and juridical terminology, qualified them and constituted them into one *collegium*.[4] Before that they had been a disparate group without any secure juridical unity.

We do not know their country of origin, except in a very general way. Virtually contemporary witnesses agree that they were "Latins," and that they called themselves "Brothers of Carmel." Jacques de Vitry (+1240)[5] , a witness who was very close to the time and place we are talking about, places them among the "pilgrims" consecrated to God, coming from different parts of the world, who were gathering in the Holy Land

---

3 Migne, PL *(Patrologia Latina)* 215:146; 215, 540; cf. also 215: 141-145. Carlo Cicconetti, *The Rule of Carmel*, Darien, IL: Carmelite Press, 1984; pp. 70-72. Albert's intervention was not, in my judgment, an act of jurisdiction in his role as Papal Legate, but as Patriarch of Jerusalem.

4 Cicconetti, *The Rule*, pp. 72-76.

5 Bishop of Acre from 1216-1228.

"attracted by the perfume of the holy and venerable places." A reference to a stage before Albert's intervention, which can throw some light on the initial project, can be found in those texts which refer to them as: "Latin brothers...living in penance" or laudably *(laudabiliter)* dwelling "in holy penance."[6]

3. The Place: Mount Carmel and the Fountain of Elijah

This site on Mount Carmel has been clearly identified today, without any shadow of doubt, in Wadi-'Ain-es-Siah, near the fountain traditionally called "The Fountain of Elijah." Both literary as well as archeological evidence, and some maps of the time, all coincide in making this identification. It is situated some 3 or 4 kilometers from Haifa, 25 km. from Acre, and 35 km. from Cæsarea Marittima.

There are two springs (fountains) at the site: an upper and a lower one. The lower spring *(fons inferior)* at the time of the Crusades was known either as 'The Fountain of Elijah,' or simply as "The Fountain." Both of these names, as well as their associations with the Prophet Elijah, preceded the arrival of the Latins to that place. Most probably it was started by a Byzantine group which had established a *"laura"'* there. "When the hermits of Carmel established themselves in Wadi 'Ain-es-Siah the place was already steeped in sacred tradition."[7] No wonder that Jacques de Vitry concluded that they had decided to follow the example of the holy prophet and

---

6 Jacques de Vitry. *Historia orientalis sive Hierosolimitana.*, Duaci, 1597; f. 85 ff., c. 51, cited by Cicconetti, *op. cit.*, p. 61-62. Smet suggests that the hermits on Mt. Carmel might have come from other groupings of hermits living throughout the Holy Land before the defeat of Hattin in 1187. These would have come seeking refuge no earlier than 1192. Cf. Smet, *op. cit.*, I:6.

Concerning the formula, *"agentes pœnitentiam"* or *"in sancta pœnitentia,"* cf. *Constitutiones Capituli Londinensis, anni 1281*, ed. by Ludovico Saggi, *Analecta Ordinis Carmelitarum*, 15 (1950), 208. Cf. also, Cicconetti, *op. cit.*, pp. 53-55.

7 Clemens Kopp. *Elias und Christentum auf dem Karmel.*, Paderborn, 1928, cited in Elias Friedman, *The Latin Hermits of Mount Carmel.*, Rome: Teresianum, 1979, p. 73. For the

solitary, Elijah; and no wonder that the Carmelites had accepted the tradition and ingenuously linked it with the time of Elijah![8]

4. Literary Genre

While not intending to enter into any philological arguments here, I would like to point out the fact that, both in the request made by the hermits (in the Prologue) as well as in the concession of Albert, our text is called a "form of life" or "formula for a way of living together" *(conversationis formula).* In the juridical language of the time, this terminology was used for statutes which were **not** Rules, *i.e.,* traditional norms for a "regular life" (monastic or canonical). Even in the fluidity of the terminology used, as well as the typology of those times when religious life was "in its birth stages," at a time of creativity, of new forms, this expression (*viz.,* form of life) reveals that they belonged to one of these relatively new forms. Moreover, this kind of "statute" was "requested," notwithstanding the claims of Albert that there were multiple forms of solutions already adopted by the Fathers for those who intended to live *"in obsequium Jesu Christi."* [9]

---

identification of the site of the first hermitage of the Carmelites cf. *idem,* pp. 52-55; 157-169.

[8] Jacques de. Vitry, *loc. cit.,* "...moreover, holy men renouncing the world, drawn by various affections and desires and inflamed by fervor of religion, chose the most suitable places for their purpose and devotion... others, after the example and in imitation of holy, solitary Elijah, the prophet, lived as hermits in the beehives, or small cells, on Mount Carmel... near the spring which is called the Spring of Elijah." Cf. Cicconetti, *op. cit.,* p. 62. Cf. also the Consitutions of 1281, *Rubrica prima,* l.c., 208. C. Cicconetti, *op.cit.,* p. 54; E. Friedman, *op. cit.,* pp. 95-103. Joseph Baudry, OCD. "Elie et le Carmel," *Carmel,* (1977), 154-168. Cf. also his "Origines Orientales du Carmel: Le Mythe et L'histoire,"*Carmel,* (1977), 327-344.

[9] For the significance of such phrases as "form of life" cf. Cicconetti, *ibid.,* pp. 76-84.

5. The Post-Albert Period: to the Time of Innocent I

As we have already mentioned, the historical context of the Rule should not be restricted to Albert's time nor to the places of origin only. In fact, the Rule "which we profess in different parts of the world up to today"[10] is that which is contained in the Bull of Innocent IV "*Quæ honorem conditoris*" from 1247, which "declares, corrects and mitigates" Albert's text and announces that all previous copies of it should be thus corrected.[11]

The present text, therefore, already incorporates the continuous experiences and evolutions which it had undergone: from the approval by Honorius III in 1226, up to the confirmation and other interventions of Gregory IX (*e.g.*, the prohibition of possessing anything, even in common, of Innocent IV—which came before the above-mentioned Bull) as well as the evolution of life and its organization (in such matters as General Chapters, itinerancy, apostolic activity).

---

[10] Constitutions of 1281, 208.

[11] Innocent IV, *Quæ honorem Conditoris omnium,* October 1, 1247. The critical edition may be found in Cicconetti, *ibid .,* 144-151, where one may also find a comparison with the previous Albertine text.

After this intervention the text of the Rule did not undergo any further correction. One further mitigation might be found via the faculty which the Pope gave to the General in 1432 to dispense from abstinence from meat, and for recreation. It is in reference to these mitigations that the Discalced speak, even today, of the "Primitive" Rule of Innocent IV. Cf. *Constitutiones Fratrum Discalceatorum Ordinis Beatæ Mariæ Viriginis de Monte Carmelo,* Rome, 1981, p. xi: "Regola 'Primitiva'...a Beato Alberto Patriarcha Hierosolimitano tradita et ab Innocentio IV confirmata." The quotation marks around "Primitiva" is the only new addition to this formula.

Concerning the mitigations of 1432, cf. L. Saggi, "La mitigazione del 1432 della regola carmelitana; tempo e persone," *Carmelus* 5 (1958), 3-29. For the issue of denominating the Rule as corrected by Innocent IV with the term "Primitive" cf. L. Saggi, *Le origini dei Carmelitani Scalzi.,* Rome, 1985; p. 17. Cf. also "S. Teresa de Jesús y 'la Regla primitiva'" in *Un proyecto de vida; la regla del Carmelo hoy,* ed by Bruno Secondin. Madrid, 1983; pp. 133-147. In the same collection cf. also Bruno Secondin, "Las 'mitigaciones' ayer y hoy," *ibid.,,* pp. 178-187. Tomas Alvarez, OCD, "Nuestra 'Regla del Carmen' en el pensamiento de Santa Teresa," *ibid.,* pp. 148-162.

A good historical introduction to the Rule is that of Hugh Clarke, O. Carm. and Bede Edwards, O.C.D., *The Rule of St. Albert.,* Aylesford and Kensington, 1973.

I do not want to claim that everything is spelled out in the Rule, but that the above mentioned points form its historical and vital context. With the massive migration (in fact, a return) back to Europe, starting perhaps in the year 1238, the cultural and environmental conditions which had determined the living interpretation of the Rule were changed. We know that there are evident traces of such changes within the text itself.[12]

II. Social, Cultural and Spiritual Context

1. In Palestine

The Frankish Kingdom of Jerusalem was already very much reduced when the hermits on Mount Carmel asked Albert (1206 - 1214) for the *Formula Vitæ*. They possessed only the coastline, about 90 miles long, from Acre to Jaffa. The major Latin settlement was at Acre, a cosmopolitan city made up of French, English, Italian, German, Frisian and Spanish (especially Catalans from Barcelona) inhabitants. The indigenous people (*i.e.* the Jews, who often came from other places, the Moslems and the traditional Eastern Christian communities) lived around the city, but were not allowed to settle inside the city itself for obvious reasons of security.

The various nationalities remained autonomous, and organized themselves in "communes" or corporations, each with its own church. The local bishop, as well as the Patriarch of Jerusalem, along with many other "local" bishops, together

[12] For the migration back to the West, cf. the Dominican writer, Vincent of Beauvais, *Speculum historiale*, Duaci, 1624 (written about 1240): "In the year of Our Lord 1238, because of the inroads made by the pagans, they were forced to disperse from that site [Mt. Carmel] to various regions of the world." The same author testifies to the approbation by Honorius III and gives some citations from Albert's "form of life." Cf. Cicconetti, *ibid.*, p. 96-97.

with their chapters, lived at Acre, because their "local sees" were situated in occupied parts of the country.

Their country of origin, their status in life, as well as their reasons for being in the Holy Land, all played a major part in the composition of the Latin population of Acre. For military and defence purposes you had knights, military orders and peasants rubbing shoulders with nobles. Following the path of devotion, there were pilgrims, hermits and monasteries dispersed all over the country. Others settled in Palestine for reasons of commerce and profit: the marine republics of Pisa, Genoa, Venice, Marseille and Barcelona were all represented there. This, at least, was the situation up to the time of the defeat of Hattin (1187).[13]

Near Carmel, in Haifa, there existed a *"signoria"*, based more or less on the European type. Carmel belonged to the diocese of Caesarea Marittima. Besides these Latin settlements, more or less stable, others came with each *"passagium generale," i.e.*, pilgrims coming every year around Easter and during the summer months: these included merchants and crusaders in addition to male and female pilgrims, all wanting to visit the "Holy Land of the Lord."

After the year 1187, and especially with the election of Innocent III in 1189, the theological motive for visiting the "Land of the Lord" prevailed over all other motives. Because of the loss of practically the whole of the Holy Land (especially Jerusalem), popular emotions ran high. Few, if any, thought of any other reason except the religious and theological motive for visiting the Holy Land. In fact, the situation of the Holy Land at that time did not favor any reason except the religious! The conditions were such that the hermits could not have been present on Mount Carmel between the years 1187 and 1192.

---

[13] Cf. Steven Runciman, *A History of the Crusades,* 3 vols., Cambridge: University Press, 1952-1955; cf. vol. 2.

2. In the West[14]

The end of the twelth century and the beginning of the thirteenth century were turbulent times; tension ran high at various levels. Yet it was also a very creative time, full of the ferment of new ideas. Mobility was the new characteristic of all the aspects of life: movement, journeys here and there, pilgrimages, commerce, social leveling, as well as interpersonal rapport, intellectual awakening, etc. The principal factors of this transformation seem to have been:

a) The demographic explosion of the twelfth century which reached its culmination in the thirteenth century. This provoked, on the one hand, a boost for economic expansion (the availability of manpower opened up new horizons), but on the other hand this skewed the equilibrium that had existed between the population and the means of sustenance. Because of other unforseeable events (*e.g.*, famine and drought) it was impossible to produce enough food for all those who lived there. In addition to these and other reasons, the new nobles, on an entirely different level, began to find it difficult to provide a good position for themselves in a land that was not their own. Masses of farmers were entering the cities looking for work. This only enlarged the great number of the poor already living there.

b) Other types of work, besides agriculture, appeared on the scene: the craftsmen and the merchants brought to the city monetary and mercantile markets. Money became an important commodity and various types of lending for interest were not very easily distinguishable from "usury."

---

[14] Emanuele Boaga, "Il contesto storico socio-religoso ed ecclesiale della Regola," in *La Regola del Carmelo Oggi* Rome: Carmelite Institute Press, 1983, pp. 37-54. One will find an ample bibliography on this topic on pp. 40-41. Cf. also Christine Thouzellier and Yvonne Azais, "La Chrétienté romaine (1198-1274)," in *L'histoire de l'Église depuis les origines jusqu'à nos jours.*, Augustine Fliche and Victor Martin (eds.), 20 vols., Paris (1946-51); vol. X, cf. also vol. IX. Also, André Vauchez, "La spiritualité de l'Occidente médiévale," in *La spiritualité du Moyen Age occidentale.* Paris (1975), esp. pp. 83-90. Jacques le Goff, *Il Genio del Medioevo.*, Mondadori (1959), pp. 14-25 and 68-75.

c) The center of life moved from the countryside into the city. New class divisions appeared: those who lived in the *"borghi"* (or suburbs), who were neither noble, nor clerics nor farmers. The craftsmen and the merchants acquired a certain importance and autonomy and became a new class, between the nobles (whether clerical or lay) and those who had no rights but lived on the fringes of society.

The "communes" appeared as a type of government, independent of the feudal lords and emperors. They promoted a new form of government within the cities. The population in these "communes" participated much more in the running of their own affairs. Rivalry and conflicts started between cities, or even between suburbs, because of their tendency to try and expand themselves and their influence, and to acquire more territory in order to enlarge their alimentary resources.

A new type of worker appeared on the scene: the full-time, intellectual worker. Schools and universities multiplied. Important works were translated. This brought about an exchange between the Moslem and the Greek cultures.

d) Feudal bonds became less stringent as the old social classifications became inadequate to include the new classses appearing in the cities. The church, faced with the threat from Moslem quarters, focused its attention on the Holy Land and continued to preach the crusades. But this type of preaching did not seem to be adequate in the new situation. On the one hand, it seemed to be very distant from the actual situation then prevailing. Because of their many and diverse practical needs, people belonging to certain social categories – i.e. merchants, craftsmen, nobles, soldiers, etc.,– lost interest in what they had held in high esteem before. On the other hand, this type of crusade-preaching was no longer accompanied by the "evangelical life," which was claimed by certain movements of the time: the pauper and evangelical movements. The church appeared to be ruined by the burden of the riches she possessed and had to administer and defend. This happened among all its component parts: clergy, bishops, monks... The church's place – among the people, and near the people – was no longer adequately filled by the monk, who now appeared to be an aristocrat, holding a place of prestige.

However, there were many institutions of every type working among the poor. The bishop himself served as "procurator" on behalf of the poor. Even the community property of the canons regular served to help the poor. The monasteries periodically distributed food and other sorts of help. The twelfth and thirteenth centuries were times which saw the refounding of charitable institutions and renewed criteria for a theology of assistance to the poor. It was at this time that the Hospitalers appeared on the scene. Pope Innocent III tried to tackle the problem of discerning between the different evangelical and mendicant movements, while searching for a way of creating new forms of religious life within the church. Meanwhile, the struggle against heresy became more incisive, even though repressive methods were at times still in use (especially against the Albigensians and Cathari).[15]

3. Spiritual Currents and Movements

Christianity was hit at the time by spiritual currents which interested all categories of the faithful, and not only the *"o rdines"* which were officially constituted among the *"oratores"* (those who pray). The common characteristic of all these currents has been called by some "evangelical awakening." The belief that all the faithful were called to live their own lives in close agreement with the Gospel gained ground. One could no longer hold that salvation came because of one's position in

---

[15] H. Grundmann, *op. cit.*, pp. 63-108. Michel Mollat, *The Poor in the Middle Ages: An Essay in Social History.*, New Haven: Yale University Press, 1986. Cf. also his *Faire croire: modalités de la diffusion et de la réception des messages religieux du XIIème au XVème siècle.*, Rome (1981).

the church, or because of one's formal adhesion to its doctrines. Salvation was to be achieved through a religious and committed "form of life" for each true Christian. In direct and quasi-literal encounters with the Gospel, each of the individual extant rules, as well as the various "forms" of religious life, was clearly understood to be limited – simply "rivulets" emanating from that "Rule of Rules, which is the Gospel." With the return to the Gospel, it was Christ who returned to the center of attention and imitation, together with his way of life and that of the Apostles.

The concrete forms through which these "convictions" passed into individual and collective lives are more or less all contained in the introduction to the Rule: the life of holy penance, the pilgrimage, becoming a hermit, poverty and the form of apostolic life according to the first community of Jerusalem. Obviously we can barely touch the outside of each of these forms which, directly or indirectly, make up the cultural and spiritual context in which the text of the Rule sank its roots, both as a whole and also as single particular themes.

a) Life in "Holy Penance"[16]

The life of "holy penance" was born of the Gospel's invitation to convert oneself and "do penance" because of the immanent coming of the Kingdom (Mt 4:17). It was an invitation addressed clearly as much to the laity as coming from the laity. This idea was inspired and, in a way, expanded by the canonical, public penance employed by the church in its first centuries. It even reached the Middle Ages, although it had then been emptied of its more powerful contents. It had been reduced to a public form of penance imposed, even against the

---

[16] Cicconetti, *ibid.*, pp. 27-34, cf. the Notes on pp. 318-319. Cf. also Gabriele Giacomozzi, *L'Ordine della Penitenza di Gesù Cristo; contributo alla storia della spiritualità dell secolo XIII.*, Vicenza, 1962. G.G. Meersseman and E. Adda, "Pénitents ruraux communitaires en Italie au XII siècle," in *RHE* 49 (1954), 348.

will of the person, to expiate grave public sins.

This free decision to "do penance," to put oneself in the condition of a penitent *(ordo pœnitentium)*, this change of life, had to be made known externally through some kind of symbol (*e.g.*, a change of dress); and the actualization of this conversion was recognized by a real change in one's social position. Often the whole process began in front of a bishop or a priest who imposed a "penance" or "way of life" (or "form of life" or, simply, a "life"). That is why both the sign and the conversion of heart it represented came to be identified with varying emphases either with "penance" or "detachment" (e.g., pilgrimages and long journeys away from home; periods of exile; being on the road; begging; being a hermit) or with physical suffering (fasting and abstinence).

Beyond binding oneself through the traditional discipline of the church, "life in holy penance" had the advantage of placing a person within the canonical order, even if he were only classified among the "*conversi*" (converted), which was one of the lesser categories of ascetic life.

Ways of living in "holy penance" were many. Apart from living inside a monastery with the monks or the canons regular, some were "solitaries" (not easily distinguished from hermits); others lived in groups; others stayed in the cities, and some even led a married life. Very often they became the beginning of a movement which frequently went on to develop other values. Peter Waldo[17] began his life according to the evangelical form after he had experienced a conversion. Francis of Assisi says openly: "the Lord allowed him to start to 'do penance;' and his first followers presented themselves as 'men of penance, coming from Assisi."[18]

---

[17] Founder of the Waldensian movement in the generation that saw Francis of Assisi's birth (i.e. 1173-1179).

[18] Manselli, *op. cit.*, pp. 96-102. Also, Magli, *op. cit.*, pp. 42-47.

b) "The pilgrimage to Jerusalem"

The pilgrimage was a form of conversion and a true rite of penance imposed "for the remission of sins." Its clear value lay in breaking one's bonds with the world – with all that one holds secure, even one's social position. It was an ancient form of penance and one particularly congenial to the condition of the people of that age. It found good ground in persons living at the time of the writing of the Rule: people of extraordinary mobility and the will to go from one place to another. Everybody seemed to be on the move in those days. The "pilgrimage to Jerusalem" (its values and motivations), was continually urged by the preaching of the crusade, which, under Innocent III especially, reached a certain theological richness along with a sure power of persuasion. From the spiritual and the religious point of view, the attraction of the "pilgimage to Jerusalem" lay principally in the fact that it was the historical place where the mystery of redemption was enacted, almost a bond uniting the whole of Christianity to the mystery of redemption.[19]

The conquest of, or the visit to, the Holy Land put one in touch with the human realities of the life of Jesus (love, suffer-

---

[19] Cicconetti, *ibid.*, pp. 39-43 with notes on pp. 321-322. Cf. also, Paul Alphandery and Alphonse Dupront, *La chrétienté et l'idée de croisade.*, 2 vols, Paris (1954-57), pp. 20-22. Frequently the pilgrimages would culminate in taking the habit or in making vows while in the Holy Land. For the traditional worth ascribed to the pilgrimage, and its biblical origins, cf. Ceslaus Spicq, *Vita e peregrinazione nel Nuovo Testamento.*, Città Nuova, 1973 [originally, *Vie chrétienne et perégrination selon le Nouveau Testament.* Paris]. Jean Leclercq, *Aux sources de la spiritualité occidentale.* Paris, Du Cerf, 1964, pp. 35-52. Raymond Oursel, *Les pélerins du moyen age.* Fayard, 1963, pp. 32-35. Here one finds this definition of the pilgrim: one who "in a given moment of his life decides to take a journey to a certain holy spot while totally subordinating the whole organization of his existence to this journey." Magli, *op. cit.*, pp. 106-116 describes the bond between the life of a penitent and the pilgrimage: "The physical encounter with the places in which the mystery of the redemption took place is certainly the oldest and most constant reason for the pilgrimage." So, too, Alphandery, *op. cit.*, p. 28. He also remarks on the attraction of Jerusalem for the pilgrim. *idem*, p. 24, and 266-277. Cf. also, Bruno Secondin, "Tentare fraternità: Il progetto evangelico del Carmelo," in *Profeti di fraternità*, Bruno Secondin (ed.), Bologna: Edizioni Dehoniane, 1985; pp. 67-101, especially notes 48 and 59.

ing and humility). It occasioned a new way of contemplating Christ: a preeminence was given to Christology in the individual and collective religious experience. Finally, it fostered the imitation of Jesus as man. It was an historical Christology which completed and integrated Pauline Christology without upsetting it. To go on the "pilgrimage to Jerusalem" was an exercise in faith; it was a practical expression of the following *(sequela)* of Christ.

The "pilgrimage to Jerusalem" was also enriched by images from the biblical tradition of the Old Testament. One pilgrim who went up to Jerusalem was Abraham who left his land behind him. The difficulties a pilgrim went through during the journey were compared with the sufferings of Job. Above all, the pilgrimage was considered to be a new Exodus. The fact that the place was occupied by non-Christians was the profanation by the Gentiles spoken of in the scriptures (Psalm 78, Lk 21:24). This biblical tradition gave meaning to physical contact with the city, the "center of the world," and with the images that were derived from it.

At the same time there was the possibility of seeing and of understanding Jerusalem through an exegetico-allegorical reading of the texts, which were already very much in use. Behind the earthly Jerusalem, which all could see and know, there was another Jerusalem – the true one – of which the earthly one was only an image. God had chosen the earthly Jerusalem to be an image of the celestial one, seen only by the eyes of faith, thanks to the prefigurings of the prophets. Jerusalem was also the place of eschatological waiting, the place where the battle with the anti-Christ would one day take place.[20]

Connected with the "pilgrimage," as a preliminary to it, was a certain form of "poverty." Especially with Innocent III,

---

[20] Innocent III, *Cum iam captis*, in *PL 216,*:744 ff. Cf. also Alphandery-Dupront, *op. cit.*, p. 31, 43 ff. For the sense of eschatological tension cf. *idem*, pp. 300-301, 344.

after his failure to arouse interest for an armed crusade among the nobles, the crusade came to be preached to the poor. The rich were "not worthy" to fight for the Holy Land. How could one follow Christ, who was naked and poor on the cross, wearing the heavy armor of the rich.[21] Quite often the "pilgrimage to Jerusalem" turned out to be the pilgrim's last journey. A glorious destiny: to die where Christ died! "Suffer for Christ, live with him and be buried with Him, so that Christ will grant you the grace of arising with him in glory."[22]

There is one last conviction I would like to mention here: The Holy Land belonged to Christ physically, because he inherited it by right from the Father and had acquired it by his blood. Therefore, it had been promised to and should be inherited by his 'faithful.'[23]

All these traits, given different emphases, were common to the idea of the "pilgrimage to Jerusalem," whether it was undertaken "just for devotion" and "atonement," or whether it had as its purpose the liberation of the city "by armed force." The "preaching of the Cross" (i.e. the invitation to take up the sign of the Cross and become a crusader) and, in a special way, the appeals of the Popes repeatedly used these motivations to spur on the princes and the Christian populace *ad obsequium Jesu Christi Crucifixi.* [24]

---

[21] *Idem*, pp. 240-244, 250, 266-272. Peter of Blois held that the Holy Land belonged to the poor, as to promised inheritors, because the Lord, by living there, had rendered it so, "according to heaven." Cf. p. 242. At this time the various sects, devout groups, penitential associations formed among the laity had made prevalent the idea that only the poor were loved by God. Cf. pp. 304-305, as well as S. Runcimann, *op. cit.*, II:784.

[22] Alphandery and Dupront, *op. cit.*, p. 24. Cf. also Cicconetti, *The Rule..* pp. 41-42.

[23] Alphandery and Dupront, op. cit., pp. 360-361. Ingenuously they put forth the intivation to the Sultan to become a Christian, and to turn over the Holy Land to its rightful owners, the Christians. Cf. Cicconetti, *op. cit.*, pp. 42-43, "The Patrimony of Jesus Christ."

[24] Cicconetti, *ibid.*, p. 41: "A pilgrim is a penitent who sets out on a trip to perform voluntary or imposed penance. A crusader includes military activity risking his life for

The conviction arose that, were the Holy Land to be won back again for Christianity, it would have to come about through the proclamation of a "holy war" against the enemies of the Cross of Christ. This created the figure of the knight/monk in either the military or the hospitaler orders.[25] At the very time when the hermits first appeared on Carmel's mountain chain, the various sects and groups of the *devoti* (such as the penitential associations formed by lay persons) introduced the idea of "election"—of a society of the poor. Slowly the idea of an armed crusade was forgotten, while the desire of a crusade by the "pure of heart" (who might win the Holy Land without the use of arms) began to gain ground. It would be a crusade which would triumph, not through the efforts of men, but through the agency of a miracle at an hour to be determined by God on behalf of the "kingdom of the saints."

"The knight/monk of the former epoch gave way to the *vir spiritualis* (the spiritual man), who is poor, weak and predestined to the glory of the saints."[26] Contemporaneously, the very idea of an **armed** crusade became the object of violent attacks from heretical quarters (such as the Cathars and the Waldensians).[27] St Francis of Assisi's decision to risk meeting the Sultan face to face and ask for peace is well known, and it fits into the overall pattern of such a change in thinking.[28] There is no doubt that the decision of the hermits of Mount Carmel to follow a "form of life" *(formula vitæ)* presented itself within the spiritual dimensions of the ideals of poverty and of an attach-

---

the love of Christ and for the remission of his sins. A hermit is a penitent who, more or less, has adopted a stable abode." Étienne Delaruelle, "Les ermites" in *La vita comune del clero nei secoli XI e XII,* Atti della I Settimana di studio (2 vols. Milano: Mendola, 1962) I:225. For the significance of the term *obsequim Jesu Christi* ,cf. Cicconetti, *ibid.,* pp. 61-65, 296-311.

[25] R. Manselli, *op. cit.,* p. 10-11. Alphandery and Dupront, *op. cit.* p. 303, 359,361.

[26] Alphandery and Dupront, *ibid* , p. 305.

[27] *Ibid,,* p. 303.

[28] Cf. the old legends cited in Alphandery and Dupront, *ibid,* p. 360-361.

ment to that Holy Land where Christ, the Master, lived and walked. I describe this spirituality as one of simply *being there, being present.* [29]

As to the official and broadly held ideology which regarded the liberation of the Holy Land, and especially the freeing of Jerusalem, as a necessity, I think it would be difficult to prove that the group of hermits who lived on Mount Carmel did not share this same vision, as well as believe in it. Moreover the Patriarch Albert, held in such high esteem by Innocent III, had been sent there with the principal aim of fostering the "recovery and integration of the land where the Lord was born." It was this man who wrote the Rule for the hermits of Carmel. It is to be expected, then, that he was especially dedicated to the "*obsequium* of the Cross" in a most literal sense.[30]

c) Hermits[31]

Eremitical life was one of the traditional forms of the ascetical life. Even given the permanancy of certain spiritual values,

---

[29] Urban IV, *Ex vestræ Religionis* (1262) pointed to their commitment to the Holy Land and their dedication to Jesus, "Who had acquired the Holy Land by the pouring out of his blood." Cf. Cicconetti, *op. cit.*, p. 305-306. Two recommendations from Pope Martin IV in 1282 and 1283 attested that the Order had existed "from time immemorial" and had been instituted "for aid," *in solatium* , to the Holy Land: *ibid*, p. 306-307.

[30] *PL 215*,:540; but cf. also 141-145; *PL 215*,:700; *PL 215*,:146. Albert of Jerusalem was praised because it fell to him, for the most part, to save the Holy Land if it were not to be entirely lost. Some exclude (which seems to me gratuitous and hasty) that the spiritual "arms" were in any way in rapport with the struggle to recover the Holy Land. It would be very difficult for the hermits, even given their grouping and the "way of life" given by Albert, to have been free from the prevailing and official ideology, which held that it was an injury to Christ to leave the Holy Land in the hands of the "infidels." Francis notwithstanding, even the Franciscans used to preach and exhort Christians to go on the crusade. Cf. Alphandery and Dupront, *ibid*, 303. They even concretized the Antichrist into the Muslims. *ibid*, 301.

[31] Cicconetti, *ibid*, p. 34-39. Jean Leclercq, *op. cit.*, pp. 44-52, 203-237. M. Mollat, *op. cit.*, 88-95, 143-144. Vauchez, *op. cit.*, 154-156. Smet, *The Carmelites...*, I:7-11. Clarke and Edwards, *op. cit.*, 15-18.

they may yet take diverse forms of organization and have different emphases in different places. The eremitical life sometimes places the emphasis heavily on solitude, while at other times the emphasis is on poverty; sometimes one finds the emphasis on choir prayer, at other times it may be on manual labor.

The desire to retire to the "desert" *(in eremis)* could only be undertaken by a those who had prepared themselves by means of a long novitiate and through preparation within the monastic life. This desire to "retire" might also be the immediate consequence of a life conversion by spending one's life in "holy penance" *(sancta pœnitentia).* One might be impelled to make such a decision at the conclusion of a pilgrimage.

The eleventh and twelfth centuries saw an awakening and a flourishing of hermits in the West. The majority of them, at least in the beginning of the movement, did not require entry into monastic life, nor even into any similar sort of organization. Their style of life did not place them among the "orders," nor among the prestigious social classes (such as that enjoyed by the monks and the canons regular), but left these hermits among the laity, and, like the "penitents," in the lower ranks and margins of social life.

Paradoxically, but only at first sight, they felt themselves closer to the simple people and to the poor. Their simple life, their relatively loosely binding structures, their poverty of dress (they walked barefoot, wore unkept beards, lived wherever they could find a place or simply in cabins), the language they used when exhorting the people to penance, all these were quite accessible and comprehensible to the people. It brought the people to love them more than the clergy or the monks. This held true for the more established hermits in groups, and also for those living alone and for those who were expressly *"itinerantes"* or belonged to the same *"forma apostolica."* It seems to me that a brief glance at what we may call a "constellation of institutions" of various kinds of European hermits does not justify the repetition of the commonly held belief that the Carmelites found a less than favorable place on Mount Carmel for the continuation of their life "in solitude."[32]

d) Mendicant Movements and the apostolic life[33]

Towards the end of the eleventh century, the idea of finding an inspiration for a way of life directly tied to the Gospels created in people a two-fold aspiration towards environments and places both quite distant and distinct from those in Europe. They sought "evangelical poverty" and "a form of life" like that of the Apostles. By renouncing all earthly goods in "voluntary poverty," they sought to renew Christian life by following Christ through imitating the "way of life" of the Apostles. This is what those who followed the two basic ideas intended: evangelical poverty, and a "form of life" according to the Apostles. These became the focal points of a new concept of Christianity. They were accompanied by explicit denunciations and criticisms of the way of life of the clergy and the monks. Sometimes they contested their right to exercize ministry since they did not live according to the "form" of the Apostles. In this way some tended to dissociate themselves from the church; but others chose this way of life with simplicity, explicitly professing their obedience to the hierarchy of the church. Above all under Innocent III they laid down the foundations for new forms of religious associations: itinerant preachers, and later, the mendicant orders themselves.

It was not the first time that the apostolic "form of life" was put forth as a requirement for a reform of the life-style fol-

---

32 Cf: also Cicconetti's bibliography, *op. cit., pp.* 320-321:

33 H. Grundmann, *op. cit.,* 15-96, 316-317, 428-436. A vast medicant movement among women, though it had great difficulty in being recognized, characterized the end of the XIIth and XIIIth centuries. Cf. pp. 147-290. Cf. also H. Vicaire, O.P., *Histoire de Saint Dominique,* Paris, 1957; pp. 77-79, 128-134, 454 ff. Also, I. Magli, *op. cit.,* pp. 14-20.

lowed by the clergy and the monks. Both groups hearkened back to the example of the primitive community in Jerusalem (viz., sharing their material possessions, life in common, unity of hearts, the anticipation of the heavenly Jerusalem, and [for the canons regular] the care of souls); however poverty, at least collectively, was not very evident, nor was it even sought after as a value. The very form in which they travelled from place to place, even when preaching, did not differ very much from the way the rich travelled: using horses and taking with them loads of equipment and manpower. There was even the obligation of providing for all the needs of a monk or a cleric while travelling, to save him the embarrassment of having to beg. But the way the Apostles travelled and lived had been described in the Gospels: carrying no gold or silver with them, no money in their purse, using no travelling bag, nor two tunics, nor sandals, nor staff. Because the worker has a right to be fed, they ate and drank whatever was provided in the houses in which they stayed. "As you go along *(itinerantes)* preach that the Kingdom of heaven is at hand" (Mt 10:7-9; Lk 10:7; 9:3-8).[34] This was the way in which the Cathari, along with the Albigenesians, presented themselves in the south of France; it was also the theme of the Waldensians and other heretical movements. Moreover, this was the way in which the "itinerant hermits" had presented themseves followed by the "Catholic Poor" of Durand of Huesca (1207), then by Bernard Prim's community of itinerant preachers (1210), and finally by the followers of Dominic and Francis of Assisi.

---

[34] C. Cicconetti, *ibid.*, 193-198, and especially the notes on pp. 338, 341. Cf. H. Vicaire, op. cit., 151, n. 65, 66. Innocent III got a living for a deposed ecclesiastic so that he would not have to beg *(ne cogatur in cleri opprobrium mendicare)* 7 May 1199; *PL 214,*:602 A; *PL 215,*:682. The same idea belonged to the Cistercians who wished to support themselves through manual labor, *"absque rubore mendicandi."* Francis of Assisi said that they ought not feel ashamed if Satan forced them to beg. Cf. H. Vicaire, op. cit., 272, 287-290, 353, 389-390, 413-417, 446-448, 451. Cf. also, Jesus Alvares Gomez, "Diversi tipi di povertà nella storia della vita religiosa," in *La povertà religiosa.* Roma: Claretianum, 1975; pp. 109-125. Also, Rudolf Maria Mainka, "I movimenti per la chiesa povertà nella XII secolo," in *idem.*, pp. 141-155.

Following the way of thinking of that time, as well as the canons of the church, preaching belonged properly to the bishops *(Ordo doctorum)*, then to the curates or others to whom the mandate had been given. The maximum that a layman could do was to exhort others to do penance (this is what the followers of Francis did initially). But the heretical movements openly held that every Christian had the obligation of announcing the Gospel (something the other groups held only implicitly). The authority for doing this came more from their poor "form of life" than from priestly ordination. The opposition of the clergy to this position lasted the whole of the thirteenth century.[35]

A characteristic of these penitential movements, as was also true of the hermits, was the affective rapport that existed between them and the faithful. They were not divided by rank or social class. They felt themselves to be "brothers" – both among themselves and with all other Christians: an apostolic "fraternity."[36] Insofar as they were "converts" themselves, the hermits of Carmel took their place among the ordinary people.[37] They did not attempt to climb the social ladder but were simply "brothers of penitence." They could not call themselves "monks" or "canons regular." The form of poverty which they had chosen was one which "prohibited" them from possessing anything, *even as a community*. Their mendicant status depended on this, along with the itinerant lifestyle which they had chosen.

The city and the villages were the places most in need of

---

35 H. Grundmann, *ibid.*, 37-44, 74-95. H. Vicaire; *ibid.*, 128-33. "According to the model which they imagined to have been that of the Apostles; they went out two by two, weakened from fasting, with unkempt beards, barefoot...with only one tunic, not taking either gold or silver in their pockets, nor taking any from the people." Cf. p. 129. For the struggle that was launched against the mendicants cf. C. Cicconetti, *op. cit.*, 213-220; and R. Manselli, *op. cit.*, 98, 137, 189, 212, 242; also M. Mollat; *op. cit.*, 150-154.

36 Cf. O. Steggink, "Fraternità apostolica", in *Profeti di fraternità;* pp. 41-65.

37 R. Manselli, *op. cit.*, 91, 119, 130-131, 178-179, 242-263. Cf. O. Steggink, "Fraternità apostolica," *idem*. Cf. also M. Mollat, *op. cit.*, 138-177.

itinerant preaching. The proximity of their listeners, along with their simple and practical form of life, allowed them to respond to the diverse social conditions of those who came to hear them. In the beginning neither Francis nor Dominic had established themselves in the city. In fact, Francis continued right to the end of his life to live long periods of true eremitical life. Both of them feared stabilizing themselves in the city. Even when they did settle there, most of the time it was on the outskirts of the towns or in their surrounding areas.[38]

The Carmelites had hitherto encountered and understood this form of life (already in Palestine from 1220 onwards). They found it again when they came to Europe – a life already affirmed, yet very strongly contested by the episcopacy. The bishops were anything but disposed to encourage them, as has been remarked in other places. Their requesting and obtaining from Pope Innocent IV "a state in which they could be 'of use' to themselves and to their neighbor" was their own autonomous decision, taken after their discernment of the situation in which they found themselves.[39]

---

[38] Cf. *supra,* n. 32. Joined to this form of chosen poverty (*viz.*, the absence of all possessions and revenues, journeys without gold or silver) was the obligation to manual labor in return for their single, daily meal. In fact the condition of the poor consisted in the fact that "these arms, once one's elementary needs have been satisfied, should hold onto nothing." So, Jacques de Vitry, cited in Mollat, *op. cit.*, 124. Again, "the poor are essentially those whom the weakness as of their means of survival leave at the mercy of everyone in society." *idem,* 141. Cf. also H. Vicaire, "Les origines dominicaines de la mendicité religieuse et la condition d'humilité mendiante selon Saint Dominique," *La vie dominicaine* 34 (1975). From the very beginning the mendicants did not settle in the city for fear of an inherent incompatiblity with the life of poverty. When they did begin to settle there, they did so at a certain distance from the city, in the outskirts. So, Mollat, *op. cit.*, 143-144.

[39] Innocent IV, *Paganorum incursus,* July 27, 1246. [This date in the *Bullarium Ordinis Carmelitarum* has been corrected in the critical edition done by Adrian Staring, "Four Bulls of Innocent IV: A Critical Edition," *Carmelus* 27 (1980), 281.] Bede Edwards had denied the authenticity of this bull in his review of my book. He was denying the transformation of the Order into a mendicant one by Innocent IV. Staring, however, shows its authenticity. Cf. *Ephemerides Carmeliticæ* 24 (1973), 428-432; cf. also Edwards' *The Rule of St. Albert,* p. 23. Here he affirms no doubt over the bull's authenticity. No special importance seems to be given to the phrase: "the desire to attain, with the aid of

e) The Marian, Elijan and Near Eastern elements

We can only briefly record the fact that Mount Carmel is very near to Nazareth. In addition to this was the great development of Marian devotion during the twelfth and thirteenth centuries, "the great Marian century!" The first chapel on Mount Carmel was dedicated to Mary. In addition, we have already mentioned Elijah. Witnesses who observed the Carmelites read rich meanings into their choice of that place. Enveloped in the Byzantine traditions of Elijah's presence, the hermits were defined as "imitators of the holy and solitary Elijah."

The Near Eastern context of the Order is less evident, notwithstanding the proximity of monasteries of Greek Christians nearby. But surely their choice of taking over an abandoned

---

the Apostolic clemency, a state in which they may, with God's help, rejoice in furthering their neighbour's salvation," expressed in this bull at least a year prior to the modification of Innocent. Cf. Joachim Smet. ibid. Thus it speaks of a passing to apostolic activity "without premeditation" as a consequence of the ever increasing choice of the city as a place of habitation. Supporting this thesis is the reaction of Nicholas the Gaul (1270), which would be inexplicable had the choice for apostolic activity occurred deliberately.

Bede Edwards then defines this passing over to apostolic activity as a yielding to the temptation flowing from frequent travelling for the purpose of begging. Cf. *op. cit.*, p. 28. With all due respect I must say that I disagree with this position completely. In fact, the wrath of Nicholas the Gaul is not explicable – not even after the Bull of Innocent IV, *Devotionis augmentum*, of August 26 1253, which gave permission to preach and to hear confessions, "because there were already many religious who are sufficiently prepared in theology accompanied by the concessions of various popes about relocating themselves in the cities." Cf. the preceding Note. Moreover Smet's hypothesis leaves that desire, linked to a Papal intervention unexplained, which could only have had any outcome and reason, if in fact they had recourse to a modification of the Rule. For a fuller treatment of this, cf. *The Rule....*, pp. 136-143, 208-212. Also, Joseph Baudry, "Le Carmel médieval devant le choix 'désert-ville,'" in *Carmel* (1977), 303-305, especially 295, n. 5. Keith Egan, "An Essay toward a Historiography of the Origin of the Carmelite Province in England," *Carmelus* 18 (1972), p. 90. It is indicative that the first foundations before 1247 (Hulne, Aylesford, Losenham and Bradmer in Great Britain; Messina in Sicily and Les Aygalades near Marseilles) were all outside of but nearby to populated areas and large cities. The same was the case for the other mendicant groups, the Dominicans and the Franciscans.

hermitage, a Byzantine *"laura,"* should give some sort of context for understanding them.[40]

III. Conclusion

In order to complete the description of the historical context we would have needed to go through all the successive contexts in which the Rule of Carmel has ever been lived, what Bernard Lonergan has called the "cumulative contexts." I am well aware, therefore, that the historical context which I have just presented is not enough by itself to supply a criterion or relevant factor for interpretation – not even as the "historical context."

Implicitly, and even sometimes expressly, I have shown what I think are the lines along which the historical context allows us to see into the Rule and, consequently, what type of reading and what kind of response the Carmelites wanted to give to the historical situation. But it is the task of the one who examines the text itself, using hermeneutical criteria, to find the true and real interpretation. Mine in only a modest contribution.

However, I think it is important to remain in constant touch with these realities which come from a past that has in some ways formed us all. A past, understood as "memory" in the Biblical sense, that is, re-encountering the traditions of 1281. To those who do not know how to reply to the questions of "when" and "by whom" was the Order initiated, we

---

[40] Ludovico Saggi, "Santa Maria del Monte Carmelo", in *Santi del Carmelo.* Rome: Carmelite Institute, 1972; pp, 111-115. Redemptus M. Valabek, "La presenza di Maria nella fraternità carmelitana," in *Profeti...op. cit.*,103-124.

Elias Friedman, *op. cit.*, pp. 91, 95-102, 200-205. J. Baudry, "Élie et le Carmel," in *Carmel* (1977), 154-168. Cf. also his "Origines orientales du Carmel. Le mythe et l'histoire," *idem*, 327-344. Sr. Eliane, (an orthodox nun), La Regla del Carmelo: puntos comunes y diferencias con el monacato ortodoxo," in *Un proyecto de vida. La Regla del Carmelo hoy*. Bruno Secondin *et alii* (eds.). Roma: Editiones Paulinas, 1985; 183-193.

shouldlike to be able to give a short formula, however imperfect – paraphrasing the ritual formulas of the feasts of Israel – one which a person can remember and transmit. "Our ancestors were pilgrims, come to Mount Carmel to live in holy penance... they received a Rule which we profess and live up to this very day."[41]

---

41 *Constitutiones 1281, Rubrica Prima, 1. c.* À propos the "cumulative contexts" of the Rule, cf. Bernard Lonergan, *Method in Theology*. NY: Herder and Herder, 1972, esp. pp. 163-164, 183-184, 312-314, 324-326. Egidio Palumbo, "Letture della Regola lungo i secoli," in *La Regola del Carmelo Oggi*, Bruno Secondin (ed.). Roma: Institutum Carmelitanum, 1983, pp. 157-165. Also in the same collection, Domenico Lombardo, "Gli strati della Reglola e loro significato," *idem*, pp. 151-155. Here one should also see the final consideration made by Bruno Secondin on pp. 233-235.

An oratory should be constructed in the midst of the cells ...

The Oratory
Wadi 'ain es-Siah
Mount Carmel

2

HOW TO READ THE RULE: AN INTERPRETATION

Constance FitzGerald, O.C.D.

I believe I have been asked to give this paper for three reasons. First of all, The Rule of St Albert has influenced my life for thirty-five years, years before and years after Vatican II. For nearly twenty years, before Bede Edwards, Carlo Cicconetti, Joachim Smet or Elias Friedman produced their studies, I heard the Rule read in the refectory every Friday. Its words and its spirit are burned into my soul as a part of my identity. Secondly, I bring the reflections and experience of a woman, a Carmelite nun, to this gathering. I come from the oldest Carmelite community in the United States – a community that has been willing to change and renew precisely because it embodies and cherishes the tradition.[1] I believe that any genuine vision for the future has to be rooted in a knowledge and love of the past. Thirdly, I am interested in and convinced of the need for good hermeneutics, serious interpretation, in dealing with the classic texts of our Carmelite tradition.[2] I assume that

---

1 The first community of Carmelite Nuns was founded in 1790 in Port Tobacco, Maryland. The nuns moved to Asquith Street in Baltimore in 1830. They moved in 1873 to Biddle Street and in 1961 to Dulaney Valley.

2 We need, in the Order, something like the *Jerome Biblical Commentary* for our great classical texts.

this, above all, is why I am here and why the uncreative sounding title "How To Read The Rule" was given to my lecture. At the two seminars given by the Carmelite Forum in South Bend I spoke on "How To Read Teresa and John: Interpretation." I hope that those of you who heard me then will bear with me while I try to situate the Rule within the context of contemporary hermeneutical theory. (Hermeneutics is the science of interpretation. The word in Greek means to make clear, to interpret. Thus the hermeneutical task consists in interpreting a text or tradition to understand it. It connotes both the search for meaning in a text and the activity of explaining to others what one has discovered.)

While the text of the Rule is much simpler, shorter, seemingly more obvious and direct in its meanings than the writings of John and Teresa, the process of reading it, or of interpreting it, is not basically different from that of reading them. The same kind of deep or close reading is demanded – a reading that cannot be confused either with one's initial encounter with the obvious meaning of the text, or even with some knowledge of its historical background. Modern critics call this process "discourse." They invite us into an ongoing conversation with the subject matter of the text whereby we actually develop a friendship or an empathy with it. Familiarity with the text can grow to such an extent in this deep reading that we seem to wear the text like our own skin.

In seeing the root of familiarity in family, we realize that the Rule has gathered into a family those who through many years of reading it have developed this familiarity and friendship with it. In the internalization of an almost intangible spirit that both encompasses and surpasses the specific points of the Rule, our collective psyche and/or soul has been irrevocably marked and we have been bonded into a community. This means that those of us who remember the days of this close reading – Friday after Friday, for example – have already embarked upon the first hermeneutical step long ago by reading and rereading the Rule.

What we are trying to do with the Rule is not foreign to us.

"Lectio" or reading is as old as monasticism itself and certainly was in the mind of Albert when he wrote and of the hermits when they read of "meditating day and night on the law of the Lord."[3] Moreover, in Teresa's 16th century *interpretation* of the "Our Father" in *The Way Of Perfection* we see an example of *lectio* or deep reading that is, in the words of contemporary hermeneutics, more text-centered or reader-centered than author-centered. The irony of the use of the term 'author-centered' here is a fruitful one because, of course, Teresa's whole reflection is Author-centered and is, in fact, a dialogue with the Author. On the other hand, it is not author-centered in its unconscious concentration on the text itself without concern for nor knowledge of precisely what Jesus meant when he spoke or what his original audience or the original readers of the gospel text understood.

When I entered Carmel, there was little available on the historical background of the Rule. However, through the method of "spiritual" interpretation which was applied to the Rule, we did come to recognize it as a "classic" or a foundational text of the Order. The experience of the "a-temporal" nature of the Rule did in some strange manner prepare the way for the text-centered approach of contemporary hermeneutics.[4] But I knew very little about what the Rule meant in the thirteenth century to Albert who wrote it, to the hermits on Mount Carmel near the spring who received and lived it, or to the church/world at large. However, with the studies of Bede Edwards, Joseph Baudry, Joachim Smet, Rudolph Hendriks, Carlo Cicconetti, Elias Friedman and others, a whole new "world behind the text" was revealed. With these first steps in exegesis and historical criticism, the project of developing a more comprehensive interpretation of the Rule was begun.

---

3 For a good description of *lectio* within the context of remaining in the cell and meditating day and night on the law of the Lord, cf. Carlo Cicconetti, O. Carm., *The Rule of Carmel* . (Darien, Illinois: Carmelite Spiritual Center, 1984), p. 201.

4 See *Ancient Carmelite Texts* printed for private circulation by Carmelite Communities Associated, 1982.

When Father Cicconetti writes of his aim to place "the background of the Rule of Carmel, both in its entirety and in its regulations, in a legislative and historical context" and thereby to rediscover "the original meaning of the Rule," he shows his awareness of the importance of historical criticism in the work of reading and interpretation.[5] We know by experience how the Rule has come alive with new and more profound meanings as we have been able to understand its original meaning, its precise and comprehensive historical context, as well as the evolution and vicissitudes of Carmelite life in the first hundred years of its existence. There is no substitute for the foundation which these historical and archaeological data provide.

What we have to realize, however, is that classic texts which have come to us out of the past do not find their *only* true interpretation of meaning in the past, as Cicconetti seems to suggest.[6] It is obvious to us that there is one exciting level of meaning in the Rule that will be accessible only to those who study, reflect upon and appropriate the historical background that is available and thereby attempt to understand what Albert must have meant and what the hermits must have understood. But there are other possible meanings in the Rule which may be even more significant, which are not dependent on or at least go beyond the standpoint of Albert or the first hermits and which will be discovered when *our* issues, concerns, questions and experiences are brought into a dialogue with the Rule.

We cannot now know the mind of Albert. Moreover, what the Rule meant to the first hermits is only the beginning of the history of its interpretation. It has long survived both Albert and the hermits and the world that produced it. By means of interpretation, it now addresses people and human situations which they never envisioned. What must be discovered and

---

5 Cicconetti, *op. cit.*, p. 7.

6 *Ibid.*

appropriated in interpretation is not so much where the text of the Rule came from, therefore, as what it helps us to understand.

The hermeneutical perspective of this presentation emphasizes, therefore, a text-centered approach which is, in the end, illuminated by and correlated with the historical research of others, but which privileges always the primacy of the actual text of the Rule. Privileging the text demands that the critic make a contemporary and sometimes personal application of the text. In other words, my theory of critical interpretation focusses on the text of the Rule itself and on the contemporary Carmelite's response to and conversation with that text.

As a woman in the church and in the world today, I come with the perspective of a woman. I come seeking to understand, interpret and evaluate the Rule and the history of its interpretation, in such a way that both its oppressive and its liberating power are clearly recognized. I come asking if this text can honestly operate for Carmelite women as a model of transformation for us and for the Order.

Unless we can discover vital values in the Rule that help us to live in and contribute to our world today, unless this Rule projects a vision for the future congruent with the needs, fears, hopes and dreams of humanity, it is a dead historical document even if we pretend it is living. Furthermore, unless this text is alive in us, it is not alive at all. If the Rule is indeed a spiritual classic, as its survival through nearly eight hundred years suggests, then it has new meanings for our age and it is up to us to discover them by a profound and disciplined reading of or dialogue with the text that is not afraid to employ the various methods of contemporary hermeneutics (*e.g.* semiotics, structuralism and even deconstructionism) to carry on the dialogue.

Pre-understanding the Text

But let us not deceive ourselves. We do not come neutral to this text of the Rule. We are influenced by centuries of interpretation – by healthy, legitimate developments and by destructive distortions.[7] If we are to be free enough to discover in dialogue with the text the new, prophetic meanings that address the questions, conflicts, issues, sorrows and joys of humanity in our time, it may be necessary to find ways of reading as well as modes of interpretation that can not only retrieve these new and genuine meanings (what is known as the "hermeneutics of retrieval"), but also to uncover the negative realities or distortions in the Carmelite tradition that *still motivate* our living, or operate as a religious justification for or ideological legitimation of oppression, marginalization and control – (the hermeneutics of critique and suspicion).[8]

If we can risk our present horizon or mind-set in new interpretation, then both the *text* of the Rule itself and our contemporary Carmelite *experience* will be challenged. This means that while we will be transformed by the values and wisdom of the text which we discover, we will also shape and enlarge the future of the text, the future of the tradition, by asking it questions neither Albert, nor the first hermits, nor previous generations of Carmelites could have posed.[9]

---

7 Avery Dulles has written best about this: "The Church may be seen as a variety of traditions undergoing constant developments and adaptation. In the course of this development the traditions are sometimes enriched, sometimes impoverished, sometimes contaminated and sometimes purified." *Models of the Church* (New York: Doubleday & Co., 1974), p. 182.

8 It seems to me we could examine harmful interpretations of solitude and the cell, of silence, of the prior's role and his responsibility for decisions regarding visitors, of obedience in terms of "the one who hears you hears me," etc.

9 See Constance FitzGerald, OCD, "How To Read Teresa And John: An Interpretation," presented at St. Mary's College, South Bend, Indiana, June, 1985, and June, 1986. These are two different papers on the same topic.

Applying Hermeutics to the Text of the Rule

In the second part of this presentation, within the context in which I live as a Carmelite nun, I want to try at least to hint at the application of this critical hermeneutical praxis to the Rule. One interesting way to begin to analyze the text is to ask WHO, WHERE, WHAT, WHEN/HOW, WHY?

Physical place or WHERE stands out in the text. It appears to be, by its prominence, more important than the specifics of WHEN or HOW the hermits do things. The text is written by Albert of *Jerusalem* to "B. and the other hermits...near the spring on Mount Carmel" who live a life of allegiance to Jesus Christ. The hermits are described or named, not in reference to a human person, nor even with reference to a mystery of God or Mary, but only in reference to a specific place – a spring and a mountain called Carmel.

A mountain, in symbolism, is situated in the heart or in the middle of the world. Rooted in the earth, yet rising into the skies, it reaches upwards, joining heaven with earth, and in its majesty is expressive of the deepest longings of the human heart for completion, for unity and for integration. It suggests both solitude and panoramic unity. Yet this mountain has not the majestic height of the Rockies nor the incomparable grandeur of the Himalayas. It has its own specific topography. It is Carmel, a garden, with a spring.

The text materially associates the hermits with the land. When one puts this beside the "allegiance to Jesus Christ" of chapter 2[10], one realizes that this land is the habitation of the human person Jesus Christ, the place where he became a citizen of this earth. The *Holy* land is *his* land; and in the light of the armor-warfare imagery of chapter 15, allegiance to him

---

[10] The enumeration being used throughout this talk is that given by Bede Edwards and Hugh Clarke in *The Rule of St. Albert* (Aylesford and Kensington, 1973). They chose to call the Prologue chapter 1. According to the copy in the Vatican Registers the Rule begins with a Prologue. Thus, chapter 2 is there enumerated as chapter 1.

can easily be read as an allusion to feudal oaths.[11] But it can also be read in terms of present day oaths of allegiance or citizenship.[12] Both assume relationships and responsibilities.

This metaphor makes the hermit a citizen tied to the place of Carmel and to the liege, Christ, whose patrimony the land is. (See chapter 6 where the word used is *locum* instead of *cellulam*.) It implies a political reality in terms of dual citizenship in the nation of physical birth and in the nation of spiritual birth. The second citizenship transcends national boundaries but is earthly and material and implies solidarity with and responsibility for the land and, by extension, for the one or ones (the people) to whom the land belongs. However, this solidarity is achieved, the text shows, first of all through "pondering the Lord's law day and night" in one's cell: the separate, solitary cell allotted by the prior with the agreement of the brothers. This more precise establishment of place links chapters 5, 8, 10 to chapters 1 and 2.

Embedded in this notion of political solidarity is a paradox; for in order to establish these outward bonds with one's fellow citizens, in order to struggle against the powerful destructive presence of evil (chapter 15), one must seek solitude and be faithful in prayer/service. The text does not say that there is only this solitude, since it admits of journeys both on land (in the "primitive" Rule) and on sea (in the Innocentian revision) and does not exclude preaching or relationships outside the hermitage; but it does indicate solitary prayer as primary.

The Internalization of Images

What happens when we internalize this material relationship to place? First of all, through the ages since the Carmelites left Palestine, Mount Carmel and the spring have been taken inside our collective heart as the great archetypal sym-

---

11 This is suggested by both Cicconetti, *op. cit.*, pp. 15-17, and Edwards, *ibid*, pp. 78 and 87).

12 See Cicconetti, *ibid*, pp. 15-17; Edwards, *ibid.*, p. 78, note 5.

bols of the Order. At different epochs they have said different things to us and perhaps now we need to probe them anew in the context of our *place.*

Secondly, if to be a hermit was, as the text demonstrates and Cicconetti proves, a form of *earthly citizenship* which could include struggle for the protection and liberation of the land, the Rule may address some challenges to our lives. For example, to be a Carmelite is to be bound to the land; it is to live an *earthly life,* not a so-called "spiritual" life on the fringe of the human. It implies a *dedication to the earth,* an involvement in the world where Jesus Christ lived as a human person, and where he continues to be embodied in people. Perhaps the symbol of PLACE calls us to be *conscious* world citizens who struggle against the annihilation of this earth and the destruction and oppression of its people (the devil who prowls around like a roaring lion looking for prey to devour). This kind of rootedness in the world with the political awareness and sophistication it implies is the experience of some communities of Carmelite women today, and is the other side of the coin of solitary prayer. We have not just decided to be this way! Rather, the experience of solidarity and the shape it has taken is a prayer experience into which we have grown out of the fullness of our life. *Place* is an apt symbol!

Application to the Cloistered Life

There is a strange irony here though. Because of cultural and historical circumstances, the nuns for five hundred years have privileged contemplation and the solitary cell which in turn has set up certain realtionships with God, with self, and with one's sisters. *Precisely because we are women* we have had **no choice** but to privilege the eremitical and community side of the charism and a material understanding of place. The text has, therefore, in one sense, functioned for our oppression and subjugation. But in consequence some of the nuns seem today to be in better possession of the charism and more able than the men to renew it in a distinctive way. The challenge for the nuns is how to appropriate freedom and equality (canonically) and yet remain autonomous enough to privilege the place of continual prayer and deep relationship.

But *place* as a symbol has its dark side. Wherever it is used to confine people in immature relationships, to deprive them of knowledge, of information and of freedom to choose and to grow, wherever it saps them of personal autonomy and responsibility for their own lives and decisions, we see a destructive interpretation of the Rule. Wherever, in the name of solitary prayer, the *material place* becomes a refuge, a place to hide, and a place where one is deprived of human relationship and contact with the world, the symbol of *place* functions destructively for Carmelite nuns no matter how it is idealized in the language of theology, spirituality, canon law or even in the lives of our saints—who are part of the history of the interpretation of the tradition/Rule.

In the concept of relationship, the WHERE or PLACE intersects with the WHO in the text. While the Rule begins with the Patriarch's salutation to his beloved *sons,* and looks back at the example of "our saintly *forefathers*" in chapters 2 and 9, the text is not situated within a father/child context. In fact, in view of the whole monastic tradition up to this time, the absence of any reference to parental relationships speaks volumes. Not even God is named Father in the text, except when the "Our Father" is mentioned in chapter 9. Instead, the Rule sets up relationships of equality and proposes a model of brotherhood, dialogue and consensus. With the exception of the greeting, the hermits are called "brothers" throughout the text. Although Albert hurries to establish leadership in chapter 3, he situates it within a community of equals. There is no reference, except by initial, to the first prior, who certainly does not give his name to the new group and who is a "brother" chosen *from among the brothers* by unanimous consent, or at least by the greater part of them.

The Organization of the First Community

Although the brothers are to promise obedience to the prior, important internal decisions are made *together:* "If the prior *and brothers* see fit you may have foundations " etc. (chapter 4a); the separate cells "allotted by the disposition of the prior *with the agreement of the other brothers,"* (chapter 5); or "*You* (plural) should discuss matters of discipline and your spiritual welfare" and lovingly correct the failings of the brothers (chapter 12). Even though some decisions are left in the hands of the prior, particularly those concerning visitors from outside the community, one suspects this is not by way of privilege, since the only ideal of leadership urged upon the prior is the gospel text "Whoever wants to be a leader among you *must be servant to the rest.*" When this text of being a servant and a slave is put beside the admonition, "You other brothers too, hold your prior in humble reverence," we can grasp the degree of mutual respect and accountability that is urged upon all the brothers (chapters 18, 19). Nor should we overlook the fact that in the all important area of forfeiture of ownership and the consequent distribution of the common goods, delegation by the prior is expected (chapter 10).

The Rule's expectation of equality and consensus is both an encouragement and an affirmation to some communities of nuns today. For those of us who have, over the last twenty-five years, slowly moved from a more matriarchal-hierarchical type of governance to what we call a "feminine, participative way of living together," it is a challenge to continue the effort to establish that kind of bondedness which makes consensual living and decision making possible.

It is interesting to note that both the Rule of the distant past and the contemporary feminist ideal of social structures call into question a hierarchy of relationships founded on levels of power rather than a network of relationships founded on bonding – on love and respect and care. When we Carmelites return to the sources, as our church after Vatican II directs, what we find, contrary to the expectations of some, is not an authoritarian framework but a situating of leadership within a community of equals and an affirmation of communal discernment and egalitarian relationships.

This egalitarianism, however, is very different from that radical socialism that aims at each person's having an *equal share* of the common goods. Rather, each is to receive from the common goods "whatever befits his age and needs." The first hermits, the text shows, were far removed from the idea of equal shares of everything, which "is itself an unrecognized product of modern bourgeois culture in which self-esteem depends on catching up with those ahead and staying ahead of those on your heels. [This] is an ideal created and fostered by a culture founded on anxiety and competition...[which teaches] its members to pull up the ladder at the same time that it helps them to 'get ahead.'"[13]

The Order is challenged in all this. It will, moreover, be strengthened when its women can openly bring into the mainstream of its life of governance and community their experience and interpretation of the Rule given to the Brother hermits of Mount Carmel, that is, their valuing of relationship and dialogical community over achievement, power, competition and control.

Looking back to Mount Carmel, looking ahead to a future where the survival of humanity may well depend on our capacity to accept diversity and profit by its richness, and standing in a present that sees a sign of the times in the mushrooming of small "base communities" all over the globe, there are some communities of American Carmelite women today who, in their attention to a community of egalitarian relationships and individual diversity and autonomy, are consciously prophetic. They realize that the movement in the world toward dialogical communities as a basis for survival, liberation and peace, in the words of philosopher Richard Bernstein,

---

[13] Joseph L. Walsh, in a book review of Kai Nielson's *Equality and Liberty: A Defense of Radical Egalitarianism* in *New Catholic World*, (September-October, 1986).

"gains 'reality and power' only if we dedicate ourselves to the practical task of furthering ... solidarity, participation and mutual recognition...in (actual) dialogical communities."[14]

Reconsidering Our Own Use of the Rule

On the other hand, in the light of the text of the Rule we need to question the recent past, and in many cases the present, where great authority over people's lives is given to or taken or held on to by the "Mother Prioress" or the "Father Prior;" where a mother-daughter relationship is descriptive not of bonding, but of power and control and the destruction of personal autonomy and consensual living. We might ask ourselves what we mean and what message we are giving if we have a father and/or mother of a *Carmelite* community.

It is precisely here where leadership and community intersect with personal autonomy that we come to the Rule's pivotal texts regarding *solitude,* which urge each one to stay in his/her own cell pondering the Lord's law day and night (chapters 5, 8). One of the greatest travesties the Rule has been used to protect is the bondage of others in the name of solitude and prayer; the usurping of another's responsibility for herself by the withholding of information, or contact or relationships. (While I do not think the text taken as a whole suggests this, I am afraid that chapter 7, which directs that the prior is to meet all who come, and everything to be done as he disposes, has sometimes functioned in the tradition for the control and domination of others.)

Solitude is the PLACE of the hermit. Five of the text's chapters are about the cell. There is no HOW to the cell except keeping watch at prayer; there is no WHEN to prayer but always. I recognize that the original text directs the hermit who

---

[14] Richard Bernstein, *Beyond Objectivism and Relativism: Science Hermeneutics and Praxis* (Philadelphia: University of Pennsylvania, 1983), p. 20. Quoted in Elizabeth Schüssler Fiorenza, *Bread Not Stone.* (Boston: Beacon Press, 1984).

can read to say the Psalms according to the custom of the church, and the one who cannot read to say the *Our Father* a specific number of times; but in allotting to each brother a cell where he is to remain "unless attending to some other duty," the text gives permission to be oneself before God. The trust is complete. The brothers are left on their own and the call to personal autonomy is inescapable. Just as certainly as the brothers are called to community, the hermit is called, within the very parameters of the Rule, to own his own life.

In my experience, nothing so characterizes the Carmelite nun as the inclination toward solitude. It distinguishes her even from other contemplative nuns. Embedded in the collective psyche, it has, as it were, almost archetypal power and is symbolized above all by the mountain of Carmel and to some degree by the spring. What is worthy of note today is that as the nuns have recovered the emphasis on community and have developed new methods of interpersonal communication, the life of solitary prayer has also matured and deepened. Far from being competitive, the two are complementary. I think this means that when one loves and is loved in community and is affirmed as a valuable, participating member of the group, one is at peace in solitude, one is at home in one's own house. Meditating day and night etc. assumes love! Conversely, it also assures it.

To the degree that one has found God and oneself in solitude, one is uncompetitive, loving and open in community. Furthermore, if one does have deep bonds in community, one is even more liable to experience oneself as personally loved by God, which is the only experience that gives meaning to "pondering the Lord's law day and night and keeping watch at prayer." If we bring anything to the story of renewal, it is certainly this learning about the relationship between solitude and community which the texts themselves validate.

Over the past twenty years it has been interesting to me to notice how often, though not always, the desire for a permanent eremitical life emerges in a person's experience when community breaks down. Moreover, in a world where the poor and crowded and oppressed cry out across the earth, we need to be certain our separated cell is the place of existential solidarity and communion, and not the place of a luxurious privacy and peace unavailable to most people.

At a more philosophical and theological level, the genuine solitary who is in real possession of her own life, understands that the true nature of our equality and community lies in the simple, human fact that we are all mortal and that we all harbor under the surface of everyday life the same existential fear of loss and dissolution and inevitable death. In the prefigurement of this death, in the solitary encounter with the abyss, the madness and the darkness, the hermits are empowered to declare themselves for the unbreakable community of final human destiny. Here in identification with the cross of the human Jesus who lived and walked, anguished and died on this earth, the *obsequium Jesu Christi* of the Rule reaches its deepest expression. It is this experience, from which the Carmelite cannot escape, that effects a solidarity – not only with one's sisters in community, but with suffering, dying humankind all over the world. Here "meditating day and night" coincides with *obsequium Jesu Christi.* Here we have circled back to some of the societal conclusions we first reached when developing the importance of PLACE in the text.

Before going on to the last section of this paper I want to mention the new phone system we have recently installed. It is a small PBX, expensive by our standards, that we foresee will not only enhance our communication among ourselves and with others outside the monastery, but will also enhance our solitude. Since everyone has a phone, the need to leave one's cell or office to communicate about community business and everyday administration is very much lessened. It removes many excuses to run around the monastery and exacts a definite discipline. We have decided this is an interesting application of the Rule.

The Rule as Living and Developing

The last point I would like to look at in the text is its flexibility, brevity and lack of detail. In this it can be compared with the Rule of Augustine but certainly differs in genre and intention from the Rules of Benedict and of Basil, and from the Rule of Pachomius – although many of the phrases and ways of saying things in the Carmelite Rule are characteristic of other rules.

WHAT the text expects is, by and large, simple and straightforward. (Perhaps chapter 15 is the only real exception with its abundance of scriptural symbolism.) The Rule establishes precise values but seldom specifies structures: that is, WHEN or HOW these values are to be lived out. Rather, the text continually recommends elasticity. First of all, in chapter 5, concerning the important issue of "separated cells," the text suggests flexibility "by subordinating this requirement to the natural terrain of available land."[15] Even the directive for "foundations in solitary places" is qualified by "or where you are given *a site* that is suitable and convenient for your observance" (chapter 4a—note the mendicant shift in the Innocentian revisions, according to Cicconetti). Scripture is to be read in the common refectory "*where this can be done* without difficulty (chapter 5a) and each one is to remain in the cell in continual prayer "*unless* attending to some other duty" (chapter 8). We must be careful to note that not even these duties are delineated nor WHERE they are to be performed – *viz.* inside or outside the place where the hermits live. Even the admonition to gather *each morning* to hear Mass is qualified by "*if it can be done* without difficulty" (chapter 11). In terms of prayer, the text, as I noted earlier, is more specific only in speaking about the canonical hours and the number of *Our Father's* that must be said by those who cannot read (chapter 9).

The sole criterion for the distribution of the common goods

---

15 Cicconetti, *op. cit.*, p. 177.

is, as I have already said, "*whatever* befits his age and needs." The meetings of the community are to be on Sundays "or other days if necessary," while the correction of personal faults depends on "*if any be found* at fault" (chapter 12). "You are to fast every day except Sunday," the text says, *unless* bodily sickness or feebleness, or some other good reason, demands a dispensation from the fast; FOR NECESSITY OVERRIDES EVERY LAW!"

Abstinence from meat always applies *unless* one is sick or on a journey or at sea (chapters 13, 14). Although the command to work is categorical, *the kind of work* is not specified in any way (chapter 16). In the original text silence is to be kept "from Vespers until Terce the next day, *unless* some necessary or good reason, or the Prior's permission, should break the silence." At other times, "the brothers are to be careful not to indulge in a great deal of talking, *although you need not keep silence so strictly*" (chapter 17). It is not *total* silence that is recommended during the day. Rather rash, careless, unbridled, superficial speech is condemned as destructive of the *quality of the communication* expected of the brother-hermits. Even though the text asssures a reward to those who do more than is required of them, it cautions in the last number: "See that the bounds of common sense are not exceeded, however, for common sense is the guide of the virtues" (chapter 20).

What is my conclusion here? While many of the conditioning phrases used in the Rule are to be found in the older rules (*e.g.* the Rule of Saint Benedict) and in the documents of the period, it remains significant that these phrases are written into this short, concise text in such abundance. Furthermore, when one unites the attitude they convey with what the text does *not* say, does *not* describe nor demand, the values of *freedom, flexibility* and *trust* are set in bold relief. Although some interpretations of the Rule in our past history seem to have had oppressive power, this text out of which we Carmelites are born can function more than I have ever before realized for the liberation of people. In this it is truly a mystical text coming, one would guess, out of an experience of God that realized there was no need to constrain or control the others who also experienced God. No wonder the Rule has lived so long in the collective soul and imagination of Carmel as its foundational myth. No wonder it is felt more deeply by so many of us even than Teresa's constitutions (at least the adapted Constitutions we read for many years). The text of the Rule can take its place beside the classic mystical texts of Teresa and John even though it is so different in genre from their writings.

The ultimate aim of reading the Rule is the appropriation of the meaning or life-direction it gives to us. In interpretation or deep reading we discover possible new ways of being and new forms of living which give us a capacity for new self-understanding. I have come to the conclusion that although this text was written in the thirteenth century by a *man* for *men*, on the whole it can be appropriated by women. Undoubtedly, as I have suggested, some of its interpretations have served through history to make Carmelite women invisible and marginal, and have legitimated their subordinate role and secondary status (the *second* Order). However, the text itself is not basically patriarchal but is, on the contrary, on the side of flexibility and freedom, community and quality, personal autonomy and respect for experience – specifically, personal experience of God. It is on the side of contemplation. For these reasons, the text of the Rule can operate as an open-ended paradigm or model that not only validates our experience as women, but challenges it and sets it in motion or structures it for further transformation.[16]

Furthermore, with this text as the basic foundational document of our lives as Carmelites, the Order as one community of brothers and sisters should be inescapably challenged to listen carefully to the experience of its women in order to make their meanings, values, insights and visions integral to the

---

16 I am indebted to Elizabeth Schüssler Fiorenza's book, *Bread Not Stone,* for some of my ideas and language here. See her "Introduction."

vision of the Order. Then this simple Rule might empower all of us in the Order today, women and men together, to explore deep and radical developments in community and in contemplation in response to the cry of humanity, the cry of God's people, for survival, peace, equality, justice and communion on this earth – the PLACE where we live out our allegiance to Jesus Christ.

You should discuss your observance and spiritual welfare ...

The Participants
Mount Carmel Spiritual Centre
Niagara Falls, Ontario

3

INCENTIVES TOWARDS A NEW UNDERSTANDING OF THE RULE

Kees Waaijman, O. Carm.[1]

When any text is presented to me to read, in terms of its origins, its structure, the meaning intended by the author, its influence on its listeners, I may completely understand that text, yet not have that text really function in my own life. I may comprehend it very well, but for the rest, it does not touch me. I have no relationship with it; it remains "outside" me.

I may approach a given text from another point of view: I may come to a text thinking that *I already know what that text contains.* In that case the text no longer offers a challenge to me because I have silenced it by my *predetermined pattern of thought.* The text no longer functions because it will only say what I *already* know.

Both of these reasons coalesced and caused the Rule to become a *dead text* within our Dutch Carmelite community. On

---

[1] This article was translated from the Dutch by Martha Alken, O.P., and emended by Kees Waaijman.

the one hand, practically everyone *knew beforehand* what the Rule contained without really reading it. One simply assumed that it concerned "Carmelite life" as one experienced it – Carmelite life at the decline of the Reform of Touraine, that is. On the other hand, newly gained insights into the historical origins of the Rule did not really permeate our province in the Netherlands. However, one can see a turning point in our province halfway into the 1970's: 1975-78 to be precise. One finds an intense confrontation between the Rule and the province, an encounter that was also occurring in other provinces. One need only witness this Congress on the Rule, which some decades ago would have been unthinkable!

Questions are once again being put to the Rule. What position did the first generations of Carmelites take in their world? What value systems directed their lives? How did they build community? What formed the core of their spiritual lives? Some even more critical questions are: Does the Rule still have anything at all to say to us? Is it not a relic of the past, out of the extinct, dark Middle Ages? These are questions enough.

The reading of the Rule created a readiness in our province to abandon our image of the Rule and take a new, fresh look at it. Supported by research that had already been completed,[2] we at the Titus Brandsma Institute had the opportunity to study the Rule anew. Based on this study,[3] we came to a new, rough translation of the Rule. During a two year period the "Religious Dimension Committee" of our province read the Rule from the perspective, "What does the Rule mean?" as well as with the question, "What does the Rule call forth in us today?" From all this came a living give-and-take between the

---

[2] Cf. Carlo Cicconetti, *La regola del Carmelo: origine-natura-significato* (Roma: Istitutum Carmelitanum, 1973). For the English version cf. *The Rule of Carmel,* (Darien, IL: Carmelite Spiritual Center, 1984). Cf. also Hugh Clarke, O. Carm., and Bede Edwards, O.C.D. (eds.), *The Rule of Saint Albert* (*Vinea Carmeli,* 1, Aylesford & Kensington: 1973).

[3] Otger Steggink, O. Carm., contributed his knowledge of our history; Jo Tigcheler, O. Carm., did the semantic research for the most important spiritual terms; Kees Waaijman, O. Carm., studied the uses of scripture in the Rule.

Rule and ourselves. Sparks began to fly! The text was being given a new chance. We were being given a new chance. In the reading the Rule appeared, not as a *law*, but as a *letter*. A letter written by Albert to us. A *letter* is to be read and answered. We wrote back to Albert.

Our learning process became verbalized in a new translation, provided with an introduction and a commentary.[4] We took it to all the groups and commissions once again with the dual question: "What does the Rule mean?" and "What does it call forth in us?" Thus the Rule received its place in our renewal process.

Now, almost ten years later, I am being asked to look back. What were the most important incentives that led to a renewed understanding of the Rule? And how does this new understanding function in the process of renewal that is going on among us? I have discovered three incentives and would like to give you a brief explanation of them.

1. The Rule as the Journal of Our Foundation-History

The first incentive contributing to a new understanding of the Rule was the insight that the Rule did not just fall from heaven, but came into existence within an historical process. This perspective was primarily formed by the study of spirituality. Michel de Certeau in 1965 had already demonstrated rather convincingly that every genuine spirituality arises: 1) within a concrete historical context, 2) with its concrete historical challenges, 3) with its own language and 4) with its own questions. All genuine spirituality meets these questions and searches for the answers in the language of the historical context itself.[5] Within the Titus

---

4 *The Carmelite Rule* (Introduction, translation and annotations by Otger Steggink, O. Carm., Jo Tigcheler, O. Carm., and Kees Waaijman, O. Carm. Almelo, 1978).

5 Michel de Certeau, . "Civilizations and Spiritualities," in *Concilium* 2 (1966), p. 9.

Brandsma Institute we consistently applied this approach.[6] Those who are able to see "contextually" discover that the Rule is the result of a growth process that covers at least 50 years. Only in 1247, when Pope Innocent IV gave the Carmelites mendicant status, was this process concluded.[7] Three important phases mark this *process of becoming*. All have left their mark on our Rule.

The first phase is that of the *Proto-Carmelites* on Mount Carmel. These Proto-Carmelites were called "hermits" by Albert.[8] They were lay hermits. In the twelfth century a growing number of persons distanced themselves from the established culture. They turned away from society and from the church. The established religious life according to the classic rules (Basil, Benedict and Augustine) did not offer an alternative for them. They left house and home and journeyed into the wilderness. They took upon themselves a sober and serious life. Some of them were *eremitæ peregrini* – solitary wanderers. The goal of their wanderings was to visit the "holy places," *visitare loca sacra*. The Proto-Carmelites on Mount Carmel were just such "lay hermits" with Western European backgrounds who had made the pilgrimage to the Holy Land.

The spiritual structure of these twelfth century hermits is clearly delineated. They were individuals who wanted to live significantly different lives *(conversio)*. They detached themselves from the establishment *(mutatio loci)*. They turned towards a life of holy earnestness and frugality *(in sancta penitentia)*.

We, who look at our own culture from this spiritual structure, discover that we, too, have our "lay hermits" and our *Proto-Carmelites*. They are the ones who have decided for themselves to live differently, counter-culturally: they relate

---

6 This reading is especially dependant on the contextual set up of the Dutch Carmelite periodical *Speling* and on the subsequent theory-forming done by Otger Steggink, O. Carm., and Kees Waaijman, O. Carm., in their book *Spiritualiteit en mystiek* (Deel 1 Inleiding, Nijmegen, 1985).

7 Cicconetti, *op. cit.*, pp. 21-207.

8 Cf. the Prologue to the Rule.

differently to others and to possessions. They relate differently to food, drink and health. They search for an alternative life-style on all levels: in personal relations, as well as in their social and religious life. Their *conversio* is marked by clear, "distancing" gestures: they are against placement of nuclear missiles in the Netherlands, in Europe and in the world; they protest against exploitation of the environment; they turn away from an authoritative, male church; they reject consumerism.

This "turning away" is simultaneously a "turning towards." A "turning towards" a responsible relationship with nature; working for peace; relating more carefully to their own bodies, respecting the Source of Life. The established orders and congregations do not offer a real alternative to these modern "lay hermits." They belong too much to the established culture. Even our present-day Carmel finds itself in the position of leading an "established religious life." We will have to begin to recall our origins among the lay hermit movement if we are again to become accessible to the Proto-Carmelites of our culture.

The second phase in re-understanding the Rule brings us once more to the Carmelites who lived on Mount Carmel. The hermits on Mount Carmel were solitaries: they lived out their personal life-choice in a personal life-style. A change entered their lives when they gathered together their personal lived experiences, when their personal *conversio* was inserted into a bonded life *(oboedientia),* when they faithfully bound themselves together in community, when, together, they chose the already lived life on Mount Carmel. Next, they asked Albert of Avogadro to give them a "formula for living" *(formula vitæ)* so as to gather together their lived, religious experience, and to insert that into the messianic movement *(in obsequio Jesu Christi)* as it was taking shape in a variety of ways. They asked for a "formula for living" corresponding to their chosen and

---

[9] *Propositum* in the Prologue = *conversatio* in the Epilogue; and *ordo* in Chapter 11.

practiced way of life.[9] Albert responded to their request and gave them the "formula for living," which we later called the Rule, sometime between 1206 and 1214. He gathered the already existing life-style of the hermits into one body; he brought it together into community; he incorporated it within the broader stream of the messianic movement; he strengthened it with supportive structures and regulations.

The spiritual structure of this second phase is one of creativity. The hermits consciously rejected adopting existing "rules" or adapting to "established religious structures." Albert and the brothers followed the strengths of their 'lived life' and attempted to faithfully incorporate them, as one body, into the greater messianic movement. From a spiritual point of view this engenders a never-ending process: the individual *conversiones* gathered together into a community-*conversio,* the personal design inserted into a common design; one's own pilgrimage inserted into the great caravan following in the footsteps of Jesus. This is the dynamic meaning of *oboedientia* which Albert recommended both before all else (Chapter 1) and after all else (Chapters 17-18) to the brothers: to involve oneself totally in the community. It is not surprising that the first thirteen chapters of the Rule consider the building up of the hermit community.[10]

This second phase leads me to think that if Carmel wants to be born anew, as the first Carmel was born, then it needs to creatively search for the strengths that lie in the modern hermit life, in the Proto-Carmelites of our culture. We should not work with a pre-conceived, pre-established "Rule." We need to do the patient, handmade work of a real "prior" – a "first brother" or a "first sister" – discovering areas of unity, building community from the concrete Proto-Carmelites, inserting this community into the broader messianic movement.

The third phase in the formation of the Rule began when, around 1238, the occupants of Mount Carmel journeyed in

---

10 Cf. *Carmelite Rule,*Steggink *et al,* notes for #3-9.

groups to Europe, a process that took several decades. In Europe they were confronted with fundamental shifts within society and within church relationships. The social and economic center of gravity was shifting from rural to urban life. The urban culture developed: home-industry came into existence; city schools were founded; citizens strove for freedom of trade and possessions; city dwellers demanded political independence, as opposed to the arbitrary will of feudal lords; the citizens organized themselves into trade unions and corporations. Within this developing urban culture there immediately arose three classes: the patricians *(maiores)*, the middle class *(mediocres)*, and the skilled workers *(minores)*.

In keeping with the mendicant movement, the Carmelites engaged themselves with the *minores*. Along with them, they had chosen a critical stance towards the church: resolutely they distanced themselves from the non-evangelical practices of the higher clergy and the established monastic life. Dominic and Francis had already designed their model-for-living that gave religious form to the spiritual power of all who wanted to live Gospel lives in this new context. Fundamental elements of their model are: mendicant itinerancy *(mendicari)*, choosing the social position of the "poor," forming a community of brothers and sisters who become brothers and sisters to ordinary people *(fraternitas)*, being itinerant preachers of the Gospel in word and deed, imitating Jesus and his disciples *(vita apostolica)*. The Carmelites aligned themselves from the inside out with this mendicant movement. They recognized its spirituality from their own experience because they themselves had come forth from the aforementioned lay movement of the *eremitæ, pænitentes* and *peregrini*. Furthermore, Albert was well aware of this growing mendicant movement.

The most important structural difference between the old monastic systems and the Rule of Carmel is that the Carmelite community explicitly situated itself in the power play within church and society on the side of the poor. The already existing messianic orientation takes the shape of a socio-ecclesial stance. A democratically structured community becomes meaningful in an urban culture that has emancipated itself from feudal relationships within a feudally ruled church. That persevering lay spirituality organized a structural counterpoint against church power holders. The spiritual structure of the third phase was a process of continual, communal transformation: the community chose a structural position in the midst of the lower class people by its housing, its religious practices and its social relationships. This process of taking a stand eventually found its juridical expression in the changes Innocent IV made in the "formula for living" in 1247. Thereby the Carmelites received their official mendicant status.[11]

If Carmel wants to really pursue this third phase of her foundation-history, which found its expression in the Rule, then the Carmelite community, precisely as Carmelite community, will again have to determine its position within ecclesial/societal power structures, especially where the poor are to be found. Moreover this entails, as we shall see further on, a never ending process of solidarity.

Thus, in its coming into existence, the Rule reflects the foundation-history of the Order. 1) Lay persons distanced themselves *personally* from the established church, the established religious life and the established society. They *personally* opted for a serious and sober life. 2) On Mount Carmel they found one another in their decision to form a community which was incorporated in the messianic movement. 3) This community situated itself in the upcoming, urban culture among the lower class people, there to form a messianic community: themselves living as brothers and sisters who became "brother" and "sister" to the bottom layer of the developing culture.

From this understanding of the Rule, I will now look at the renewal process that has taken place in the Dutch Province during the past twenty years. The starting point in that process of change was, and still is, abandoning the established

---

[11] Cf. Cicconetti, *op. cit.*, 167-207. Also, *Carmelite Rule*, #5-9.

religious life. These are *personal* processes. During the Provincial Council of 1969 personal stories surfaced for the first time: it seemed that many had already taken *personal* leave of the established "Order."

The Order had become too clerical. In a certain sense we have returned to our lay stance, to our origins. This process of "distancing" moved parallel to, or sometimes was caused by, a sharpened awareness of the signs of the times. On the one hand this awareness was confirming (*e.g.*, insofar as there occurred the breakthrough to a culture-of-dialogue). On the other hand this awareness was critically "distancing" (*e.g.*, insofar as the industrial, technical culture continued to destroy human life and the environment). *Personal* choices were demanded. It was as if the first lay hermits had arrived again on Mount Carmel! There was no real cohesion. That grew only gradually. During the 1970's, one by one, dialogical communities began to take form. In mutual brother- and sisterhood they determined to place themselves in the service of the Messiah: living "around the Gospel." Gradually these communities learned to determine their position within the cultural power play, a process that is still going strong. By going through the process of becoming Carmelites ourselves, we pursued the Rule, as it were, with our own lives, and "reversed" the Rule. Its coming-into-being gave the language and the direction for our renewal process.

If read from a process orientation, I think the Rule also provides a blueprint for persons seeking affiliation with the Order. Some already live as lay hermits of Mount Carmel: these have distanced themselves from the culture, and *personally* chosen a *conversio:* they have turned towards a sober and earnest way of life. They are the brothers and sisters who, today, group themselves around "Brother B." Some of them have decided to form "community." Here we need to be careful. We need to do as Albert did: bring together the strengths of these lives, while giving form, formulation and orientation to the lives that they live. Only afterwards does the never ending process begin: the process of determining one's position within the power play of our culture, the preferential option for the poor. At the core of all this is the fact that all three aspects (*viz.*, *personal* choice, brother-sisterhood, and determining one's position), discovered *together* in their dynamic ensemble, are continually relived. Only then can one speak of a real growing-into Carmelite life, a never ending process of transformation.

2. The Rule Envisions a Process of Transformation

The second incentive that brought about a new understanding of the Rule was the slowly regained insight that spirituality envisions a process of change in which the chosen, central values touch and transform the deepest layers of the person. Much of spirituality existed in the fact that the basic values of Carmelite life were only accepted cognitively. One harbored a "perfect" value system, but a closer look revealed it to be only a "veneer" poured over one's personhood. One had not struggled with it, as had Jacob with the angel. One did not carry the scars on his body; it remained external.

It is essential for spirituality that the basic values become flesh and blood, entering into the deeper psychic layers of the person.

> It is not only the content of a spirituality which is important, but also the way it is given shape in life. In other words, spirituality is really to be the deepest reality out of which a person lives, the life-model offered is to be internalized completely. It is not sufficient that the 'truth' and 'value' of the content are assented to intellectually, anymore than that the person's outer actions are adapted to the requirements of this spirituality.[12]

The concern of spirituality is that the basic inspiration works so deeply into the kernel of my being that it transforms

---

[12] Hein Blommestijn, "Spiritualiteit en hoe je jezelf kunt bedriegen," *Speling* 29 (1977), 99-114.

my actions from the inside out, creating new forms. Only thus can "central values" work deeply into my being, and vice versa: only thus can my unique contribution further these central values.

Whenever I read the Rule again from this regained, new insight, I begin to see that the purpose of the Rule is not really aimed at bringing about the formulation of a value system. That value system has already been determined, in a certain sense, for "everyone, to whatever state of life he may belong or in whatever form of dedicated life he may have chosen."[13] One has to "live in the footsteps of Jesus." But that, strictly speaking, is not the Rule. Albert takes us further after this general orientation: "But since you ask us to give you a formula for living in accordance with your way of life, to which you are to hold fast from now on *(propositum)*, we ordain..." Then follows the Rule, or rather, the "formula for living."

Albert wants to provide a formula for living by which the already-chosen way of life can be permanently exercised. He wants to articulate a process of transformation which precisely stimulates, orients and structures the practices already chosen by the hermits. As he says at the end of the Rule: "These things we have briefly written to you, thus laying down for you a formula according to which you are to live." A dynamic way of reading this Rule brings us closer, I think, to the very purposes of Albert. I want to highlight this with three passages from the Rule. They have been chosen so as to present once again, and more deeply, the aforeoutlined area of tension: *personal* decision, community building, and cultural positioning.

1. The first passage that has begun to speak anew is Chapter 14. In it one talks of the armor of God: Carmelites must make an effort *(studeatis)* to clothe themselves with the "armor of God" *(indui armatura Dei)* with the greatest care, to accept it as their new form. The basic symbol of the armor will now be

---

13 Prologue.

further elaborated in the various symbols. To begin with: "Your *loins* are to be cinctured with the *girdle of chastity*." The loins are the symbol of our human needs. These deeper layers, where our needs and desires move, have to be purified. The Rule does *not* ask that we "retain purity," but that we *become purified* unto the deepest levels of our emotions. The Rule continues: "Your *breast* (must be) fortified by *reverent reflections*." The breast is the seat of the most contradictory emotions: anger, jealousy, excitement, calculation – but also, tenderness, respect and true compassion. The Rule wants us to clothe ourselves with the breastplate of selflessness, of purified intentions. Furthermore, our spontaneous defense mechanisms, our "harness," our "shield" and our "helmet," must be transformed into "justice in love", "trust" and "liberation." Apparently it is possible to be armed with egocentrism, distrust, oppression. The Rule envisions a transformation process: to transform our defense mechanisms in order to be disarmed and to become dis-arming. Finally, our offensive weapon – the "sword" – needs to be transformed by continual intimacy with scripture.

What do I learn from such a passage? I learn that the Rule does not want to place upon me a "value system" that is designed for me, as it were, from the outside. It wants me to *become* that value system; that I really clothe myself with it *(indui)*, that it become *part of me*: unto my loins, unto my breast, unto my aggressions, unto my defense mechanisms.

The *personal* choice of the hermit now appears to have been a first step on a never ending road: to allow my total personality to be transformed by God. It is God with whom I have to be clothed, through whom I am to be purified, directed and transformed into justice, love, trust and liberation. I am to allow divine "patterns" to enter my person, so that they give orientation to all my activities from the inside out.

If I look back upon our lives with this in mind, then I see the importance of training directed towards the deeper layers of the person: intensive spiritual direction, counselling and personal therapy; retreats, personality training, ongoing formation, etc. All these means call for patient handiwork: to allow our "value system" to really enter into the deeper layers of our person.

2. The second passage that has begun to speak anew is Chapter 11, in which Albert advises us to discuss weekly "the preservation of your life together and the well-being of the individuals." Already in the first monastic rules there is a format for religious dialogue (the *collatio*). These "conversations" form a definite framework within which religious life and community life are deepened and, if necessary, corrected. In the words of the Rule: "Excesses and shortcomings of the brothers, if these be found in anyone, should be corrected with becoming charity."

The first Carmelites apparently operated from the assumption that "life together" (community building) and "personal well-being" needed to be *preserved*. Therefore they gathered together weekly. Probably the critical questions were: Is our community *still* a sacrament of the Reign of God? Is our messianic character *still* visible? Is the Eucharist *still* a true expression of the breaking and sharing? The one who says that the community needs to be "preserved" is completely aware of its vulnerability. Albert knows that a community is a living organism, prone to decline and to disintegration. Community is never finished!

The one who "preserves" acts as a shepherd or as a breeder, envisioning growth, taking no satisfaction in the actual manifestation and the beautiful appearance, but always raising up possibilities and searching for authenticity. Those who "preserve" know that religious community is a vulnerable and continually threatened ensemble of structures and personalities. Those who "preserve" know that the concern is to become community, to grow towards community from week to week.

What counts for the community, counts for the individual person as well. The Rule wants the full growth of the person, the freed wholeness of the psyche *(salus animarum),* to be the object of dialogue. Am I still going the way of continuous transformation into God without exaggerating or weakening? The one who speaks about well-being – the essential liberation of persons – reveals a knowledge of our vulnerable psychic structure, of our broken entity, of a possibility of hardening to the core of our being. Well-being, wholeness and liberation are not products of nature! They need to be freed, in a continual wrestling, from our psychic structures.

This concern for the life of the community, and for the liberation of the person, is being practised in a number of dialogical communities which have grown up within our province since 1972. At this moment about ten of these dialogical communities exist. In these communities life together and the growth of each individual is carefully discussed by means of "facilitated conversation," through common meditation on Scripture, in days of reflection, in house meetings and in weekly exchanges. This dialogical life-style determines also the manner in which we, on a provincial level, speak with one another about the well-being of persons, of groups and of our province.

3. The third passage that began to speak anew is Chapter 3, the "added chapter" about dwelling places. When the Carmelites were still in the Holy Land, they chose to abide in solitude, in places often difficult to reach. However, when the Carmelites returned to Europe and took up the mendicant way of life, their place was thereby already given to them: with the poor. This change in the way of life is expressed in Chapter 3, approved by Innocent IV in 1247. In an earlier letter from Innocent we learn of the motive behind this addition. The Carmelites wanted to live in such a way as to "serve, not only themselves, but their neighbor." As was mentioned before, the passage towards a mendicant way of life meant openly determining one's position within the developing urban culture. The Carmelites left their position of community-in-solitude (the wilderness) and consciously situated themselves among the poor in the developing urban culture so as to be accessible to ordinary people in their need.

This change in position of the community as a whole is also reflected in the other alterations made by Pope Innocent.[14] These can be summarized as: the community of brothers (and sisters) expresses in word and deed the brotherhood (and sisterhood) of all people; it does that not by demanding or dictating, but through begging, asking, receiving and being available to the most ordinary city dwellers.

Whenever I reflect on this additional chapter concerning our dwelling places, I am confronted with the tension between the group itself choosing the place to live in solitude, and allowing the place where one is to live to be "determined," to have a place "be given," to have a place "appointed." This tension is inherent in our lives. On the one hand, we ourselves, are choosing where to live; on the other hand, we have our place appointed by the poor (in the urban culture). In other words: to choose our position from out of the group, or to allow our position to be determined by the needs of the poor. This tension involved a process of transformation for the first generations of mendicant Carmelites: from a community that determined its own place in solitude to a community that received a place within the cultural power structure of an urban community among the poor.

There is a comparable transformation process occurring, not without great tension, within our own province, just as it is in the whole Order. There is a powerful movement afoot! I point only to our Filipino brothers and the related Filipino groups in the Netherlands, who emphatically see that our place within our capitalistic culture must be the position of the poor. For them it is the Lord himself who, through the poor, gives them their *place.* A "place" here includes the whole architecture of our life: housing, life-style, use of possessions, relationships, etc.

If I view this tension (between determining my own place and having my place appointed) from the perspective of trans-

---

14 Cf. Chapters 2, 4, 9 and 13.

formation, then I mean to say that each moment – even if I live among the poorest of the poor! – I have to allow my "chosen position" to be transformed into my "received position." The one who says, "This is my place," overestimates him/herself and gambles away the mendicant spirit. We go back to a place "in solitude." "The way chose me," said Dag Hammerskjold. That meant for him that the call, "Farther!" forced him at each moment to leave the "known patterns" and his own initiatives. To make our "home" *(domus)* as community among the poor calls for a continual transformation: our "home" is more and more open to others; our possessions are seen as "begged;" we are made more and more into "brother" and "sister" by others. We change from place to place *(mutatio loci)* because we are moved by others!

3. The Rule: A Mystical Way

It may seem strange that I connect the Rule with mystical processes. Yet this connection is less arbitrary than it may appear at first glance. Mystical processes concern a dynamic transformation that is so profound as to completely transform the inmost core of the person through the central symbol that has permeated one's life: through God, or whatever name we give to the One who is all-transcendent/immanent. Being touched and transformed by God is so overwhelming that it appears to the consciousness of the mystic that absolutely nothing of one's earlier life survives.

When looking at the Rule from the perspective of this mystical transformation, one does not necessarily look for the word "mystical." The Rule can very well envision a mystical transformation without using the word "mystical" or "contemplation." The question rather is: Does the Rule envision a dynamic transformation that operates so profoundly that the core of one's being is completely and radically transformed by God in such a way that one lives out from God? When I attune myself to the Rule in this way, I begin to see its mystical power of expression and discover its mystical orientation. Here one will discover the central value of the Rule. I want to illustrate this approach with two passages from the Rule.

1. The first passage is the well known chapter 7: "Let each one remain in his own living quarters or nearby, pondering day and night the Word of the Lord, keeping vigilant in prayer, unless engaged in other lawful occupations." I want to concentrate on the core of this passage: "*pondering* day and night on the Word of the Lord." These words have been taken from Psalm 1. In the context of the Psalm and against the background of the time in which it was written,[15] *meditari* (*hagah* in Hebrew) points to a process of mystical transformation. One "murmured" the Torah, "ruminating" it until the text had completely become own's own, and began to "sigh from within" as the cooing of a dove. One made the Torah his own bodily, emotionally, cognitively, memorizing it so that he ultimately became one with Torah. One motive for this was not simply the holiness of Torah. One experienced this transformation so as to become one with the One who forms the "Be-ing" of Torah: Yahweh, the Lord.

In clothing oneself with Torah at all levels of existence, more intimately than one's own body can, one becomes, as it were, Torah oneself, and thereby "language of God," "body of God." *In lege Domini meditantes* means: allowing oneself to be clothed with his Word, so as to be clothed by him, to become his language until he speaks in the individual from the inside out. This Torah-mysticism, retained unbroken in the Jewish mystical tradition up to Hassidism, remained alive within Christianity until far into the Middle Ages. For persons in the Middle Ages, meditation was not one or other abstract form of prayer. They meditated with the whole person. They read the text with their whole existence: murmured it aloud, learned it by heart, deliberated with their understanding, and with their

---

[15] Cf. Kees Waaijman, O. Carm., *Psalmen bij het zoeken van de weg.* (Kamoen, 1982), pp. 8-18.

will ready for action. "In this manner, meditation absorbed the whole individual and planted scripture in the whole person."[16] Meditation is not only saying the Psalms, but saying and saying them until their power of expression speaks precisely in my saying them. A love experience wherein my activity (speaking, reflecting, considering) is transformed into a deep passivity: it is not I who speak, but he speaks in me. Thus, meditation is not just the study of scripture in order to be able to help the faithful by teaching and preaching.[17] It is primarily a mystical transformation in God.

2. The second passage I want to speak about in relation to this theme of the Rule from the perspective of mystical transformation is the chapter about silence, Chapter 16. If you read this text carefully, several times, you will notice that the *silentium* functions on various levels in the Rule. The most tangible level is the nightly quiet *(silentium nocturnum; silentium summum).* Here "silence" suggests an *atmosphere of rest and quiet.* All noise is to be avoided. This atmosphere of rest and quiet must also be preserved as much as possible during the day *(silentium diurnum).*

However, *silentium diurnum* brings forth a second level of meaning: silence during the day serves not only to create an atmosphere of rest and quiet in the physical sense, but it fosters a manner of relating with one another, creating an atmosphere of respect within the community, an atmosphere in which each person can come to his or her rights. This level of *silentium* envisions a culture of justice, of respect among us *(cultus justitiæ). Silentium* is broken wherever one opens wide the door for injustice, whenever one offends others and, thus, oneself. *Silentium* forms an attitude of caution and respect.

When this attitude has permeated one's activities, then we come upon the third level: one's actions are stilled; stillness is the soul of my behavior. Certain statements, especially from

---

16 Cicconetti, *op. cit.,* pp. 309-310.

17 So Thomas Aquinas held.

Isaiah, call this level to mind. They point to a stillness that forms the inner side of work: patient and stable activity, not short of breath, but carried on by the deep breath of Yahweh himself. Having come to an inner rest, all our activities are permeated with intense concern for one another, for the future and for remaining soberly true to one another.[18]

This third level of a completely internalized *silentium* takes us, finally, to the mystical level: *"In silentio et spe erit fortitudo vestra."*[19]

To comprehend the real meaning of this reference to Isaiah, we need to recall the dynamic structure of biblical "stillness," *doemia.*[20] Biblical *doemia* covers a whole process. *Doemia* primarily means the "deep shock" that comes from being taken by an overwhelming experience. One is petrified, struck dumb. Next, *doemia* is a consciously held silence to enable one to come to own the shock, silence as a means of processing shock. One works with this overwhelming experience, accepts it, interiorizes it. One practices this silence so as to allow the shocking experience to enter more deeply. Finally this *doemia* becomes "stillness:" a quiet outlook, a quiet awaiting. This is the essential, inner side of silence.

This is the fourth mystical phase. Silence is totally interiorized: I am merely "watchfulness" in the night, sensitivity for the other, discerning that which is different, quiet attention for the amazing fact of life, for that ever surprising event. I become simply an eye, an ear, an open being: awaiting. It is this mystical stage that Isaiah has in mind with his *silentium et spes:* silently expecting, quiet that is only awaiting. This process of quieting is a mystical process because the all-overwhelming experience was caused by Yahweh himself. He upsets us with his incomprehensible presence. Quiet inter-

---

18 Cf. Is 30.

19 Is 32:17

20 Kees Waaijman, *De profeet Elia.* (Nijmegen, 1985), pp. 67-68. Cf. *A Hebrew and English Lexicon of the Old Testament,* ed. by F. Brown, S. R. Driver, C.A. Briggs. (Oxford: Clarendon Press, 1953), pp. 198-199.

iorizes this "still-shocking" presence: a quiet that finds its flowering in a pure reaching-out-towards-him; becoming quiet because of him, and finding therein only quieting. Becoming quieted by being-desire only. This naked ecstasy (the only way to union with him) is experienced and intensely verbalized by our mystics, John of the Cross and John of St Sampson. They saw that the very core of *silentium* is quiet, as completely lived-through detachment; as pure and essential love, as "the night that unites the lover with the belovèd." It is this "quiet" that constantly transforms our actions from within to selflessness, justice and respectful patience. It is this "quiet" which flowers into justice among our brothers and sisters. It is this "quiet" which truly fills the quiet of the night.

Conclusion

I have brought forth the mystical dimension of the Rule by using these two passages. They are only two paradigms. Whoever reads the Rule in this way will never finish discovering unexpected aspects of it. The confrontation with the Rule is only just now starting. New aspects, which transcend the Rule as a formula or as a model, are continually being discovered. "Living in the footsteps of Jesus" (Prologue), "a dedicated life in Christ" (Chapter 14), now come to mean: becoming totally transformed in God, allowing oneself to be so disarmed as to be clothed only with God.

The "chastened heart" of the Prologue calls to mind the Beatitudes: "They shall see God." For God has "planted his eye in our heart."[21] Moreover, to restrict oneself (through fasting, abstaining from meat, silence) no longer signifies "being stuck" in mortification, but becomes a symbol of the annihilation of each and every external foothold. Vigilance in prayer (Chapter 7) turns into quietly watching in the night, without a

---

21 Sir 17:8.

foothold. This watching, which is night itself, is "more than necessary" *(supererogaverit).* In mystical transformation the Rule itself is transcended for its own completion: we lose all footholds so that he can give us a place. Yes! He is our "place" and we are beggars. We beg for him, the Fountain of our life.

Those who know how to say the canonical hours ... should say them according to the pratice of the holy fathers and the approved usage of the Church ...

Chapel
Mount Carmel Spiritual Centre
Niagara Falls, Ontario

4

WHAT IS THE HEART OF THE RULE?

Bruno Secondin, O. Carm.

More than seventy commentaries on the Rule are known.[1] Practically all of them consider Chapter 7 to be the central nucleus of the text, and of the way of life it proposes. It reads: "Let all remain in their cells or nearby, pondering day and night the Law of the Lord and being vigilant in prayer, unless engaged in other lawful occupations"*(Maneant singuli in cellulis suis, vel iuxta eas, die ac nocte in lege Domini meditantes et in orationibus vigilantes, nisi aliis iustis occasionibus occupentur.)* At least implicity the current Constitutions of the Order retain this position (cf. nos. 10 and 59). One can, therefore, speak of a traditional and almost universal conviction about what constitutes the "heart" of the Rule.

Only recently have doubts begun to be expressed about the centrality of Chapter 7.[2] Egidio Palumbo, a young Carmelite

---

1 See Joachim Smet, "A list of Commentaries on the Carmelite Rule," in *The Sword*, 11 (1947), 297-302. See, also: A Martino, "Il commento alla Regola nel Carmelo antico," in *Eph. Carm.*, 2 (1948), 99-122; Victor of Jesus Mary, "La exposición canónico-moral de la Regla carmelitana según los commentadores Descalzos," in *Eph. Carm.*, 2 (1948), 123-203; Egidio Palumbo, *Letture della Regola del Carmelo*, Thesis ad Lecentiam, Claretianum, Pontificia Universitas Lateranensis, Roma, 1983.

2 The numbering used throughout is that found in the Vatican registers which

who has studied commentaries on the Rule from the varlous centuries, writes:

> We have to ask ourselves if the centrality of Chapter 7 is a "necessity" arising from the text of the Rule, or whether it is a subjective understanding on the part of the reader who is conditioned by the idea of the perfection of Christian life as seen in its solitary and eremitical forms. The history of the interpretations of the Rule does show one fact: when the centrality of Chapter 7 shut out other "truths" of the text, which did not belong to the subjective vision of the reader, this preconditioning was changed into a prejudice and the reading of the Rule became restricted and static.[3]

We are convinced that the centrality of Chapter 7—especially as it is understood in the tradition as emphasizing solitude and prayer—has to be profoundly rethought and transcended. According to recent Italian studies, the center of the Rule's way-of-life is to be found in the group of chapters from seven to eleven, with Chapter 10 (the oratory and daily Eucharist) being the theological and central focus. The Rule does not refer principally to isolated persons praying in their cells, but rather to a *fraternity*; that is, a group of "brothers" who are totally committed to a journey in unity, in co-responsibility, and in dedication to the Lord, even though they may have different backgrounds and personal needs.

Here then is our topic and what we wish to illustrate and demonstrate today.

I. The Road to the New Interpretation

Working from 1981 to 1983 a group of Italian experts brought forward a new interpretation of the Rule. They sought

---

begin with the Prologue, then proceed to Chapters 1 - 18, and then concludes with the Epilogue. This notion is central to the symbol employed throughout this article.

3 E. Palumbo, "Letture della Regola lungo i secoli," in *La Regola del Carmelo oggi*, (Bruno Secondin (ed.), Roma: Institutum Carmelitanum, 1983), p. 165.

an interpretation that would be truly based on its text and on its historical origins. They wished to respect fully the intrinsic unity of the text as well as all of its individual parts, even fragments that might seem banal or secondary. They used the new hermeneutic methods available from the disciplines of anthropology, history, linguistics and theology.[4]

They did not begin with the idea of finding a confirmation of some pre-construed meaning; however the traditional assertions about Chapter 7 were not taken as an absolute. The aim was to recover the vital *logos* contained in the text, even if this were not always explicitly expressed. It was only in this way that one could hope to rescue the Rule from being a quasi-archeological, lifeless curio—the state to which it had been finally reduced—so that it could once again be the bearer of a vital and inspirational vision as well as of fresh impulses, always open to new historical realizations.

It is of the nature of a *Rule* that it condenses and organises in its language, structures and intellectual framework of a particular epoch, a way of life that is destined to motivate later generations which are historically and culturally quite distinct from those of its origins. The richness and fruitfulness of a *Rule* are to be found more in the power of its vision, in its capacity to show direction, and values, than in its restrictions through norms or rigid forms. The interpretation of a *Rule* should have the ability to invigorate its hearers so that the written words be transformed into a source of new undertak-

---

[4] The results have been presented in the following works: B. Secondin, *La Regola del Carmelo: Per una nuova interpretazione,* (Roma: Edizioni Institutum Carmelitanum, 1982; Spanish ed.: Madrid: Libreria carmelitana, 1983); *La Regola del Carmelo oggi,* (B. Secondin, ed., (Rome: Institutum Carmelitanum, 1983); *Un proyecto de vita: La regla del Carmelo hoy,* B. Secondin *et. ali,* eds. (Madrid: Ed. Paulinas,1985); B. Secondin, ed., *Profeti de fraternità, Per una nuova visione della spiritualità carmelitana,* (Bologna: Ed. Dehoniane,1985, in particular pp. 67-101). Also forming a part of the work accomplished in these years: Michael Brundell, *"Vivere in Christo:" Biblical Spirituality in the Rule of Saint Albert of Jerusalem,* (Thesis ad Licentiam, Pontificia Universitas Gregoriana, Roma 1982); V. Mosca, *Profilo storico di Alberto patriarca di Gerusalemme,* (Thesis ad Licentiam, Pontificia Universitas Gregoriana, Roma 1983)

ings which enshrine the vital *logos* which lies hidden in the text.[5]

Such richness seemed lost or very weakened in the recent history of the Order, notwithstanding efforts at new critical and systematic reflection on the Rule. There have been investigations of various kinds: historical-juridical studies[6] examined its nature and meaning in the context of the crusades, and its similarity to the monastic tradition of the Desert Fathers;[7] it has been scrutinized in relation to the eastern monastic tradition;[8] the reasons for the mitigations have been carefully explored,[9] along with the "Teresian" interpretation of the "Primitive Rule."[10] But none of these studies has given rise to any new inspiration. They have, indeed, extended our historical and empirical knowledge. They have left unsatisfied, however, any desire for a dynamic, visionary or vital reading

---

[5] Cf. D. Rees *et al.*, *Consider Your Call, A Theology of Monastic Life Today*, (London: 1978; esp. pp. 43-56). Some other interesting ideas are found in the article "Regola/Regole," in *Dizionario degli Istituti di Perfezione*, vol. 7 (Roma: Ed. Paoline, 1984, 1410 - 1617); cf. also A. De Vogüé, "*Sub regula vel abbate: Étude sur la signification théologique des règles monastiques anciennes,*" in *Coll. Cist.* 37 (1971), 209-241.

[6] For example, the studies of Elias Friedman,O.C.D., *The Latin Hermits of Mount Carmel, A Study in Carmelite Origins*, (Rome: Institutum Historicum Teresianum, 1979); C. Cicconetti, *La Regola del Carmelo: Origine, natura, significato*, (Roma: Institutum Carmelitanum, 1973; English tr. *The Rule of Carmel*, Darien: 1984); Ambrosius a S. TERESIA, "Untersuchungen über Verfasser, Abfassungszeit, Quellen und Bestätigung der Karmeliter-Regel", in *Eph. Carm.* 2 (1948), 17-48.

[7] This is one of the characteristics of the Dutch commentary. *Carmelite Rule*, (Introduction, translation into Dutch and annotations by O. Steggink, J. Tigcheler, K. Waijman; trans. into English by Th. Vrakking in collaboration with J. Smet; Almelo, 1979).

[8] Soeur Eliane, O.C.D, "La Règle du Carmel et la tradition monastique orientale," in *Carmel* 8 (1974), 354-372; Soeur Eliane (Orthodox), "La Règle du Carmel. Points communs et differences avec le monachisme orthodoxe", in *Carmel* 14 (1980), 221-231.

[9] Ludovico Saggi, "Mitigazione del 1432 della Regola carmelitana. Tempo e persone," in *Carmelus* 5 (1958), 3-29.

[10] P. Garrido, *El hogar espiritual de Santa Teresa*, (Institutum Carmelitanum, Roma, 1983); L. Saggi, "Santa Teresa de Jesus y la 'Regula primitiva,'" in *Un proyecto de vida*, pp. 133-147; L. Saggi, *Le origini dei carmelitani scalzi: 1567 - 1593, storia e storiografia*, (Institutum Carmelitanum, Roma 1986): T. Alvarez, "Nuestra 'Regla del Carmen' en el pensamiento de Santa Teresa," in *Un proyecto de vida*, pp. 148-163.

that would do justice to the text itself, taken as a whole, or answer the needs and sensibilities of our time.[11]

1. Unity and Stabilization of the Text

Let us consider, then, the way in which the Italian group set about its task. The members first sought to discover the unifying inner principles of the various parts of the text. It would be a faulty reading of the text which would focus attention only on some chapters (for example 7, 14, 16) and, as a result, would minimize or ignore the value of the remainder, or reduce it to incidentals. This latter way of interpreting the Rule does violence to the unity of the living experience which predated the work of legislation. Codification is added to this unity which furnishes the vital foundation for the work of legislation. The presence of several experiential *stages*[12] in the internal composition of the Rule led us to study the dynamic of this accumulation in order to get a sense of the *whole*, rather than a mere historical illustration of the reasons for the different strata of the text.

The current theology of charism[13] guided us in our reading.

---

[11] The following were generous but incomplete attempts: Kilian Healy, "The Carmelite Rule after Vatican II", in *Analecta O. Carm.*, 29 (1981); 31-52. Stephano Possanzini, *La Regola dei Carmelitani: Storia e Spiritualità*, (Florence, 1979). Carlos Mesters, "Fundamentação biblica de espirituadidade carmelitana," in *Carmelus*, 26 (1978), 77-100. V. Wilderink, "Compromisso carmelitano na Igreja de America latina," in *ibid.*, 12-49. Also lacking this sense of vital inspiration is the work of J. Jantsch and C. Butterweck, *Die Regel des Karmel: Geschichte und Gegenwart einer Lebensnorm*, (Afchaffenburg: Kaffke, 1986).

[12] A synthetic presentation of these stages is to be found in D. Lombardo, "Gli strati del testo e loro significato," in *La Regola del Carmelo oggi*, pp. 151-156.

[13] Cf. *Il carisma della vita religiosa , dono dello Spirito alla Chiesa per il mondo*, (Milan: Ed. Ancora, 1981). *Carisma e istituzione: Lo Spirito interroga i religiosi*, (Rome: Ed. Rogate, 1983). F. Ciardi, *I fondatori uomini dello Spirito: Per una teologia del carisma di fondatore.* (Rome: Città Nuova, 1982). B. Levesque, "L'ordre religieux comme project rêvé: outopie et/ou secte?" *ArchScSocRel* 41 (1976), 77-108.

Moreover, the way a charismatic impulse matures gave us the key to the unity of the text. The theology of charism shows that a text like the Rule is the result of a genetic and evolving process which begins from a stage of birth (*statu nascenti*) in which it is indeterminate and unexpressed. It then passes through the stage of being a "lived identity," though not yet codified. There follows an organic elaboration of the principal elements of the identity. Finally, there is a definitive, mature and conclusive stabilization of the genetic process. A sign and fruit of the stabilization is a definitive *official text,* which is called a rule, constitutions, statutes etc. Today this thesis or explanation is quite clear and developed. It can explain the process that takes place when isolated persons, or small units of persons, move to establish themselves as a religious group and attain a collective consciousness of an identity that is preserved in a definite form and authoritatively acknowledged. This is the genesis of religious institutes, and also the key to understanding their foundation history—from the initial birth-pangs to the clear and definitive identity, canonically recognised.[14]

In our case the application is clear. The global way of life of the Rule is to be read in the *final stage* of its evolution and clarification, that is, in the form we call "institutionalized." In fact, the Carmelite Rule gathers together, expresses and codifies a reality which reached its definitive and stable form only in 1247 with the approbation of Innocent IV. There is evidence of earlier phases in the text: directly or indirectly, expressly or in its aims, symbolically or structurally, the text testifies to intermediate stages in a process of maturation. These phases cannot be considered as a "more perfect form" of its identity.

More must, I think, be said. When one speaks about the different versions of Albert and of Innocent IV, as if it were a

---

[14] Cf. F. Alberoni, *Movement and Institution.* (New York, 1984). L. Moulin, "Pour une sociologie des ordres religiuex," in *Social Compass,* 10 (1963), 145-170; L. Cada, *Shaping the Coming Age of Religious Life,* (New York: Seabury Press, 1979).

matter of some "loss of rigor" or of some *process of mitigation*, one is clearly superimposing on the historical facts some deeply held ideological positions which have neither historical nor theological foundation.[15] The intervention of Albert is undoubtedly most important, but it is *a stage* in the transition towards full identity.

Albert had three roles: 1) He had a *social* role, in so far as he united in one association *(in unum collegium)*, now juridically autonomous, a group which hitherto recognised **B**[rocardus] as leader, but without the necessary legal requirements. 2) He had a *cognitive* role, in that he gave the group's existence a rational structure. He enriched it with symbolism; that is, he pointed out and codified an aim which went beyond the merely visible, material facts. 3) He had a role of *affective orientation*, because in using the word "brothers" *(fratres)*, he channeled the feelings of the "hermits" in the direction of a warm, shared fraternity. In other words, through Albert the *ethos*, which had been lived without organic thematization, assumed a nature as well as institutional, linguistic and symbolic forms which were allied to the social and ecclesial needs of the time.

After Albert there came the return of part of the members to Europe. They faced the immediate difficulty of an ecclesial situation in which new forms of institutionalized presence were emerging. Events showed, then, that the process was not complete and that the (Albertine) Rule did not yet correspond fully with the needs of the group's life. At the instigation of those who were now "Carmelites," acting through a discernment process at the highest level (general chapters), the popes successively revised the text and its interpretation which had not yet reached mature form. This last arrived with the defini-

---

15 See, for example, the inexact statement about the various "Rules" (Albertine, Innocentian, Eugenian) by T. Alvares, "Nuestra 'Regla del Carmen' en el pensamiento de santa Teresa" in *Un proyecto de vida;* pp. 148-63, especially pp. 154 ff. A different vision in found in L. Saggi, *Le origini dei Carmelitani scalzi*, pp. 10-33. Also of interest is O. Steggink, *Arraigo e innovación*. (Madrid, 1976).

tive text in the bull *Quæ honorem Conditoris* of Innocent IV, on October 1, 1247.[16]

Perhaps providentially, editions of the text before 1247 have been lost. Later reconstructions of the Albertine formula (the so-called "Primitive Rule") from the middle of the 14th century are hypotheses which are reasonably founded, but lacking in full historical certainty. The literature on the "Primitive Rule,"[17] and attempts to return to the primitive model as the authentic one, must today be seriously demythologized, and thus refuted as being historically uncertain and theologically misleading.

This is the first path of research which we followed. It can be seen to be quite new and revolutionary when compared with existing models of interpretation. Furthermore, this way of approaching the Rule has the possibility of ending the complexes about primitivism and mitigationism that color relations between the O. Carm. and O.C.D. branches of the Order.[18]

2. The Rule: From Process to Way of Life

The demand for a global unity of the text led us, secondly, to distinguish in the Carmelite Rule between the traces of a *process* to a collective, codified and stable indentity, and the way of life (project) which the rule codifies and transmits. Thus we began to speak of the *Rule as process* and of the *Rule as project* or *way of life.*

---

16 A color reproduction of the text, preserved in the Archivio Segreto Vaticano, *Reg. Vat.* 21, ff. 465^{v}-466^{r} is to be found after page xxi. A complete history of the bull is found in Carlo Cicconetti, *The Rule of Carmel,* chapter 7.

17 This is to be found in Philip Ribot's anthology (dated about 1379), *Decem libri de institutione et peculiaribus gestis religiosorum carmelitarum,* in the *Epistola Cyrilli,* ch. 3. We have published the "Albertine redaction" presented there, taking the text from the most authoritative manuscript, *MS 779,* Bibliothèque de l'Arsenal, Paris, ff. 57v-59r, in *La Regola del Carmelo: Per una nuova interpretazione,* pp. 91-97.

18 This is a chapter of history which one hopes has now been transcended. For the actual situation Cf. "Le mitigazioni oggi," in *La Regola del Carmelo oggi,* pp. 272-279.

In the technical language of linguistics, "codification" is a second degree language (a meta-language); it is an *objectifying discourse* marked by a historicity that is bound up with existing conceptualization. Though it serves to explicate profound experiences and vital meanings, "codification" cannot either explain or reveal them fully. For an exact interpretation of a text like the Rule it is precisely these vital meanings that have to be recovered, so that fidelity to them can in the future give rise to new, existential forms of life.

To grasp this project we made abundant use of different interpretative schemata that are provided by the various hermeneutical theories of our time, such as cultural anthropology, collective imagination, linguistics, the function of symbol, myth and culture, the history and sociology of institutions, the role of models and utopias etc.[19] There was, naturally, a special place for a knowledge of the history of spirituality, of the monastic traditions of the time, for the symbolism of the crusades and for the inspirational force of the movements of evangelism and of the Christocentric eremitism of the 12th and 13th centuries.[20]

---

19 Among the many titles that exist we mention the following: Paul Ricoeur, *The Conflict of Interpretations.* (Evanston, 1974). Also his book *The Rule of Metaphor,* (Toronto, 1977). I. Barbour, *Myths, Models and Paradigms,* (London, 1974). C.A. Bernard, *Teologia simbolica,* (Rome, 1981). G. Durand, *Les structures anthropologiques de l'imaginaire.* Ernst Cassirer, *Symbol, Myth and Culture: Essays and Lectures of Ernst Cassirer, 1935-1945,* (New Haven: Yale University Press, 1979). Umberto Eco, *Trattato di semiotica generale,* (2nd ed., Milan: Bompiani, 1984). E. Goffman, *The Presentation of Self in Everyday Life,* (New York, 1959). E. Ortigues, *Le discours et le symbole.* (Paris: Aubier, 1962). J. Trabant, *Elementi di semiotica.* (Napoli: Liguori, 1980). V. and E. Turner, *Image and Pilgrimage in Christian Culture.* (New York: Columbia University Press, 1978).

20 *L'eremitismo in Occidente nei secoli XI e XII,* (Atti della 2ª Settimana internazionale di studio, Mendola, 1961, Milan: Università Cattolica del S. Cuore, 1965). *Istituzioni monastiche e istituzioni canonicali in Occidente (1123-1215),* (Atti della 7ª Settimana internazionale di Studio, Mendola, 28 August-3 September, 1977, Milan, 1980). Jacobus de Vitriaco [Jacques de Vitry], *Historia orientalis,* in J. Bongars (ed.), *Gesta Dei per Francos,* (Hanover, 1611). G. Fedlato, *Perché le crociate: Saggio interpretativo,* (Bologna: Ed. Patron, 1980). H. Grundmann, *Movimenti religiosi nel medioevo,* (Bologna: Ed. Il Mulino, 1975). M. Cohn, *The Discovery of the Individual, 1050-1200,* (Church History Outlines 5; London: SPCK, 1972). R. Pernoud, *Les hommes de la croisade,* (Paris: Fayard-Tallandier, 1982). J. Prawler, *Histoire du royaume latin de Jerusalem,* (2 vols., Paris: CNRS, 1975). A. Vaucher, *La spiritualité du moyen âge occidental,* (Paris, 1975).

It is particularly useful to hold together the various hermeneutical elements of a text. By this I mean: 1) the multiple experiences of Albert and of the group; 2) the legislation that was ordered to the way of life (the project); 3) the fact that the Rule was given in the literary genre of a letter; 4) the active reception of the rule by the brethren; 5) the decoding of what is signified by signs; and 6) the open and dynamic process of identification. This work was very extensive and very complex. We had to grasp exactly the single project of life which itself was the fruit of various personal and collective experiences. All this is condensed in a single text which is quite limited by its style and development, by its background and subjective exponents.

In fact, we tried various hypotheses for a unified reading. Our concern here was that the hypotheses would have the capacity to retain their interpretative value throughout the various historical levels of the text, and the different collective and ecclesial situations of those involved in the project. Many of the classical interpretations give the impression of being *ideologically superimposed* on the text. This goes for the eremitical interpretation, as well as for the symbolic (prophetical/Marian), historico-juridical and ascetical ones. These restrict the meaning to a few isolated elements which are then partial truths. The rest is emasculated and rendered insignificant.

Not many people take into consideration the fact that an obstacle to correct interpretation is the traditional way of dividing the Rule into short chapters (eighteen altogether, along with a prologue and an epilogue). Even the titles which were given to these chapters are a secondary element, and are in fact misleading when one attempts to understand the structure of the text, its literal meaning and the thrust of its words. These headings reflect a juridical preoccupation, even in the way they are formulated. They encourage a fragmentary, moralistic and legalistic reading of the Rule. They are a categorization much later than the origin of the Rule, to be precise from the 16th century

(1585).[21] Since they reflect a canonico-legalistic mentality, they can with profit be set aside and rejected in favor of other titles that are more faithful to the text and more inspirational.

By avoiding a preoccupation with the old titles and the subdivision into chapters, we were able not only to find new titles but also to bring to light deeper unities between groups of chapters, which then became an instrument for a new interpretation of the text. (See the proposal in *Figure l.*) This is the general scheme we adopted: we respected the subdivision in chapters as it was well-known and easily perceived; we gave new titles, which are for the most part renewed translations of the older ones; we blocked various chapters in sections.

3. A Central Nucleus as Heart of the Rule

From this work a central nucleus appeared which is comprised of Chapters 7 to 11. In it we find reflected the classical form of community in the Acts of the Apostles (2:42-47; 4:32-35). It seemed clear to us that through a communitarian activity articulated in structures, themes, institutions and living collective experiences, there is a desire to reproduce a way of life which would have its orientation from the Jerusalem model.

If we compare the configuration of the primitive community in Acts with the contents of Chapters 7 to 11, we find a clear parallel. It appears evident, therefore, that the Rule is conditioned by and wishes to reproduce this model in a quasi-perfect manner. The values emphasized in both texts are the following:

a) fidelity to the Word (Chapters 4, 7, 14, 17, 18; Acts 2:42);

b) perseverance in prayer (Chapters 7-8; Acts l:14; 2:42,46; 4:24-31);

---

[21] The chapter divisons first appear offically in the edition of the Constitutions of the prior general Giovanni Battista Caffardi (1586), but they had already been used by John Soreth (+1471) a century before in his commentary on the Rule, *Expositio paraenetica*.

Figure 1

	Constitutions 1586	Contitutions 1971
	Prologus	Prologue
I.	De priore habendo et de tribus sibi promittendis	The eletion of a prior and the profession of the brothers
II.	De receptione locorum	Foundations
III.	De cellulis fratrum	The separate cells
IV.	De communi refectione	The common refectory
V.	De non mutando nec permutando cellulas	The allotted cells not to be changed
VI.	De cellula prioris	The prior's cell
VII.	De mansione in cellulis	Solitude and continual prayer
VIII.	De horis canonicis	The canonical hours
IX.	De non habendo proprium	Individual property and common possessions
X.	De oratorio et de audienda Missa quotidie	The oratory and daily Mass
XI.	De capitulo et correctione fratrum	Fraternal discussion and correction

Secondin

PROLOGUE

Greeting

The following of Christ

STRUCTURES
OF THE COMMON LIFE

1. The prior and the sacred bonds

2. Places to live
3. The cells of the brothers
4. The common table
5. Fidelity through stability

6. The prior's cell

LIVING FOUNDATIONS OF FRATERNITY

7. The Word, fulness of solitude
8. Celebration of praise through the Psalms
9. Communion of goods and poverty

10. Place for prayer and daily Eucharist

11. Dialogue and fraternal correction

XII.	De ieiunio	Fasting
XIII.	De abstinentia carnium	Abstinence
XIV.	De armis spiritualibus	The soul's armor
XV.	De assiduitate operationis ad evitandam otiositatem	Work
XVI.	De silentio	Silence
XVII.	De humilitate ad Priorem exhortatio	The prior to serve his brothers
XVIII.	De honorando Priorem ad fratres exhortatio	The prior to be honored as Christ's representative
Epilogus		Epilogue: Generosity to be guided by common sense

c) sharing of goods (Chapters 4, 9, 15; Acts 2:44-45; 4:32-35; 6:3);

d) fraternal unity (Chapter 11; Acts 2:42, 44, 46; 4:32);

e) the centrality of daily worship in the temple, the place of the mysterious presence of the Lord (Chapter 10; Acts 2:46; 5:12).

This last value is highlighted by the setting of the place itself. The "oratory in the middle of the cells" (Chapter 10) evokes a whole prophetic symbolism concerned both with ancient Jerusalem (Ez 46:13; 48:8; Hg 2:9), and with the Savior in the midst *(be-qereb)* with his fruitful and consoling presence (Zep 3:14-17; Zec 9:9 f.: Sir 24:10-12).

From the historical point of view we know that the spirituality of the time discovered, and later emphasized, a series of values clustering in the idea of Jerusalem: the ever-inspiring primordial experience of Christianity; the goal of pilgrimage to the Holy Land; a model of evangelical life in fraternity; also, a utopian dream with some apocalyptic expectations.[22] It would not be at all strange, therefore, if the hermits of Carmel made Jerusalem their own by inserting it into the center of their project of life.

One must allude also to a certain monastic spiritual tradition which was taken up and underlined—particularly in the 12th and 13th centuries. According to it, fasting and abstinence were values which the Apostles practiced fervently

---

22 Cf. M.L. Gatti Perrer (ed.), *"La dimora di Dio con gli uomini" (Apoc 21:3); Immagini della Gerusalemme celeste dal III al XIV secolo.* (Milan: Ed. Vita e Pensiero, 1983, with a complete bibliography on pp. 256-283). G. Olsen, "The Idea of the *Ecclesia Primitiva* of Twelfth- Century Canonists," in *Traditio* 25 (1969), 61-86. G. Leff, "The Apostolic Ideal in Later Medieval Ecclesiology," in *JoThSt* 18 (1967), 58-82. J.M. Howe, *Greek Influence on the Eleventh-Century Western Revival of Hermitism,* (Ph.D. dissertation, Los Angeles: University of California, 1979). M.H. Vicaire, *L'imitazione degli Apostoli: Monaci, canonici, mendicanti, IV - XIII secoli,* (Rome: Ed. Coletti, 1964). G. Miccoli, "Ecclesiae primitivae forma," in *Chiesa Gregoriana.* (Firenze: Ed. Nuova Italia, 1966; pp. 255-299). P.C. Bori, *Chiesa primitiva: L'immagine della communità delle origini - Atti 2:42-47; 4:32-37 - nella storia della Chiesa antica,* (Brescia: Ed. Paideia, 1974). E. Peretto, *Movimenti spirituali laicali del Medioevo. Tra ortodossia ed eresia.* (Roma: Ed. Studium, 1985).

(cf. for example Acts 13:2-3; 14:23; 2 Cor 11:27).[23] In this perspective one should add, therefore, Chapters 12 and 13 (fast and abstinence). These chapters, too, could be understood as a call to "apostolic community." The modifications to the text of Chapter 13 in the approbation of Innocent IV did not weaken, but rather reinforced in a new form the summons to apostolic community. This is so because it adds the model of itinerant preaching ("frequently beg while travelling," *frequenter mendicare itinerantes*), which is a typical imitation of the mission of the disciples (cf. Mt 10:1-42; Lk 10:1-16).[24]

This discovery of the *Jerusalem community archetype* is accepted today almost unanimously by the experts who have studied those of our writings which have propounded it.[25] We can thus consider it to be a new acquisition for the interpretation of the Rule. It is not, however, a completely new idea in the spirituality of the Order. We have found traces of it in the most ancient texts of our spirituality, such as *The Fiery Arrow* (the *Ignea sagitta* of Nicolas the Gaul, 1270)[26], in the earliest extant constitutions (London, 1281),[27] and in other texts of Carmelite spirituality, for example the Carmelite Rite, the Teresian project, Mary Magdalene di Pazzi, etc.[28]

---

23 Cf. Vicaire, *L'imitazione degli apostoli*, pp. 51-57.

24 One should note the presence of phrases and concepts proper to the monastic tradition of the Fathers (e.g., Chs. 8, 9, 12, 15, 16, Epilogue), and of the new types of legislation, such as the permission to eat meat at the table of one's host (Chapter 13), which come from the Constitutions of the Dominicans (1241).

25 Cf. the reviews of *La Regola del Carmelo oggi* by Gh. Flipo in *Revue d'Histoire Ecclésiastique* 80 (1985), pp. 177-181; and by M. Conti in *Antonianum* 60 (1985), 531-534.

26 Cf. the edition of Adrian Staring, "Nicholai prioris generalis ordinis Carmelitarum *Ignea sagitta*, in *Carmelus* 9 (1962), 237-307; c. 1,22s; c. V, 70-77.

27 Cf. L. Saggi (ed.), "Constitutiones capituli Londinensis anni 1281," in *Anal.O.Carm.* 15 (1950), 203-245; the reference is to the *rubrica secunda*, p. 208, *"e x praecepto sanctorum patrum iubemur habere cor unum et animam unam in Domino."*

28 Cf. B. Secondin, "Tentare fraternità: Il progetto evangelico del Carmelo," in *Profeti di fraternità*, pp. 67-101, esp. pp. 73-74, 87-89.

4. A Unitary Project

The third stage was to place this central nucleus in an organic relationship to the rest of the text. In this way other complementary meanings would come from the other parts which would then be seen to take on significance in terms of the dynamic unity of the whole text. When we studied the themes of the other sections, we arrived at the conclusion that the Rule not only proposes a unified way of life (project), but it also furnishes criteria of discernment for evaluating fidelity to the project.

One could illustrate it visually as an arc. At the two ends of the arc are the two principles: 1) the following (*sequela* from the Prologue) and 2) the awaiting of the Lord (Epilogue). The apex of the arc is the presence of the Mystery (Chapter 10). Between these three reference points all the rest of the Rule rotates, either as a consequent actualization or as dynamic referent. (*Figure 2* gives the complete scheme of the general project in a graphic illustration.)

I. The **basic principle:** following Christ (*obsequium Jesu Christi*). This is to be generous, without ambiguity either individual or communitarian (Prologue). A profession of fidelity to Christ the Lord with the support of the Holy Spirit (the salutation) nourishes this foundation and guides the authoritative discernment requested from Albert.

II. **Structures of the common life**: the presence of a representative authority chosen from within and elected by the collegium of the *brothers;* the reciprocal bonds (vows); the material disposition of places; co-responsibility in matters deemed important, that is, in decisions that influence the life of the group in a significant way; the administration of goods. All these structures are found in Chapters 1 to 6 and also 9.

III. **Living foundations of fraternity**: Word and prayer; fraternity in the community of goods; periodic verification of fidelity; fraternal reconciliation. Central above all is the paschal memorial (daily Eucharist) in the "center" of the community. All these are found in Chapters 7 to 11. In them we

Figure 2

The "Arch" of the Rule

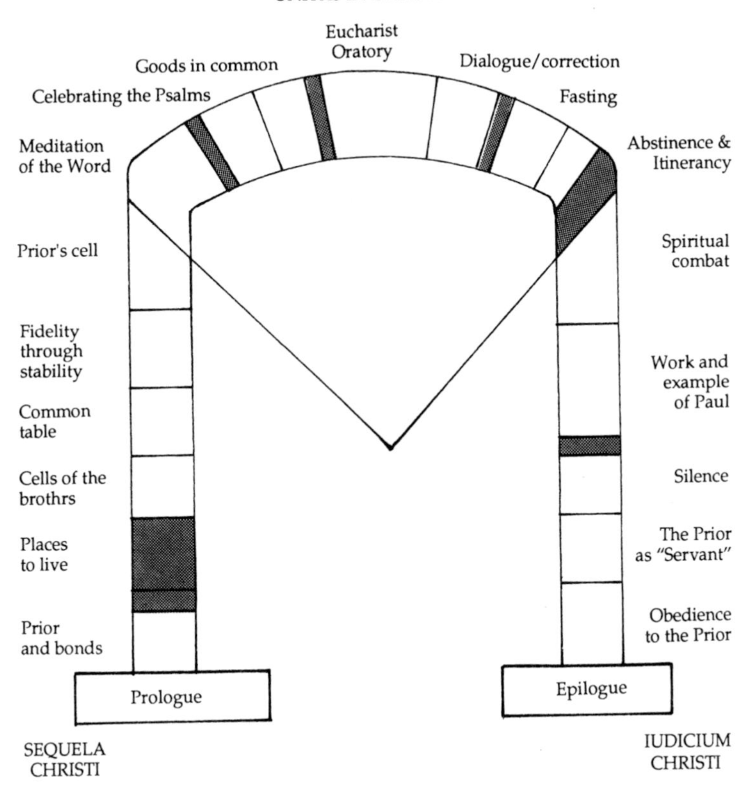

see reproduced the model of the Jerusalem community, and implicitly also the Jerusalem utopia of the prophets and the apocalyptic literature

IV. **Strengthening the inner person**: some necessities for a full and renewed spiritual life.

- *bodily asceticism:* fast and abstinence (Chapters 12 and 13) to arrive at an existence free from hedonistic tendencies, and to imitate "apostolic" asceticism.
- *profound integration* for an *authentic "life in Christ "* (in the Pauline sense, 2 Tm 3:12): the necessary path is spiritual warfare, sharing in common work, imitation of the Apostle Paul, the wise use of speech in interpersonal relations ("silence favours holiness," *cultus iustitiæ silentium*). These are the matters treated in Chapters 14 to 16, which we have called the "spiritual code" (and which is probably of pre-Albertine origin). In this section concern for personal spirituality is harmonized with attention to others: love of God and love of neighbor lead to a "devout life in Christ" (*pie vivere in Christo*—Chapter 14), which remains faithful even in difficulties.

V. **Maturity of fraternity**: the verification of the maturity achieved is found in the role which the Word has in all. The Word is embodied and fruitful in the role of service, which characterizes the prior, and in the spirit of the faith of the brothers towards his authority (Chapters 17-18). The project is realized fully if the Word is heard and put in practice by all ("have in mind and put into action," *habeatis in mente et servetis in opere* Chapter 17).

VI. **Discernment and generous fidelity**: discernment and generous fidelity (Epilogue) are further signs of a path which, if successfully pursued, leads to wisdom of heart and serene stability. But it is also a disposition for mental openness to what may be new, seen in the perspective of Christ who will return, and of the Spirit who guides with the gift of discretion.

5. Intermediate Conclusion

It is clear that we are dealing with a model of life of a dynamic and open type, that is, it favors the transformation of the structures of the individual consciousness of each one in order to introduce him into the global whole of the collective meaning that is being sought. But this latter meaning remains open to being expressed in new possibilities according to changing historical and socio-cultural contexts, and to the unforeseen action of the Spirit who calls for the embodiment of new experiences.

One should note the following about the new interpretation which we have offered, especially with respect to other readings or commentaries. It partly confirms them in that all include certain fundamental elements, such as the following of Christ, interiority, prayer, mortification, silence, work; but it partly transcends them in its new, more complete and dynamic synthesis. This is because it gives a dynamic value to every fragment of text in the perspective of a project open to a new and developing fidelity.

It seems to us, therefore, that this interpretation shows clearly that the heart of the Rule and its way of life cannot be found in Chapter 7, taken in the traditional concept of solitude and prayer. A centrality of Chapter 7 gives pride of place to an anthropocentric, individualistic, and eventually isolationist, reading of the Carmelite path. In our interpretation the center appears as the result of a multiplicity of "concentrations," or concentric circles. (See *Figure 3* for diagram)

Structurally, it is not the personal cell but the oratory that is at the center, the heart of the way-of-life of the Rule. The construction of a common center, where people are to come together (*con-venire*) for the daily rite, appears as a symbolic element which is capable of transforming radically the collective ego in the direction of the Mystery. In theological terms the rite or Mystery is celebrated in community; each one comes to it from his solitude to open himself for communion with the Lord. This celebration daily generates and renews

Figure 3: **The Rule as an Open System**

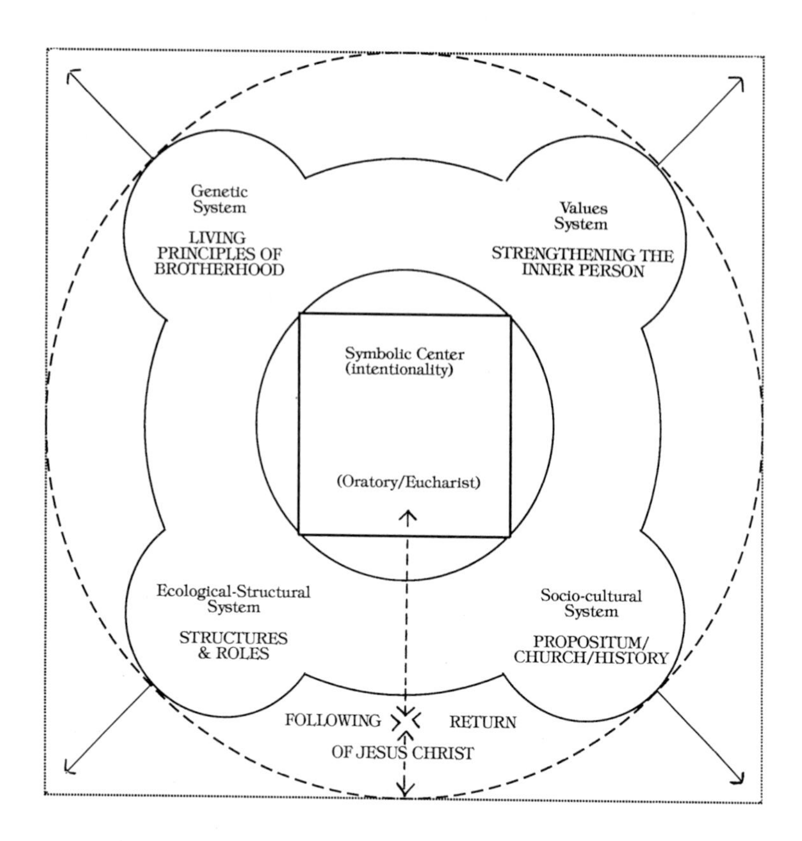

The *circle* (dynamism), the *square* (static state) and the *diagonal arrows* (depth and development) indicate the achievement of harmonic maturity (continuous lines) — involving both novelty and stability — and openness to ever-new horizons (broken circle) which nevertheless preserve identity (external square indicating a continuum).

From the center of the colective 'ego,' charged with vital energy, emerge centrifugal forces in the four fundamental directions: by means of this communication, this coming and going back and forth between synchronicity and diachronicity (between continuity and innovation), personal structures of consciousness are transformed, and what has been experienced by the group receives a variety of expressions and adaptations from individuals.

personal ethical fidelity which deepens the life of each one later in and through the cell.

II. Consequences for Spirituality and for the Project of Life

It is clear that this general outline of the Rule does not reduce it to a cold, distant or purely ideographical historical memory—like the map of a territory. Rather is it inserted well into values which form every Christian life even today, and must become the living foundation of the spiritual life even for us. At the same time it demands developing a new commentary on the Rule which, unlike almost all previous ones, is *not* constructed on individual chapters *taken in isolation.* What is needed is a development of the *wholeness* of each single value: from Christocentricism to the experience of prayer; from the celebration of the Mystery to spiritual warfare; from intracommunitarian relationships to the concept of relationship with Christ and with history. Recently we have begun trying to develop this new type of commentary which goes through the text in a global way. It requires a delicate theological and spiritual sensibility to be able to rescue the text from an earlier overly rigid and moralizing interpretation, and hence to place it in a wider perspective.[29] We will now try to show concretely, with examples, how one can draw new consequences from a fresh reading of the Rule in line with our new interpretation.

---

[29] Cf. the works already cited: *Profeti di fraternità*, esp. pp. 7-14, 84-101; *La regola del Carmelo: Per una nuova interpretazione*, esp. pp. 28-42, 76-86; *La regola del Carmelo oggi; Un proyecto de vida: La regla del Carmelo hoy* (a revised and expanded version of the preceding book). There are also some new developments in the series *Documentos carmelitas* (Ed. Libreria carmelitana, Ayala 35, Madrid); *Herencia y nueva profecia*, n. 4, 1983; *Costruirse en comunidad*, n. 5, 1984; *Caminos de vida*, n. 7, 1986.

1. The Following of Christ

The first thing to be said about the new interpretation is the great prominence it gives to the theologically solid value of the following of Christ (*sequela Christi*). Hitherto the phrase at the beginning "in obedience to Jesus Christ" (*in obsequio Jesu Christi*) was emphasized and defined as the specific aim of our life. We know well that the phrase represents a declaration of intent about our life and that it reflects our continuity with the great tradition of historic monasticism. Rather than defining what we are, however, it defines where we are in order to find the foundation and the total meaning of our life, that is, in the historical conviction that following Christ is a law common to everyone.

This historical and spiritual law is taken as the supreme and fundamental norm also for the hermits of Carmel. One senses the concentration here on the essential Christocentricity of the Christian life of a Stephen of Muret or a Francis of Assisi. The early "Carmelites" were men of their times. As Cicconetti has pointed out, we find also the concepts of the crusades and of allegiance (*obsequium*), and of service (*servitium*), fidelity (*fidelitas*), "way-of-life" (*propositum*), etc.—all of which were characteristics of the time.

A first observation, therefore, on "following" according to the Rule is that it is to be understood as a global principle, unifying both life and the spiritual tradition. The rest of the Rule makes no sense unless one arrives at an authentic following which, though gradually realized, proceeds from a loyal and profound commitment: "from a pure heart and faithfully in clear conscience" (*de corde puro et bona conscientia fideliter*). The remainder of the Rule has value and meaning only in the perspective and framework of "following" Christ. A word about the phrases "pure heart" and "clear conscience:" from a "pure heart" (*de corde puro*) indicates a disponibility arising from the depth of our basic life orientation. From a clear conscience (*de bona conscientia*) suggests a way of acting that chooses appropriate steps and means of realization. Otherwise we remain in the area of the vague and the superficial.

Continuing still in general considerations, we come to the most important summons of the way of life (*propositum*). The Latin word indicates the commitment typical of the crusade movement (a pledge to go to the Holy Land); it is also a way-of-life, which is already present in deeds, but will have henceforth a greater solidity and clarity. It is the synthesis of multiple experiences of both individuals and of a group.

Albert took account of this lived reality which had to be subject to the universal law of following Christ, and which also had to condition the actual concrete forms in which the following was to be actualized. It was not a matter of some utopian ideal, of some generic or vague statement. To the universal and traditionally esteemed value of the following, he added their own specific experience, their life, their rule-of-life as already being practiced ("according to your way of life"—*iuxta propositum vestrum*, Prologue). The procedure here is very important: it indicates the necessary personalization and concretization, as well as an attention to contexualization and adaptation. As a result, the whole Rule has to be read as an adaptation of the universal law of the "following" to a particular group with its experiences and needs (the way of life—*propositum*). In other words, the concrete reality is concerned with this "following," the primacy of Christ is lived in a particular way.

This is the perspective in which we are to read the injunctions about the material surroundings (Chapters 2-6, 10), about the relation of members within the structures (collegial decisions: Chapters 1-4, 7, 10, 11, 15), about the way in which the realization of values is conceived, such as authority, the Word, prayer, reconciliation, celebration, work, subsidiarity and a practical pluralism. We have also to consider relationships *ad extra* in the same context of the "following" being concretized in the Rule according to the way-of-life (*propositum*). Here we consider the fact of benefactors, the arrival of visitors, generous hosts, social conditions (journeys), the ecclesial tradition of lived reality, and the mentality and culture of the time.

From all this we can easily deduce that the law of the "following" is transformed in the perspective of the Rule into four main themes.

Firstly, there is a *community of authentic discipleship* under the guidance of the *Master* who teaches and presides, who is at the center of their daily and weekly meetings. His law accompanies them in their solitude, he judges all activity, and he is the mysterious power that sustains all activity. He will come at the end, but he also comes each day, and remains with the one who "lives in Christ." The material surroundings should also favor this formation of a *community of disciples.*

Secondly, there is the orientation of a style of life. There is the ascent towards Jerusalem which is now rethought in new formulæ, not solely in terms of geography, but in terms of interiority. There is the following which acquires depth in the whole of existence and not merely in an earthly or social sense. There are Paschal events: daily in the Mass, weekly in chapter, and annually in the fast. These last indicate that time finds its vital meaning in Christ. The style of life is evaluated in terms of "a warfare to live in Christ" (Chapter 14), a powerful notion which calls to mind the structure of baptism, which is here being brought to fullness. There is also the fact that work contributes to the formation of authentic disciples of the Lord, since it is proposed and esteemed by that great witness to Christ, the apostle Paul. Indeed, to work is to follow a holy way ("this way is holy and good"—*hæc via sancta est et bona,* Chapter 15); work is journeying and following.

Thirdly, there is an aim which is clearly and often repeated: it is to serve Christ faithfully (*fideliter,* Prologue); it is to be a servant in the community as an expression of fidelity to Christ (Chapter 17); it is "to live in Christ," and so merit a favorable judgment when "the Lord will return" (Epilogue). The return of the Lord overshadows the whole project of the Rule: it acts from within both to relativize all self-sufficiency and to look forward to a future "judgment."

Fourthly, St Paul is also found in this project of the community of disciples. The law of serious manual work and the avoidance of idleness are proposed according to his example. In addition to the value of work, Chapter 15 clearly shows Paul as a model of life and the exemplification of a set of values which are to be realized through perseverance. Thus, he is described in Christological terms ("in whose mouth Christ speaks"—*in cuius ore Christus loquebatur,* Chapter 15). There is, moreover, the final exhortation to walk (*ambulare*) in this way in order to serve Christ and the Gospel without duplicity.

It should be noted that the Rule does not propose an "imitation of Christ" in the way spirituality was to be taught for so many centuries after St Thomas. The Carmelite Order would later devote much attention to the imitation of Christ and to a multiplicity of associated devotional forms, for example, devotions whose focus was the Child Jesus, the Crucified One, the Precious Blood, the Scourging at the Pillar. The Rule, however, clearly and decisively proposes a more dynamic and open way, namely the following of Christ. "Following" indicates attention, adhesion, open accord, creativity, diversification. Only in Chapter 13 do we find an emphasis on imitation, but the context there is itinerant preaching, and thus there is the question of a typically mendicant element assumed in the transfer to Europe.

In the Rule, then, we find a Christology which esteems discipleship and revolves around a "life in Christ," prayerful listening to the Word, celebration of the Mystery, a vision of meditation as a way of imprinting Christ into one's life (e.g. Chapters 14, 16, 18 and Epilogue), and the awaiting of his return. The same way-of-life (*propositum*) as a dedication to the Lord in the Holy Land, which might have been characterized by a self-giving that is concretized in particular historical or geographical frames of reference, is now transformed into an open journey to be undertaken in any place or time

2. Fraternity as the Acting Subject.

The network of interpersonal relationships is so strong in the Rule, and further developed and explicated in the modifications of the popes, that we can speak of a kind of "creation of brotherhood"—or in the terminology of the sociologist Max Weber, a *Verbrüderschafftung*. It is, in fact, an internal law of fraternity and of personalized community which is stronger than the needs of individuals, though these latter are respected and acknowledged.

The Rule will not allow the individual "brother" to live according to any personal needs which would have an absolute value. Solitude (Chapters 3, 5, 7), personal meditation (Chapters 7, 14, 17), silence (Chapter 16), having one's own separate cell (Chapters 3, 5, 6), all have meaning *only in terms of* a journey by brothers-in-community. The one who dwells apart (Chapter 7) is a "brother." He receives a personal space according to the *collective judgment* of the community. To keep to this place, without falling into a frenzied desire to change it, is a sign of fidelity in the common project. This is the true meaning of Chapter 5 which forbids the changing or exchanging of cells.

The true "brother" is not one who uses solitude to escape his brethren. Indeed, he cannot understand his solitude except in terms of *multiple relationships* with them. He isolates himself not ultimately for the purpose of being himself, but rather in the depths of his being to be a person-in-relationship. Stripped of all egoism, blockages and superficiality he becomes both "brother" and "disciple" without either ambiguity or hypocritical formalism. He is thus a person capable of *total communion*. In the Rule, the cell is the school of communion and fraternity, and not just a place of personal encounter with God.

Thus we have to conclude that the subject involved in the Rule is not an isolated person, but the assembly (*collegium*) of brothers, namely fraternity, in the sense of a group of brothers living together in a stable way and in close interpersonal relationships. The officially given new name is "brother." Albert always uses it: after the formal greeting to the hermits-in-community, he employs it for the prior (Chapter 17) and for the others (Chapters 2, 3, 5, 9, 11, 18). The whole language used shows that it is not a matter of a generic title, but rather a project of fraternity and of *koinonia,* which is, therefore, reflected in the vocabulary used. The word "brother" is not used in isolation, but in relation to the other members, and hence in relation to the group. It indicates, then, the relational character of their way of life. Signs, structures, elements of structure, roles, values, models and symbols are all manifestations of an intense and authentic project of fraternity. This whole socio-cultural world and its symbolic outreach must be rooted and expressed in faith as well as in prayer, in poverty as well as in work, in asceticism as well as in service, and in respect for tradition as well as in openness to what is new.

If fraternity is to reach its full intensity, there are spiritual needs common to all which must engage the depths of the *whole person.* The *body* is concerned through abstinence, work, physical permanence, the movement towards the oratory—all of which have connotations of community and fraternity. The *psyche* is also involved through the values of detachment, silence, disponibility to change, the judgment of coherence and of feelings. The *anima* is engaged through the values of communion, total and proven fidelity, faith, service, following, eschatological expectation, love and humility.

Both by its institutions and language the Rule warns against amorphous and deadening uniformity (Chapters 9, 11, 12, 13), which would then lead to an hypocrisy that feeds individual egoism. Rather does it seek loyal conduct ("a way of life according to which you shall afterwards live"—*conversationis formulam quam tenere in posterum,* Epilogue). This loyal conduct between brothers penetrates everything, making them grow together in *justice,* which is fidelity to the command of love of God and of neighbor (as Chapter 14 indicates).

The conclusion of the Rule alludes to a generous "giving more," undoubtedly echoing the phrase of the good Samaritan when he provided hospitality for the wounded man (cf. Lk 10:35). For us there is a suggestion that the Rule is not all. It is always incomplete and short (*breviter* of the Epilogue) in the face of lived experiences. It is also insufficient for all future needs. But this "more" should not be a disincarnate or narcissistic "more," but rather should be in the line of service, welcome, and attention to others and to history. It is impossible to go to God without loving the brethren and welcoming them with attentive generosity. This interpretation coheres with the internal movement of the Rule which we have already shown.

3. The Spirituality of Communion

We can give another example. The spirituality proposed by the Rule is, at its most profound level, a spirituality of communion (*koinonia*) according to the Jerusalem model (Chapters 7-11), integrated with Pauline (Chapters 14-16) and with Gospel intimations (Chapters 13, 17, 18, Epilogue).

Communion is *interior* (*ad intra*) with Christ the Lord (Prologue, Chapters 10, 18), under the guidance of his Word (Chapters 7, 14, 17, 18), of his paschal mystery (Chapters 10, 14), and of his Spirit (the greeting and Chapter 14). It is in dialogue (Chapters 1, 2, 3, 5, 9, 11), in fidelity to obligations assumed (Chapters 1, 5, 9, 11), in mutual forgiveness (Chapter 11), in sharing (Chapters 9, 11, 15), in spiritual warfare (Chapters 14, 15), in participating in the common law of work to earn one's bread (Chapter 15), in the avoidance of every kind of self-appropriation (Chapter 5, 9), in service (Chapters 6, 9, 17), and in obedience to the word of the Gospel (Chapters 17-18).

Communion is also *exterior* (*ad extra*). There is communion with the whole great ascetical and prayer tradition of the ecclesial community (Chapters 8, 9, 12, 13, 16), with people on the road through itinerant preaching (Chapter 13). There is communion in the acceptance with grateful hearts either of table hospitality or of something to be shared (Chapter 13) such as daily food (Chapter 4), or the gift of a place (*locum*, Chapter 2). Besides all this, there is communion with people like the apostle Paul, with the proclamation of the Word and the testimony of work so as not to contaminate the Gospel

(Chapter 15), and there is a communion with the wisdom of the ages (Prologue, Chapters 12, 13, 16).[30]

Emblematic and symbolically evocative is the role of the prior who takes his place at the entrance (Chapter 6). He preserves the fidelity necessary for such a withdrawal from the world. But he is also there to receive and to help. Furthermore, he motivates the whole group to face reality (represented by those who come by). Reality, too, is a path to communion: to solidarity, to being neighbors, as suggested by the text of Luke's Gospel (Lk 10:25-37), which is allusively evoked twice in the chapter on spiritual arms, and in the Epilogue. The exegetical meaning of this passage has to take account of the context of the journey *from* (and implicitly *towards*) Jerusalem, and which bears therefore a vital resonance for Carmelites, originally pilgrims to the Holy City. This journey and this aim are now transfigured in a way of life which takes the form of a journey of the heart (*itinerarium cordis*) to the "lasting city which is to come" (cf. Heb 13:14). Those who in Chapter 6 are said to come are not just occasional strangers; there are also generous hosts and companions on the journey (Chapter 13). All this demands fraternal attention on the part of those who serve the Lord as brothers and who believe that in him alone is salvation (Chapter 14).[31]

A spirituality of communion must then be a spirituality of welcome, of dialogue, of solidarity, of service, of universality, of encounter with all the dispersed children of God (cf. Jn 11:52).

> Where a Christian cannot any more be a Christian with other Christians, he must be a man with other men...Fraternity towards those outside must frequently be manifested through a tolerance which can be defined as a

---

[30] Cicconetti's *La regola del Carmelo* [*The Rule of Carmel*] has shown the many links, both juridical and spiritual, with the monastic tradition. Cf. note 24 *supra*.

[31] The work by David Blanchard, O. Carm., *Models in the Muddle: Carmelite Origins as a Hermeneutic Problem*, (Washington Theological Union, 1983), offers interesting suggestions for further development with the help of more ample documentation.

respect for the "otherness of the other," and for the secret which God shares with him.[32]

In the context of communion one can understand why there is a complete absence in the Rule of a penal code (*codex poenarum*), that is, an indication of penalties to be inflicted on the brethren. All punitive judgment is left to the Lord on the Last Day (Chapters 14, 16, 18, Epilogue): the brothers are to correct one another with love (Chapter 11); they are to respect the diversity present amongst themselves (Chapters 9, 12, 13); they are to accept one another despite minorities and majorities (Chapters 1, 3)—without any rigid zeal about detailed prescriptions (Chapters 2, 4, 7, 9, 10, 12, 13, 16) and without absolutizing either law (Chapter 12—"necessity has no law"—*necessitas non habet legem*), or unanimity or uniformity (Chapters 1, 3, 8, 9, 12, 13).

The times in which the Carmelites were born are known as the "Age of the Crusades," that is, the years of waging wars to reconquer the Holy Land. Worldly enterprises in those times took place under the guise of religious pretexts; cruel massacres were justified by what they called service (*servitium*) of the Lord of the Land, Jesus the Savior.[33] Against this background we find the Carmelites—at least as described and demanded by the Rule—having, as their way of life, to live out their fidelity to Christ the Lord with a *dis-armed mind*, with a love of peace, with respect for the fragility of each one, and with endurance together of the burden of fidelity (*fidelitas*) and communion. Their warfare is against the deceits of the Evil One, whose temptations would lead them into confusion, into division, and into interior and exterior disquiet (Chapters 5, 14-16).

In other words, they chose a form of life based on respectful cohabitation, on dialogue and trust, on forgiveness and

---

[32] J. Ratzinger, "Fraternité," in *Dictionnaire de spiritualité*, V:1165.

[33] G. Fedalto, *Perché le crociate: Saggio interpretativo*. (Bologna: Ed. Patron, 1980). M Erbstösser, *The Crusades*, (Newton Abbot: David & Charles Brunel House, 1978).

pluralism, on acceptance and co-responsibility, and on service and fraternal correction in love. We can, therefore, certainly speak of a *culture of peace and non-violence.* It is a lesson, and an important role, for our times. A prophetic call is laid upon us, which we must recapture and actualize. From this point of view we see that the original "Carmelites" felt themselves to be church in a way that was innovative: having elements of *opposition* to the views of their time, so that they were in part a *counter-culture.*

But there is more. The "Carmelites" vehemently opposed the conciliar canons of the Fourth Lateran Council (1215) and of the Second Council of Lyons[34] (1274), which attempted to impose a standard typology on all new groups. Eventually they obtained an acknowledgement of their specific autonomy and of their original Rule. Here we see that for them belonging to the ecclesial communion also included respect for their own charismatic individuality; juridical approbation could not be sought at the price of a loss of identity. The ecclesial form (*forma ecclesiæ*) which they embodied did not follow the ecclesiastical categories that were emerging, namely centralization and control, clericalization, and confusion between spiritual and temporal powers; integralism and sacralized institutions, along with stifling rigidity. It was not, therefore, by chance, but by a *deliberate counter-cultural choice* that the Carmelites preserved their identity. Other religious groups at the time felt an urgency to do likewise.

They wished for, and believed in, a church of communion: a church that would be poor and free in fidelity; a church which listened, prayed and received; a church which celebrated and purified itself; a church which loved, suffered, and served; a church which awaited the Lord who was coming, but which ran to encounter the new world already knocking at its door; a church which retained the wisdom of generations of spiritual teachers, but at the same time knew

---

34 For a recent synthesis with bibliography see the articles in the *Dizionario degli Istituti de Perfezione,* "Lateranense IV", V:474-95, and "Lione II," V:574-678.

how to inculturate itself within new contexts according to its own specific character, which would guide it in distinguishing between the essentials and what was merely contingent.

The tendency of the Rule to relativize almost everything is to be interpreted as the project of a fraternity which did not espouse harshness or excessive enthusiasm, but rather knew liberation at the heart of its fidelity (cf. Gal 5:13) through a living encounter with the living God. He is present and operating in the community of "brothers" through the Word and the Mystery, through the Spirit and the material structures as well as ecclesiastical institutions, through commended experiences ("way of life"—*propositum*) and events as yet unknown. Everything must express the centrality of the Lord: the place, activity, rites and rhythms of life, values and aims, models, projects and expectations. Everything must be brought under the Lordship of his law (Chapters 7, 14) and given over to his faithful service (Prologue).

4. The Vocation of Carmel to Prayer

In addition to following Christ and being in communion, we can give a third example of how one can develop the new interpretation in a classical area of our spirituality. The whole Rule proposes in a logical fashion a journey to maturity, as we have already seen in the outline. But there are also expressions which recall more directly this perspective, such as to meditate (*meditare*), from a pure heart (*de corde puro*), to please God (*placere Deo*), in obedience to Jesus Christ (*in obsequio Jesu Christi*), to live devoutly in Christ (*pie vivere in Christo*), the reward of eternal life (*æternæ vitæ mercedem*), everything is to be done in the word of the Lord (*quæcumque ... in verbo Domini fiant*).

Centuries of tradition have delineated the make-up of Carmelites in terms of Chapter 7—prayer and solitude. This chapter defines us as men and women of spirituality, of the interior life, and of prayer. It is frequently said today that our communities are "praying fraternities." How can we square this datum of tradition with an interpretation of the Rule which places its center in Chapter 10, and orients the whole project (including therefore Chapter 7) to this tenth chapter?

We would have to say that the emphasis given by tradition to Chapter 7, understood as an injunction to solitude, meditation and prayer, is excellent. But it does not correspond exactly to the literal meaning of the text, much less to the meaning this chapter has in the dynamic symbolism of the whole Rule. Chapter 7 remains fundamental, but it is because of the Word which must be so absolutized that it fills solitude and the whole of time ("meditating day and night"—*die ac nocte meditantes*), and is transformed into a thirst and a craving ("vigilant"—*vigilantes* in the strong sense of the word). The power of the Word is at its greatest in the Eucharist which is the foundation of all truth proclaimed and communicated, and which gives a sharing in the vitality of the Risen One. The way-of-life is regulated and modelled precisely on eucharistic sacramentality, rather than on solitude and meditative prayer.

Unfortunately, tradition concretized (in solitude/isolation, and in prayer, in a generic sense) an injunction which has its power **not** in solitude itself, but more precisely in meditation on the Word and in what follow this meditation: prayer, fraternal communion, celebration of the Mystery, and other activities which result. There was a concentration especially on being alone and on a vague or weak notion of prayer. Meditation on the Word did not enjoy the primacy which belongs to it, but was rather on the same level as other modes of prayer, including devotions. The result has been an emphasis more on the prayer of solitaries than of the members in fraternity; and on an individualistic spirituality rather than on ecclesial communion.

The prayer to which the Carmelite is to be dedicated is described in the Rule as a "watching in prayer"(*vigilantes in orationibus* , Chapter 7), that is, an existential response to the Word which has been meditated and assimilated. To pray is, then, to pass into the secrets of the heart of God revealed by the Word; it is to stretch towards the One who dwells in the Word in various modes of response (prayer and activity), but it is not limited by it; it is to stretch towards the One who draws us. To watch (*vigilare*) becomes an attentive regard of the whole of our being and of our whole soul towards God through solitary prayer and the prayer of the Psalter, through fraternity of goods and of hearts, through work and silence, through fasting and service, and through discernment and observances. All these are taken up and completed in the celebration of the daily Passover that synthesizes the aims and historic fruitfulness of the Word, and that is the leaven of unity and the proclamation of the reality which is to come.

In the community of the primitive church we find prayer as a fundamental and frequently noted element (Acts 1:14,24; 2:42; 4:24-30; 6:6; 8:15; 9:40; 10:2; 13:3; 21:5). This prayer is born from a listening together to the Word, it is gathered up in the celebration of worship, and it is consolidated and crowned in the life described as "having one heart and one mind" (Acts 4:32). Such should be the prayer of Carmelites. It must be an experience of church, and therefore be a building (*oikodome*—Eph. 4:16; Col 2:19) of the *koinonia* between the brethren which is perfected and animated by prayer. Prayer has also to be a living watchfulness on the part of people who await their God, desire to see his face, and feel him in their midst as guide and as Lord.

When we speak of Carmelites as "called to prayer," we have to make sure that this phrase is not taken as a call to an individualistic experience, to a set of secret and self-centered acts set apart in rigid places and times. Nor is it some kind of assent to God through solitary or unique paths. This would lead to a form of spiritual narcissism and to a prayer that is all too close to psychological introspection. I should prefer to speak of a call to make the church alive, to make it vibrant as the Body of Christ.

According to the Rule, prayer for Carmelites is not just a dedication to do something, to think in a certain way, at a certain time. These may form the components of prayer, but they remain valuable only as secondary elements which depend on cultures and persons. Prayer depends on making the forms of the church one's own. It must lead to allowing oneself to be called forth and loved, judged and saved by the Lord of this community. One responds to his activity with the Word and life, with actions and solitude, with struggle and deliberation, with praise and supplication, with silence and memory, and with invocation and vigilant awaiting. It follows, therefore, that the Carmelite itinerary to maturity is authentic only when it respects the principles of ecclesiality, and is conformed to the needs of an authentic ecclesial experience.

Again, the ascetical and penitential life, so highly valued in the Carmelite tradition, must not be lived as an individualistic asceticism, but as an ecclesial journey. It is suffering "fidelity," the pain of an integrity which seeks "to live devoutly in Christ" (cf. 2 Tim 3:12), in the context of a church which knows that human frailty obscures its face, but which seeks in the Lord alone (Chapter 14) liberation and splendor (cf. *Lumen Gentium* , 48).

To be capable of being "vigilant in prayer" (Chapter 7) as the praying church, we have, at the same time, to be the church of reconciliation and service, the church of discipleship and witness to the Word, and the church of the broken bread and of the consolation of the Spirit. Only in this way is prayer authentic.

The place "to be constructed in the middle of the cells" in the Rule is architectonically in the center both of the space and of the text itself (Chapter 10). The oratory has a power to evoke values and meaning which go beyond every other element, and it has the power to draw them all to itself as to a summit and a measuring gauge. The oratory, indeed, orients everything in its own direction: all is pointed towards what is celebrated there, and what is expressed in a daily coming together (*con-venire*) is a summons to come out from solitude, and from the danger of self-sufficiency in the separate, personal cells (Chapter 7), in order to encoutner the "brethren" in the place where the Lord lives in his Mystery. There they are called upon to listen (*ad audienda,* Chapter 10) and to foster communion towards a total unity.

We could use an idea which we find in the oldest extant text of Carmelite spirituality, *The Fiery Arrow* (*Ignea sagitta*) from 1270 by Nicolas the Frenchman. He refers to the text in 1 Peter 2:4-5, and states that we are called to be as living stones dressed by grace to build up "the glorious edifice of the celestial city, Jerusalem."[35] Applying this idea to the Carmelite project we can say that our journey of the heart (for Teresa, *The Way of Perfection,* for John of the Cross, *The Ascent of Mount Carmel*) reaches its perfection when the adhesion to Christ the living stone (the "following" of the Prologue), and the growth of the seed of the Word of God transforms us ("day and night meditating on the law of the Lord," Chapter 7; Chapter 14—"let the Word of God abound in your mouth and hearts"). Thus we become as living stones for the building of the house of the Lord (cf. 1 Pt 1:23; 2:4 f).

III. Final Conclusions

We return to the general title, "What is the heart of the Rule?" The response is clear: it is the daily celebration of the Eucharist in the topographical "center" of the dwellings. All the other elements converge on this experience, and on the place where it is accomplished. Such celebration constitutes the summit and source, the fullness and the model for the whole project.

We have also shown how this new interpretation can be developed as a commentary. Our way of doing a commentary is based on historical, theological, structural and intentional criteria which are carefully and scientifically evaluated. Yet this way of interpreting slips into the text in a natural way, almost as the implicit demand of the Rule's meaning, and as a

---

35 *Ignea sagitta,* I:22-23.

development of the most valid aims of the Rule. In recent years we have demonstrated a large number of other applications, as well as shown how it is able to comment on the text.[36]

We thus venture to think that in this way the possibility has been shown of remaining faithful to the full text, of finding value for each single part, and at the same time of avoiding fragmentation or reductionism. But it has been equally shown that it is possible to derive new, vital proposals for our time which are in harmony with the ecclesial and cultural needs of today. The Roman document *Mutuæ relationes* (1978) states that the charismatic experience of the founder is "transmitted to disciples because they live it, preserve it, deepen it, and continually develop it in harmony with the Body of Christ, which is in perpetual growth" (n. 11). This, in fact, is what we have tried to do.

The values of a "fidelity-in-becoming" seem to be clearly absent in the traditional forms of commentary, even in almost all the most recent ones. One reason is that they set out with preconceived interpretations which are external to the text, on the basis of which they twist the text to conclusions which it does not support. An example would be the eremitical or Marian readings of the text, or ones that would insist on the spirituality of the Desert Fathers. Another reason is that not knowing how to find a global movement in the whole text, they reduce it to bits that are juxtaposed without any justification, and finally they impose on the text quite meager moralistic meanings. Again, the reason may be that the power of symbolic and intentional language is forgotten, even though it was quite dominant at the time of the Rule's composition. Finally, the reason may be the failure to distinguish adequately between the Rule as a process in the formation of a text, and the Rule as a project, an open way of life. This last omission has borne fruit in useless and improbable projects at being faithful to the "Primitive Rule," and unfortunately also in

---

36 Cf. the works cited above in ftn. 28.

quite un-Christian intolerance between the Carmelite families.

The final moment of the process of the formation of the text (1247) is also the beginning of the history of interpretations of the "way of life" through commentaries both written and lived. Other generations have shared in this history of exegesis—generations different from ours in their problems, mentality and aspirations. We, too, are called upon to give our contribution, not as external spectators, but as active protagonists especially by the way we live. There will, therefore, never be an end to investigations of the Rule. It is only through a plurality of perspectives and competences, of spiritual sensibility and committed journeying, that the Rule will keep its inspirational role and enable us to bring from the family treasure "things new and things old" (cf. Mt 13:52).

5

THE CHALLENGE OF THE CARMELITE RULE

William McNamara, O.C.D.

All I have with me is the text of the Rule ... and a clock.[1] I was going to carefully prepare a text, but I decided against it, since I arrived—decided to risk it—which is always a terrible risk. But risking it is, of course, one inescapable aspect and dimension of the human adventure—of the spiritual life. But, before I say anything else, I want to beg your forgiveness. Since I do not have a text, I am not sure of what I am going to say. And, therefore, I am worried. And I had been so impressed with this convivial assembly and to have seen all these different kinds of Carmelites gathered together into oneness. I don't want to introduce a nugatory note.

I do know that the Carmelite vocation is to disrupt and disturb, but do forgive me, if I end up following that particular vocation into the terrible truth. That is where we all want to go: into the awful, numinous presence of the Terrible Good. And then we will know joy. And then we will know oneness, in the infinite and eternal mode. But, *in via, en route,* I do believe we must suffer together some disruptions, and some radical disagreements.

---

1 This talk has been transcribed from cassette tape by the Editor.

I was glad to see the recent letter of our Father General—and I love that word *father*—to the Sisters in which he begged the Sisters to receive and interpret and respond to him, radically. Radical in the deepest and most profound sense of that word: getting to the roots, acknowledging the roots—and then doing something about it. It is not enough for us to think; it is not enough for us to try; we have got to change. For the sake of the poor, broken world which we love in Christ, *we have got to change!*

And so I came to this affair, thinking of it in terms of a "life and death" affair. A number of cloistered, Carmelite nuns wrote to me and asked me if they should come, and I said "No! How dare you even think of it? Unless you are convinced that it is a matter of "life and death." Then come! So I wouldn't like to see us slip... slide, in a solipsistic sort of way... into everydayness. We have got to leap from where we are into where we've never been. And be led there, into that place we know nothing about, by the Holy Spirit, with the help of the scriptures and the Fathers and the Mothers of the desert, and our long, mystical tradition. But leap we must into that new place. Move we must, steadfastly and daringly and boldly, into deeper and deeper levels of being. Where we are now is dead. The literal meaning of "ecstasy" is to "move out of a dead place." Where we are now, at least institutionally, collectively, is dead. And so, we must support one another in this exploration into him.

One of the reasons I decided to risk it and address myself directly to you—and get from you what to say—is so that there would be no impediment to an I-Thou[2] relationship. And it is only in an I-Thou relationship that the "Holy Other,"[3] that most "Mysterious Thing," that God, that Life, that One—the Holy One—erupts!

So here's the Rule. I happen to think that this document is

---

2 Martin Buber, *I and Thou*. (NY: Charles Scribner's Sons, c1958).

3 Cf. Rudolf Otto, *The Idea of the Holy*, a study of the non-rational element in religion.

about the simplest, most pellucidly clear document I have ever read. In fact, it was a stroke of genius when Albert, Patriarch of Jerusalem, wrote this Rule! It is the summation of all the deep, profound, mysterious living of the prophets in the Old Testament, culminating in Mary, Mother of Carmel and of Jesus Christ, Our Lord, himself, and then of all those Fathers and Mothers of the church who dared follow him into unknown, unmanageable solitude, silence, passion and then, resurrection.

So here we have this utterly simple document. It seems to me that all we have to do is to look at it, especially if we are at all intuitive, to understand it immediately. The trouble is—living it. I think that women should be particularly adept at understanding it, because they tend to be more intutitive than men. You know, I know that we are equal—we are not *as equal*, but we are equal—but we are very, very different. Men, of course, have to become more and more "womanly" to understand the Rule. More and more insightful; more and more intutitive. And women have to become more and more egoless and more and more Christ-like. Not be distracted by the side-shows of the present age. After all, modern society is a conspiracy against man: males and females. All of us together have got to take a strong, silent, solitary stand against the bad results of the military-industrial complex, the techno-barbaric juggernaut. Otherwise, we will all succumb *nicely* to the bland barbarism of the bourgeoisie.

We who are Carmelites—have this Rule. I just want to trip through it to a couple of things I want to say. In paragraph 8[4] it says: "Each one of you is to stay in his own cell, or nearby, pondering the Lord's law day and night, keeping watch at his prayers unless attending to some other duties." That I see as the key to the Carmelite life and to the Carmelite spirit. Really *pondering* the Lord's law day and night—not just "day," but

---

4 The numbering of the Rule used here is from the edition of Bede Edwards and Hugh Clarke, *The Rule of St Albert* (Aylesford and Kensington, 1973).

"night!" I have noted that more people *sleep* at night. That's one of the "fat habits" we've gotten into. But that word "pondering" means that it is not enough to read the law; it is not enough to read the scriptures in a "pious coma." (The more we read something, the more likely we are to read it in a "pious coma.") Unless an idea catches fire, it does us no good. All the great classical ideas of humanity will do us no good, unless they catch fire. That's why the Fathers of the East always talk about the mind "descending into the heart." It is not enough to cogitate or to speculate. Cognition is not enough. There's got to be contemplation. If anyone is going to contemplate, it must be a Carmelite. Then the mind, and whatever is in the mind, must descend into the heart. Then you have the conflagration. That goes all the way back to Elijah. What "fun" he had with his fire! That lies right at the heart of the Carmelite tradition—fire!

The "I-in-the-mind is the fire-in-the-heart." I think I heard Fr Noel say that—I think I read it in one of his marvelous little books. That the "I" of the mind is the "fire" in the heart. Everything must come together: the mind and the heart and the emotions, the conscious and the unconscious. We must bring it all together. We must "re-collect" all our scattered and dispersed forces, and focus and concentrate them on the living God. That living God is not a separate God. That living God is utterly distinct and utterly transcendent, but not separate. So that if I come into touch with the living God, if I, with my whole being, come into passionate love of the living God, and respond to him the way Elijah did ("Behold the living God in whose presence I stand"), then I come into touch simultaneously with all the living beings in the world, and I bring them peace. I bring them love. I draw them into that "terrifying Unity" that is God-in-love-with-man; that is the "roaring" of God and the "hounding" of God in the whole world, in all the earth, in all the creatures. That is what you find in the poems of St John of the Cross. That's what you find in St Teresa. That's what you find in the whole Carmelite tradition.

It is not so much man's search for God, but, as one of my

favorite theologians, now dead, Abraham Heschel,[5] said: The really big, essential thing is God in search of man. That's the passion! There is God, in Christ, at the very center of the universe, seeking with infinite desire, by the power of his Spirit, to transform every single individual, every single animal, every single creature, into Christ. And I do think we must include the animals and all the other creatures. In fact, one of the ideas I had when I came to this conference was to talk about animals. We have a lot of false assumptions. One of them is that in the "hierarchy of being" we are uppermost. I am not so sure. Having lived in close proximity with bears and deer (I mean "nose to nose" and "eye to eye"), they seem to be better mannered; they seem to be more "in tune" and in touch with the living God. They seem to be more themselves, while we seem to have all these masks and personas and hide behind all kinds of psychological armor, whereas they seem to enjoy the wild. One of the reasons that we are so unhappy—in fact, most of us are miserable most of the time—is that we do not participate in the "wildness" of God. We were created and are now graced to participate fully in the wildness of God—God who has no limitations and no boundaries. So there is a connection between "wilderness" and the "wildness" of God.

There is a practical question that keeps coming to my mind: "Is it possible to pull off this supernal goal in a big building, in a city? Can you be a Carmelite solitary and silent enough? Can you be passionate enough? Can you be mystical enough? that is, enjoy the consciousness of your union with God?" You've got it! The question is—Can you enjoy the consciousness of that union with God in a big building in a city? I have a categorical answer: No!

Don't go! I can qualify it. I know that most of you live in big buildings, in big cities, and that you are holier than I am.

---

5 Cf. his book *Man's Search for God*.

What I want you to do, when I say categorically, "No! You can't do it!"—what I want you to keep in mind—is a very important statement by the greatest philosopher in the history of the world, Aristotle, who said: "That which is impossible and probable is better than that which is possible and improbable." So the very fact that you are faced with this kind of impossibility, referred to by Aristotle, heightens the challenge—but does not excuse you. I am very lucky to live in the wilderness, to live in a hermitage, and to live with a community of hermits who support me in my passionate search for the living God; who lift me up every time I fall. That's a lucky night. "O happy night."

Most of you are not that lucky, but are more challenged and more graced and more blessed. To pull it off—the consciousness of divine union, the mystical life, the highest aspirations of Elijah, St Simon Stock, St Teresa of Avila, St John of the Cross, St Thérèse of Lisieux, and all the great Carmelite saints and all the great Fathers and Mothers of the desert—it is impossible to walk in the big city, and to live in a big building in any one of the proliferating, megalopolitan monstrosities of our world, called "cities." Because we stake our whole being and our whole adventure on God, it is a supernatural adventure. Therefore, you can thrive among the ziggurats. You can thrive mystically in the city.

I do see this paragraph 8 as the key to the Carmelite spirit—wherever you are, and whatever you are doing. In fact, no human being can become human, let alone Carmelite, without lots of solitude and without lots of silence to cope with the mystery. After all, what is a mystic? A mystic is the only normal man or woman in the world. A mystic is one who has been drawn into the mystery. A mystic is one who knows God, no longer by hearsay, or by information, or vicariously or derivatively. The mystic is one who knows God by experience—the way the friend knows the friend and the lover knows the beloved and the spouse knows the spouse. The mystic is drawn into the fulness so that nothing is left out. That temptation might occur if the mystic thought of God as a "separate God." But as he is drawn into the living God, and is overwhelmed and possessed by God, then he or she comes to enjoy, on the deepest possible level, all "human" beings and all creatures: dogs and cats and hippopotamuses and grass and sun and moon. Remember what the Buddhists say: We are liable to be trapped—we are so intrigued by our doctrine and our words and our symbols that we get stuck there—we muck around in *eros* all our lives, and we never end up in *agape*. So the Buddhists say: You must remember that all your words and all your symbols and all your signs and all your doctrines are fingers pointing to the moon, but what you must look at, gaze at, contemplate, participate in, is the moon. Now you can't just skip those indispensible means. We need structure, we need institution, we need doctrine, we need signs and symbols and words, in fact the richer that religious world is, the richer that Catholic world is, the more liable we are to become real: to become human, to become mystical. Nonetheless, we have got to move beyond the words and the doctrines and the set-ups (and that's all they are). All we can do is to try to create a climate and an atmosphere in which to become human.

We are not humanized until we are divinized, until we are so open, so disposed, so vulnerable, so open to the transcendent, so...so...nothing—that we have gotten out of the way of God; and God has touched us at the very core of our being. That's contemplation! What we have got to do is to get out of his way, and that's a de-egotizing process. We come closer and closer to nothingness. And then, what happens? The archetypal invasion! (It's fun using those words!) Which simply means that God takes hold of you, possesses you, and by the power of his Spirit transforms you into Christ, so that you act like Christ, you think like Christ and you love like Christ.

So ... those thoughts grow out of pondering the Lord's law day and night ....

And "keeping watch at prayers." That's a good word, "watching." That's different from "saying prayers." In fact, I've noticed (I've tried to read as much as I could since Vatican II, and since the Carmelite General Council) I've noticed that the words that are most commonly used, not only by us, but by all the orders as they are reassessing and trying to renew, are "prayer," "community" and "apostolate." Now there is something very curious and very peculiar about that. Because those three things happen to be the things we can do nothing about!

You can't schedule prayer. You can't program prayer. All you and I can do is "meditate"—and meditate we must. We think it's a big deal to meditate a couple of hours a day. It's nothing! Those people who take "enlightenment" or "at-one-ment" seriously (like so many of my Buddhist friends) spend 6, 8, 9 hours a day "sitting," doing nothing, just sitting—meditating. Now we, who are Carmelites, need to develop the art of meditation, hoping that it will turn into prayer. It turns into prayer when God comes. Strictly speaking, that is the only miracle. So, maybe there should be less talk about prayer. I would never try to teach prayer.

Our Lord Jesus Christ never tried to teach prayer, until one day his disciples begged him to. Then he taught them the *Our Father*. What Jesus did, and seemed to plan on doing all of his life, was something better than teaching prayer. If you teach prayer, chances are you will come up, or your students will come up with something, or your followers or disciples will come up with something artificial, or arbitrary, or concocted. That isn't real prayer. So Jesus didn't teach prayer; he did something better: he *seduced* people into life and into love—knowing that, if people would really live, live at "full tilt," live passionately, and bear gloriously all the burdens and responsibilities of being a lover...they will pray. They will pray out of desperation, out of the depths. And it will be real prayer, because they will be in touch with the living God. That's one of the key words that we have to accentuate, "practising meditation." Practising stillness; that Marian stillness; that stillness of Our Lady. The re-collecting of our forces and just being still. So that prayer might happen. So that God might come, for the sake of the world.

Then the other word we find used is "community." We

can't create "community." All this talk about community! It's one of the things you can't create. It's an indirect by-product of something else. The only communities I know of in the whole world (this is just my limited experience) are communities of solitaries. And this is true of marriage! The only "married communties" I know of are "married solitaries." It doesn't work! Unless each one of the partners is a solitary, the marriage cannot possibly succeed. Well over 70% of the marriages in North America fall apart because neither one contemplates; neither one enjoys the mystical life. Neither one is enjoying the mystical dimension of one another. And so they do not draw one another into the unknown, darksome, delightful, unfathomable depths of the real. And no one can survive on the surface. No one can survive on the edges of the church. All the people I know who have been hanging around too long on the edges of the church have died there, even though they are still walking around and talking and making a lot of noise and going to a lot of workshops. But they're dead! I would, in fact, dare to say that in most cases a priest—a nun—would be better off planting a flower or playing with a dog than going to most workshops offered by most universities in North America. (That's just a little opinion of a little man.)

Community grows out of, and enriches, solitude. "You cannot give what you do not have." I think that the greatest human need, not just religiously but politically, in North America right now is the need for solitude. Blaise Pascal, one of the most intelligent men in the history of the world, said that most of the problems of most of the world occur because so few of us are capable of going into a room and staying there *alone*.

He reminds me of another Frenchman that we all know—Nicholas.[6] He is my favorite! I do think his words were

---

6 Nicholas of France ("the Gaul"), Prior General (1266-1271), author of the *Ignea Sagitta*, or *The Fiery Arrow*. (Cf. the edition by Adrian Staring in *Carmelus* 9 (1962), 237-307. English translation by Bede Edwards in *The Sword* 39 (1979), 3-52. Nicholas argued against those who left the "safety" of the desert for life in the city.

not acerbic enough, and his conclusions not compelling enough, but he did all right. However, he was not heeded. So—community is a possibility only to the extent that we are solitaries; which doesn't mean "Pecksniffian spooks"—which doesn't mean that we live necessarily in a cave or a hermitage. It means that we are "rooted," first of all, in the ground-of-our-being, self-possessed, but above all, rooted in the *Urgrund.* That is a word one of the great protestant mystics used to refer to something deeper than the ground-of-our-being. Today, ever since Paul Tillich, we have been talking about the ground-of-our-being, and kind of identifying that with God. It's not good enough. We've got to get to the ground-of-our-being. We've got to enjoy self knowledge; we've got to discover the self, but it's not good enough. When we get there, to that firm ground, then we've got to leap into the *Urgrund,* into the "underground" of our being; and that's who God is. The One who sustains us from his infinite and eternal love, by his infinite and eternal love.

The other popular word is "apostolate"—or even more popular, "ministry"—which, for the most part, usually means a "mini spree." The apostolate actually means what it says: literally, it means "to be sent." Therefore, the only authentic, valid apostles—preachers of the Word—of what Malcom Muggeridge is fond of calling "vendors of the Word"—are those who have "been sent." And the only people whom God sends into the world with his blazing Word are people whom He has already touched and transfigured, begun to transfigure at the core of their being. Who are the apostles? Touched sinners. Who are the only people that you ought to listen to? Touched sinners. We are all sinners. No human being in this world is not. But we have got to be *touched* sinners. We have got to come, sinful as we are, and stand in the awful, terrible, wonderful, bewildering presence of God and say: "Here I am. Take me, use me up, and then, if you will, send me into the marketplace to represent you. 'Behold the living God in whose presence I stand.'"

Those are the three words: "prayer," "community," and

"apostolate," that we seem to be worried about and are using an awful lot in trying to reassess and renew our Carmelite lives. I would rather talk about and see us concentrate on the practice of meditation, so that we are readied, prepared and disposed for infinite possibilities. So that we are ready to be "Goddened," so that we are ready to be "Christened," so that we are no longer satisfied with side-shows, but go to the "big tent," and move right in to the "big tent" and face him! And all the devastating demands of his love. That is a terrible challenge. Rather than talking about prayer, I'd rather that we concentrated on the practice of meditation, and how to do it, and how to get ready for him. The Holy Other. The *Thou*.

And then, instead of community, I would rather see Carmelites go deeper and deeper into solitude. It takes a long time to be born into this instant; that's what the poet said. We have hardly begun to be solitary. People talk about being Carmelites for forty years; even those old geezers have hardly begun to be solitary. We've got to move deeper, deeper and deeper into solitude. We have no idea of what God can do to us, if we will rid ourselves of all the baggage and all the bondage of the world. When we move out of the world—we move out with no disdain for society—but with great compassion and love. What we move out of, by the grace of God, is what characterizes the dead society, "the empire," that is, power, all kinds of power. That was Our Lord's whole message! Every encounter, every confrontation he had with Peter was about power. "Peter, you don't understand. I have come to shift the whole of life from the axis of power to the axis of love. So stop striving and straining for privilege and power, and just be."

You can't pull this off by yourself. Get out of God's way and let God be God. So we move out of power and the power-struggle; we move out of compulsions. That is the great human problem: acting compulsively. When we live in the crowd we almost have to act compulsively because we become driven. The herd instinct predominates. That, of course precludes freedom: the freedom simply to be; the freedom to engage in utterly useless acts. The freedom to waste your time, which is the highest, purest, kind of human act. All the highest, purest human acts are "useless" and "wasteful." That is why God commanded us (knowing our proclivity to be half-dead and to be moved from distraction to distraction) to waste at least one day a week. That's minimal! That is the meaning of Sunday. It doesn't mean to go to Mass! It means to waste the whole day! In other words, God is so good and so absorbing and so captivating and so enthralling that you must do nothing gainful, nothing useful for one whole day. God requires that of you. Then as you move beyond that minimal humanity, and become more and more human, become more and more free, become more and more divinized, you waste two days, three days, fours days, and, finally, all week.

I would not encourage you to begin with the week. Begin with just the obligation of wasting one whole day! Then, gradually (almost surreptitiously) begin to waste two days, three days, so that you don't notice it too much.

Recently, the bishops were trying to discover what are the chief problems in the church, and they discovered three: bigness, business and bustling liturgies. This was a survey conducted by the bishops in America. The three chief things that prevent us from becoming free enough to become men and women governed and ruled and transfigured by the Spirit (living the life of the Spirit in, through and with Christ) are bigness, business and bustling liturgies.

Thomas Merton diagnosed our society as a "shipwrecked society." Then he went on to ask the question: What do you do when you suffer shipwreck? You do not simply float. You do not simply drift. You swim for your life! And once you have reached safe, sound ground, then—and only then—are you in a position to help and save the others. That, I think, is a very good insight.

I worry about the overriding notion since the General Chapter of "enculturation." Who wants to collaborate with, or be drawn into and assist, gargantuan collossalism? A vulgarism! Here is something that I am able to notice, precisely because I am a hermit and just make these occasional forays into the ordinary world. Because I am not used to hearing and seeing things, they impress me deeply. On the way here, the first thing I saw when I landed in the airport in Boston (and this always happens) is this extraordinary display of magazines, which is a picture of the North American culture. I saw Cindy Lauper, and I saw Tina Turner, and I saw Michael Jackson, and I saw Miss America (not only Miss America, but nowadays, Mr America). In one glance you have a picture of American culture, which has collapsed. So it would be a bad thing to try to accomodate oneself to a dead culture. I would rather talk in terms of "creative subversions." That is what monasticism always has been. That is what this Rule is: creative subversion. How do you live in a mad, derailed, dissipated society with sanity? How do you become holy amidst the chaos of the world? That is the question. This Carmelite Rule is suppposed to be one of the answers to that question.

I was very much impressed by this little paragraph 10. It is the first time that poor monks were allowed to own their own asses. I love that paragraph! Of course, it has been misinterpreted by many people down through the centuries, either in terms of callipygian cupidity, or callipygian stability. Callipygian cupidity simply means "slavering gulosity" or, in other words, that one is inordinately preoccupied with the shape and form and peculiar movements of another's behind. That's callipygian cupidity! I think that is one of the ways that this has been misinterpreted. The other is callipygian stability. In the last three monasteries that I visited I would ask the superior, the Father Prior, "How are things going?" In each case the Father Prior said the same thing. He said: "Everything would be going fine, if only the monks (or the "friars," if you like) would stop this callipygian stability." Each one of the priors used a more quaint provincialism—a parochialism—than that. But that's what they meant! What was spoiling things and stopping people from moving into deeper levels of being and from coming to know God by experience was this "callipygian stability." In other words, they were stuck in a kind of deadness.

Monos, as you know, means "alone." *Monos* means "high monogamy." If there is no "high monogamy," then we are bound to compensate. We come up with all sorts of punctilious, fastidious idols. We engage in all sorts of questionable activities. The only proper activity for a monk is "spousal relationship" with the Holy Other through "intimate relationships" with others. There are certain things you cannot skip. There are certain things you should skip! I saw a movie once in which Steve McQueen, the actor, went to visit his "friend" and he said: "Let's skip all the mini-moves and move into the big love affair." That's a perfect expression of true monasticism! Skip all the mini-moves, and all the flatulent effluvia of "words, words, words," and all the fatuous inanities, and the gestures that don't really allow one to leap into the beyond. Skip all the mini-moves and get into the big love affair! That's *monos*—high monogamy!

Monochos means "alone" and "sad." *Monos* means "alone" and *achos* is the Greek word for "sad." That's why St Jerome said that "The vocation of the monk is *to weep.*" So the first thing that we have to do when we move into the monastery, when we move into solitude and move into silence and move into simplicity is "to weep" over our sins. That we have ever disturbed the universe by our sins. That we have ever offended God. That we have ever *not* been totally in tune with the Sacred Heart of Christ at the creative center of the world. That we weep over the conditions of the world. Think of the atrocities of today! This is the worst of all centuries! This is the century of death! This is century of murder! This is the century when we have discarded millions of human beings—and without much guilt, and with no apology. The church should be apologizing. President Reagan should be apologizing. Our Holy Father, the Pope, should be apologizing. There should be apologies all over the place. That is why I began with an apology. And I hope you accepted it.

The other thing I noticed in the Rule is the accentuation on "work." Anyone who has done much work in psychology, or has done much retreat work with priests, knows that one of the basic problems among priests in North America is their sedentary existence, the total absence of manual labor. When the Rule refers to work, it implicitly refers to manual labor. Then it cites St Paul, who worked by the labor of his hands. Just as it is almost impossible to become human without silence and solitude, it is also almost impossible to become human without work—hard work. It is a spiritual discipline.

That's about it. I think. I want to remind you again that the thing at the heart of Carmelite life is fire. From Elijah to now: fire! Look at what Our Lord said: "I came to ignite fire on the earth, and O how I long for that fire to be blazing!" So all of our ideas, all the things that we talk about, have got to catch fire. All that is in the mind has got to descend into the heart, so that we become fire!

Remember the story of the young monk who went to the Elder, the Father of the Desert, and he said: "You know, I am keeping my law; I am fasting; I am disciplining myself; I am doing all the things that monks should do. What else can I do?" And the Abba Joseph said: "Why don't you become fire?"[7] It is not enough to go through religious routine motions; in fact, that is deadening. More people are killed by "a little religion" than by anything else! Remember what that great solitary in Concord, Massachusetts,[8] said: "Most men live lives of quiet desperation." It's not a spectacular kind of suicide, but it is suicide. It's "everydayness." That's why I love Walker Percy, the greatest Catholic novelist in America. Every one of his characters and every one of his protagonists represents this

---

7 Cf. "The Wisdom of the Desert" in *The Fire and the Cloud,* ed. by David A. Fleming. (NY: Paulist Press, 1978), p. 25: "Abbot Lot came to Abbot Joseph and said: 'Father. according as I am able, I keep my little rule, and my little fast, my prayer, meditation and contemplative silence; and according as I am able I strive to cleanse my heart of thoughts: now, what more should I do?' The elder rose up in reply and stretched out his hands to heaven, and his fingers became like ten lamps of fire. He said: 'Why not be totally changed into fire?'"

8 Henry David Thoreau (1817-1862), the author of *Walden Pond.*

"everydayness." That's the central malaise of our nation, our society, our country—"everydayness." It kills us. That kind of sameness; that kind of levelling egalitarianism. We have got to leap out of that and leap into the fire.

Remember, one of the great spiritual writers and directors (who is going to become popular again) is Dom Marmion,[9] who said: The difference between the saints and the rest of us slobs is that the saints plunged into the fire and came out consumed by the fire, by God's love. The rest of us get close enough to be warmed by it, but stay far enough away never to be burnt again. And that's "lukewarmness;" that's "mediocrity." That's what we seem to be guilty of. We're "pretty good." Being "pretty good" is very vulgar! We are mediocre! Instead of being towering human beings, instead of being saints, instead of being touched sinners, we just eke out our existence on the surface, on the edges of the church. That is where deadness prevails.

So, fire! As Chardin put it: "Some day, having mastered the winds and the tides and the waves and gravity, we will harness for God the energies of love. And then, for the second time in the history of the world, man will discover fire!" [10] That's what we have got to do. Amen!

---

[9] Abbot Columba Marmion, O.S.B. (1858-1923). Born in Dublin, Ireland, and ordained for the diocesan clergy, he joined the newly founded abbey of Maredsous in Belgium in 1887, because there were no Benedictine abbeys in Ireland at that time. For many years he lived at Mt St César Abbey, while teaching at Louvain. He was elected abbot in 1909.

[10] Pierre Teilhard de Chardin (1881-1955). The theme of fire was a frequent one with him. Cf. "The Mystical Milieu," in *Writings in Time of War*. (NY: Harper & Row, 1965), and "The Mass on the World," in *Hymn of the Universe*, (New York: Harper & Row, 1961).

6

THE SPIRITUALITY OF THE RULE

Redemptus Maria Valabek, O. Carm.

Is Carmel's spirituality to be garnered from its Rule? It is not just an archeological oddity that for centuries the primitive Rule of the Order was considered to be the *Institution of the First Monks*.[1] Was this so because the Rule of St Albert was thought to be too concise and fragmentary? Acutally it is an answer to a set of questions posed to the ecclesiastical superior, rather than a logically developed rationale of life as lived by the Latin hermits on Mount Carmel. The very fact that the nature of our text is not a Rule in the classical sense, but a *formula vitae*—a program of life set out in a hard-to-find order—could lead a person to question the validity of basing Carmel's spiritual striving on such a document. Moreover, various prosaic, practical, almost juridical injunctions could turn a person off the Rule as a source for the life of the Spirit which the name "Carmel" evokes in most Catholic minds.

Even more important than the written Word of God is the living Gospel, *viz.* the Word of God incarnated in the lives of

---

1 The *Institutio primorum monachorum* was written by the Catalonian Carmelite Philip Ribot (? - 1391) about the year 1370.

the followers of Christ; so too, more vitally important than the text of the Rule is the spirit which animated and contenues to animate those who live by Carmel's mystique. The fact that the Carmelite Rule was written by a non-Carmelite, by someone coming rather from the Augustinian tradition, should already warn us not to make of it a sacred cow. Undoubtedly St Albert formulated a way of life as dictated to him by the actual hermits living in the Wadi 'ain es-Siah on Carmel, but still it must be said that the Carmelite experience comes to us in filtered form. St Albert did not live on Mount Carmel; he could not have had the experiential knowledge of the life of the Latin hermits in the same way as is reflected in the often neglected work, *The Fiery Arrow* of Nicholas the Gaul, written in 1271, some sixty years after the Rule. In this latter work, if one has the patience and wisdom to sift through some pessimistic and dire prophetic warnings, a vivid and even attractive spirituality emerges. However, this very work assures us that to take the Carmelite Rule as the basis of the Order's spirituality is a correct posture. The whole second part of the document is a commentary on the Rule, seen of course through the eyes of a staunch proponent of the eremitical dimensions of Carmelite life.

Although it would be erroneous to look for a full-blown spirituality in the Rule, it would be equally erroneous not to recognize the foundational principles of Carmelite life in it. Although it contains some very concrete prescriptions, still it contains no catalogue of the "do's and don't's" of Carmelite life. Although it contains some juridical pointers, it is not basically a juridical approach to Carmel's charism. The basic layer of the Rule's spirituality is eremitical: however it must be immediately added that the group *(collegium)* of hermits were desirous of ecclesiastical recognition. They wished to be able to elect their own superior, which would give them juridical status in the church. This entailed a decision on their part to forego some of their individual options, of which as hermits (mostly laymen) they could have availed themselves, in favor of a common bond which would necessarily entail coenobitical elements. In fact, intertwined with the first layer are the coenobitical elements which later papal interventions merely reinforced. The 1247 revision of the Rule, approved by Pope Innocent IV, never abrogated the eremitical elements, but it did add coenobitial elements which the hermits-gradually-turning-into-friars could adopt.

This brief overview is necessary in order to understand the unique situation that Carmelites came to hold among the other mendicant orders as they were assimilated into that apostolic form of religious life. Out of a desire for survival, and also out of their desire of being useful to their neighbor, Carmelites came to be numbered among the friars of apostolic brotherhood, who had as their goal a simpler and more Gospel-oriented way of life, as compared with the opulent monks and career-bent clerics.

However, whenever a Carmelite would return to his Rule he encountered the original eremitical elements, intimately woven into the fabric of his *raison d'être*. Thus of all the groups of friars who aimed to return to the pristine simplicity and purity and zeal of the Gospels, the Carmelites have been those who could not help reevaluating the original elements of their charism. Of all the mendicants, the Carmelites, especially in their reforms and renewals, returned to their primitive ideal of *vacare Deo* (to leave oneself free for God, to enjoy the time spent with God; or as St Thérèse would put it, *"à faire plaisir au bon Dieu")*.

1. The Christocentricism of the Rule

True to the medieval mentality, the Rule refers in the very first place to Christ Jesus when it speaks of God: *"in obsequio Jesu Christi."* A religious must "live in allegiance to Jesus Christ and serve him faithfully with a pure heart and a good conscience." St Albert immediately seizes on the essential: religious are *not* in the first place bound to a well-described, scheduled way of life, but they are bound to a person: Christ

Jesus. In fact, the Rule is pervaded by this presence of the person of Christ both in word and in sacrament. Although *obsequium* was used by St Albert in the obvious medieval sense, it is useful to recall the context in which it appears in St Paul's letters.[2] The fact is that Paul considers an authentic follower of Christ as a *doulos*,[3] something of a slave or servant. Christ expects a total attachment to himself, exceeding attachment to any other person ("Do you love me more than these?")[4] Captured on the road to Damascus by the overpowering presence of Christ Jesus, St Paul never ceased inculcating in most realistic and concrete terms the radical belonging to Christ which a disciple accepts. The thrust of 2 Cor 10:5, in which our text is found, is basically: faith requires that we submit our wills to the wishes of Christ. The context well suits the troubled and skirmish-filled existence of the Christians in the Holy Land, and certainly Carmel's hermits who were committing themselves to a fervent life in the land made holy by the redeeming Blood of Christ. In fact Paul assures the disciples that God makes the Christian strong in his service. God knows how to level the fortifications of enemy camps. Paul has concrete persons in mind as he assures the Corinthians that God will overturn the kind of sophistry that tries to repudiate and minimize the teaching of the Gospel. He will captivate all for the service and following of Christ.

This implies a *Weltanschauung* which absolutizes the person of Jesus, not just in one's thoughts but in the whole of one's existence. The self-surrender to the person of Jesus implies that he become ever more firmly the important person in one's life. As Lord of heaven and earth, everything is subordinated and relative to him. He is the Absolute, not in the sense of rules

---

[2] St Albert explicitly calls on a dedication to St Paul in order to lead an authentic Carmelite life.

[3] *Dou'lo* was a term used by Paul to describe himself and his associates in the ministry, cf. *Theological Dictionary of the New Testament*, II:261-280; esp. 276, section c.

[4] Jn 21:15

and regulations to be followed in obedience, but much more radically and demandingly in the sense of vital dependence on him for one's very life. Christ is not a mere ideal or exemplar or idea or archetype, but rather the sharer with us of his very life as Son, well-beloved Son of God. St Paul seems to be at wits end to make this truth relevant; he seeks out various ways to express its radicality. He calls out in desperation that we are Christ's property: "You are not your own property; you have been bought and paid for. That is why you should use your body for the glory of God."[5] It is the inner world of a disciple that is captured for and by Christ.[6] And for the radical change *(metanoia)* which the yoke of obedience to Christ Jesus demands, a fleshy, worldly way of judging and acting must be transformed into a Christ-centered dynamic: "Your mind must be renewed by a spiritual revolution so that you can put on the new self that has been created in God's way, in the goodness and holiness of their truth."[7]

The medieval mentality within which St Albert would have been using the term *obsequium* gave it other overtones. In a feudal society everyone was expected to live in the service (*obsequium*) of someone insofar as he was bound to a sovereign: either to a temporal ruler or to God. There was a personal rapport, causing one's person to be regarded as a "bound" person with the promise of good and faithful service. This duty of "service" towards the patron demanded corresponding protection on his part for those who placed themselves at his disposal. These concepts were regularly applied to monks and clerics (and to all Christians) in their "duty" to regain the Holy Land for their Lord and King Christ Jesus. In this hallowed land a person became a special "subject" of the place by *hereditary right* because Christ was of the House of David; and by *the right of conquest* because he had shed his

---

5 1 Cor 6:19-20.

6 2 Cor 10:5.

7 Eph 4:23-24.

Blood to acquire it. The fact that Carmelites made their vows in the physical land which was the kingdom of Christ on earth meant that they were his vassals in a special way and wished to live on this land which was his very own.

This "allegiance" or "belonging" to Christ results in "serving him faithfully with a pure heart and a good conscience." In the rest of the Rule Albert spells out how this faithful service of the Lord should be lived out by the hermits of Carmel, given their particular concrete charism. On Mount Carmel this service would have been largely centered on prayer, both in the divine services, to be celebrated in the chapel to be built in the midst of the caves and cells, and in the prayerful atmosphere which meditation on the law of the Lord and vigilance in prayer[8] implied. Had any of the hermits been crusaders, they would have served the Lord in a very different way: risking their lives in battle for the conquest of the Holy Land, Christ's heritage. Now their battles on Christ's behalf turned on the ways of peace: to prepare a pure heart and a good conscience in order to further the divine intimacy which prayer presupposes. The recitation of the Psalms (soon to be transformed into the choral recitation of the Divine Office in their chapel) was a potent means of putting on the mind of Christ. The medieval person did not look on the juridical obligation to the Divine Office as we do; for us it is often considered to be a dampening of the Spirit. In medieval times it was the attempt to serve Christ in a deeper way, to assimilate his thought patterns, his ways of praying. The Psalms and the scriptures were read aloud so that they might be riveted in the person's memory and serve as the normal way for expressing their experiences. Something that we might consider repetitious and uncreative, the medieval person considered inspired by the Holy Spirit. The words of scripture were more divine than human, and so would transform the inner person most surely into Christ, thus making it possible to serve him faithfully.

---

8 Chapter 7 of the Rule.

Christ is to be served "with a pure heart." So often we limit this reality to a being "free from sin," or to innocent spotlessness.[9] Certainly this aspect is part of the integral meaning, but for St Paul it would have broader connotations: "heart" designates more often than not the inner spirit. A pure heart connotes a spirit which is simple, upright, sincere, unswerving in the pursuit of good. It is opposed to teachers of false doctrines, who indulge in idle, sophisticated talk, and whose attitudes are too often merely external and superficial.

Christ is also to be served "with a good conscience." The New Testament uses this expression in other contexts[10] to denote a positive attitude which spontaneously responds to the demands of the moral law. Conscience is the power to judge and evaluate, with emphasis on the interior dispositions. In fact these two expressions describe interior dispositions which express themselves in concrete manifestations of love and service of Christ Jesus and of one's neighbor. They orient the disciple to Christ—to his will and activity.

Christ Jesus is present in the hermit community in many ways, and according to the Rule he permeates the whole life of a Carmelite. His presence in his Word is paramount. The Rule is a concatenation of scripture texts, many of them Christ's own words by which he speaks to his followers. St Albert explicitly reminds the hermits that it is Christ who is speaking to them in the teaching of St Paul. In the context of the obligation to work assiduously, he states: "In this you have the teaching as well as the example of St Paul the Apostle, by whose mouth Christ speaks, who was constituted and given by God as the preacher and teacher of the gentiles in faith and in truth. If you follow him you cannot go astray."[11] Christ is present among his own in the Eucharist which is to be celebrated daily, as far

---

[9] *The Rule of Carmel,* ed. by Otger Steggink, Jo Tigcheler and Kees Waaijman (Almelo, 1979), p. 15.

[10] 1 Tm 1:19; Hb 13:18; 1 Pt 3:16.

[11] Chapter 15 of the Rule.

as this is possible.[12] Reflecting the strong sense of hierarchical authority in medieval times, St Albert explicitly mentions Christ's presence in the superior. The confreres are told to honor the prior "thinking more of Christ than of him. Christ placed him over you and told the superiors of the church: 'He who hears you hears me, he who despises you despises me.'"[13] Hearts and minds should be fastened on "the one and only Redeemer" from whom they should "hope for salvation. He saves his people from their sins."[14] And it is the Lord who will be the final judge, the searcher of hearts and minds, who will give judgement not according to appearances but according to one's authentic response to his call. "If anyone does more than here described, the Lord himself, when he returns, will reward him."[15]

The prophet Elijah and the Blessed Virgin Mary, who are such prominent archetypes in Carmelite spirituality, are only implicity present in the Rule: 1) in the Prologue, when St Albert mentions the fountain (of Elijah) near which the hermits had congregated; and 2) in the chapter on the oratory which was to be built in the middle of the cells and which was dedicated (as we know from non-Carmelite sources) to the Blessed Virgin. Yet it is not so strange that the followers of Albert's Rule (which was simple, direct and aimed at the faithful following of Christ) should opt for symbolic figures who embodied all they were striving to live. The person of Christ Jesus was the model for every type of religious. Subordinate models such as Elijah and Mary would serve to concretize those elements of Christ's rich reality which Carmel's hermits found particularly described in their Rule. And so the prophetic dimension of their life was epitomized in the ideals of the prophet Elijah, while the embodiment of the perfect disciple and servant of the Lord was seen in his mother Mary.

---

[12] Chapter 10.

[13] Chapter 18.

[14] Chapter 14.

[15] Epilogue.

The emergence of these two figures in Carmelite spirituality followed from the very realistic way in which the original hermits understood their following of the person of Christ Jesus. his presence and his cause were dominant; the Carmelite family gradually came to appreciate how incisively Elijah and Mary gave flesh to the ways in which Carmelites pledged their allegiance to their Lord Jesus.

Recent studies on the Rule have stressed the fraternal and communal dimensions of the life described by St Albert. Without doubt the *propositum* ("project of life") given by the hermits to the Patriarch included coenobitical elements, symbolized by their vowed obedience to a superior or prior. In their quest for ecclesial recognition they were willing to surrender some of the independence inherent in a hermit's way of life: they would continue to live as a religious group marked, certainly, with elements of traditional heremitical life, while at the same time intent on avoiding the perils of self-delusion which is only too real a danger for anyone living on his own and beholden to no one. The ancient Desert Fathers had much to say on this subject.

In the 13th century various renewal movements called for a return to the Gospel pure and simple, without the centuries' overlay of human additions. The ideal community proposed was the apostolic one described in the first chapters of the *Acts of the Apostles* (hence the name apostolic fraternities was given to those new, charismatic movements). It comes, then, as no surprise that the Carmelite *formula vitae* also reflects this contemporary conviction. Chapters 7-11 of the Rule are intruiguing parallels to Acts 2:42-47. With regard to sharing things in common and the abdication of property, verses 32 and 35 are also relevant.

Every reform movement in the church aims to present the Body of Christ as a true instrument of God's grace. Over the years various spiritual elements in the church become overshadowed—and even contaminated. One of the principal thrusts of every religious family is to address this situation and to *restore* the church to the beauty it had when it came from the hands of the Lord himself. A large part of its witness has to do with the way in which fraternity is lived. Religious movements usually are concerned that a fresh, uncomplicated "style of life" be re-established; that in it the unique position of Christ as Head of his Body be clearly manifested; and that the fraternal bonds among the members of that family be not only established but also be a clear witness to the value of "brotherhood" both in the church and in society. In other words, reform or renewal movements are attempts to show that the Spirit of Jesus is indeed still very active in Christ's Catholic Church.

The "brotherhood" of Carmel, then, should be seen as part of the Christocentricism of the Rule. Christ Jesus is not found alone—he is inevitably found within the members of his Body. Christ Jesus did not appear in our lands for his own sake or glory, but "for us and for our salvation." By his very nature he is "for others," giving them, in the power of his Spirit, the Father's gifts of life and love. This is why the Second Vatican Council can teach that all Christian fraternity begins around the Eucharistic table of the Lord.[16] Religious families are not in the first place fraternities such as we find on college campuses or among persons of a single intent. Apostolic fraternity is not man-made in its origins, nor is it sustained primarily by man-made laws and means. It is effective insofar as it lives by the life-giving presence and activity of the Spirit of Christ Jesus. Just as the church is not adequately distinguished from Christ (*i.e.* the church is simply unthinkable without the dynamic presence of Christ the Head and of his Spirit), so a religious community finds the consistency and intensity of its communion in Christ and in his Spirit.

The physical presence of Carmel's hermits in the Savior's land would surely make a return to the spirit of the apostolic community of Jersualem doubly congenial. Like the first generation of Jerusalem Christians, so Carmel's hermits were

---

16 *Presbyterorum ordinis*, § 6.

to be noted for faithfulness to the Word,[17] community praise,[18] sharing of goods,[19] daily Eucharist[20] and "fraternal" communion.[21] This "brotherhood," both in Jerusalem and on Mount Carmel, was based on the primacy of the Word: "whatever you are to do, it should be done in the Word of the Lord."[22] Reechoing the insights of Luke, Albert enjoins on the hermits a following of Christ by following the ideals and values of the apostolic Christian community. The conviction in both cases is that committed Christians are so filled with the Holy Spirit that they not only live the strongest bonds of communion with one another, but are also able to give wholesome witness to the gifts that animate them from within. Prayer was an extremely important and constant factor, but it reached its culmination in the effective and sacrificing practise of charity towards one's brothers.

Carmelilte tradition is consistent with this principle: the authenticity of prayer can be measured by the effective charity which follows from it as a necessary complement. Both in the Acts and in the Carmelite Rule, the "brotherhood" is marked by an underlying, deep resolve to act for the common good. Insofar as the Spirit of Jesus is allowed to dominate one's life, a person becomes capable of letting go of individualistic hankerings and attachments and at the same time of committing oneself to a strong sense of responsibility for others. The love of God "poured forth into our hearts"[23] makes one desire to share one's goods—both material and spiritual—with one's "brothers." This is not the result of rules and regulations, but of the overwhelming desire to be conformed to the will of

---

[17] Chapter 7.
[18] Chapter 8.
[19] Chapter 9.
[20] Chapter 10.
[21] Chapter 11.
[22] Chapter 14.
[23] Rom 5:5.

Jesus. Prayer, observance, charity: these cannot be legislated, at least not in their deepest meaning; they must be the result of heart and will and mind, overwhelmed with the Spirit of Jesus.

The original Rule, while clearly for hermits, contains other community elements—which should not surprise us because St Albert himself was a religious (a canon regular) and had been commissioned as papal delegate for one of the original renewal movements, the Humiliati. In the Rule St Albert goes beyond eremitical, desert spirituality, though this is not lacking. Particularly in the first part he wishes to give a structure to community life, in contrast with the preoccupation of the Desert Fathers to build up the spiritual maturity and strength of the individual hermit. A superior is to be elected by the brothers themselves or at least by some of them.[24] The prior and community should *mutually* assign the places which the hermits are to inhabit.[25] Even the prescription that cells or caves are not to be changed unless the prior give permission has to do with the common good and the surrender of the individual hermit's right to detemine his own dwelling.[26] In Chapter 11 the weekly community meeting is described. Interestingly, the superior is *not* told to give a discourse, but rather *all members* are expected to come together to dialogue about the common life and the spiritual welfare of each member of the community.

In the original Rule these "fraternal" elements were harmonized with the eremitical elements. As time went on, and Carmelites entered the European scene, the communal elements were emphasized further as the men from Mount Carmel were more and more amalgamated into the growing mendicant movement. Interestingly, the additions of Pope Innocent IV in 1247 do not touch the eremitical thrust of Carmel, but they do strengthen the fraternal or coenobitical elements:

---

[24] Chapter 1.

[25] Chapter 3.

[26] Chapter 5.

foundations no longer need be only in desert or solitary places, but could also be accepted in cities and towns.[27] Meals need not be taken in solitude, as seems to be the intent of the primitive Rule, but there is to be a common refectory. Meals are to be taken in common, accompanied by the reading of sacred scripture, as was the common practise of the day.[28] The question of possession of goods was resolved in the mendicant way: while individuals may not possess things, the community can.[29] Explicit mention is made of "begging" and of itinerancy, of having to eat outside one's own community[30]—which again conjures up the rationale of the then vibrant mendicant movements, whose roots were in "brotherhood."

Tensions and conflicts inevitably accompanied the spreading adaptation to a more communal way of life. As witnessed by men like Prior General Nicholas of Gaul, there was a vocal element among those early religious who resisted the encroachment of this mendicant mentality. In fact the Rule as it stands today does not resolve that tension. It still bespeaks an eremitical, contemplative way of life—which is still incarnated in a few instances today—together with a strong "fraternal" strain that has usually been the more predominant thrust of the Order.

2. The Contemplative Dimension of the Rule

In the popular mind, Carmel stands for a "fortress of contemplation."[31] Largely because of the outstanding Carmelites who had contemplative experiences and were gifted with the ability to describe them, the name Carmelite evokes the image

---

27 Chapter 2.

28 Chapter 4.

29 Chapter 9.

30 Chapter 13.

31 Cf. the Constitutions of Montpellier from 1268.

of prayer—and even of the highest degrees of mystical contemplation. Surprisingly, there is no mention of contemplation in the Rule. However, in the medieval context this would have been something redundant. It was taken for granted that eremitical life should be a life a loving communion with the Lord, whose presence was discovered permeating all of creation and reaching even to the depths of the human spirit. The Rule, then, formulates the ordinary means to foster and facilitate the "contemplative attitude"—namely that of openness to the divine dimension.

Silence and solitude were not required in order to produce a vacuum for the elimination of earthly sounds and distractions. They were stressed in order to make it possible to go beyond the obvious externals to the deeper reality of things; in other words to highlight the "divine milieu" in which all things in heaven and on earth exist. One of the longest chapters in the Rule is the one on silence. In one scripture quote after another St Albert seeks to reinforce the need for quiet in order to achieve the goal of Carmelite life—*viz,* to allow every person, situation and thing to be appreciated in its rapport with God and his saving grace. In order to hear "the sounds of silence," a person must be able to stand back from the many and varied sounds which usually clamor for his attention and interest. What can be harmful to anyone (and doubly so to a hermit) is idle chatter, which dissipates the spirit and provides an escape into useless or peripheral matters. The silence required for the contemplative life stands opposed to muteness, just as solitude is opposed to isolation. Muteness and isolation cut off from others and so impede community life. True silence is awareness of the Other—and of others—with all the dignty and beauty that is theirs. It makes one discover the true face of the Other while at the same time evoking disinterested love for the "brother." Silence allows others to make themselves known authentically, without trying to dominate them by overriding loquaciousness or to reduce them to what one thinks they ought to be. Solitude provides for this sure milieu. Relationships between persons are adequate images of one's relationship with God. Both silence and solitude allow one to identify the all-embracing and overwhelming sense of God's presence—which so often goes unheeded because of complex and attractive noises. These, then, are not the "passive" attitudes that an overly moralistic or juridical approach would make of them. Rather silence and solitude are the *humus* in which new and deeper experiences of God can flower.

The word "passive" evokes negative reactions today in a society that lives off the dynamic and the creative. But "passive" in the spiritual life implies openness and receptivity. When God wishes to share his gifts, and even himself, this note of openness and of receptivity is supremely important because God is neither limited nor chained down to human categories. He offers himself through the contemplative experience in ways that often stagger a person into "unknowing" when compared to the normal processes. In any case, one finds oneself unable to express his experiences adequately. In this sense the Carmelite Rule evokes the more "passive" virtues: obedience and humility are stressed insofar as the mind of Christ was centered on these attitudes. If a person wishes to follow Christ and serve him, these two basic attitudes of Christ's life cannot be lacking. Obedience allows him to attach himself wholeheartedly to the will of God, which was Christ's nourishment. Humility allows him to be true to himself and to accept himself *as God knows and loves him.* These attitudes are essential for the contemplative experience, for they demand that God be allowed to act freely. From the human viewpoint it means that the main initiative comes from "on high," while human collaboration becomes dynamic and creative only insofar as it gladly accepts and puts the divine initiative into practice.

The same might be said for the spirit of simplicity, and even for the spirit of austerity that obtains in the Rule. The important thing is not the absence of many material things, but rather the cultivation of an atmosphere in which these material goods are not allowed to crowd out and distract from the more important spiritual realities that are the cornerstone of the Kingdom. The vows themselves[32] are encompassed in this vision: they are meant to free a person from overpreoccupation with self and leave the self open to the ever surprising and creative action of the Spirit of the Lord. A person's will, affections, material goods are all submitted to whatever God wills to do with them. The underlying attitude, made sacred by Carmelite tradition, is detachment—not in the sense of non-interest, but in the creative sense of letting the Lord be Lord-of-the-whole-person. It is not then a question of minimal prescriptions for how poverty, chastity and obedience are to be safeguarded, but rather a wholesome and contemplative attitude of spirit by which the person is able to become sensitive to the stirrings, guidance and fire of the Spirit of Jesus.

The Rule embodies this spirit in the prominence it gives to the *Word of God*. Brief as it is, the Rule contains about a hundred explicit or implicit biblical texts. The scriptures are the prime source of Carmel's contemplative mystique. How is one to know whether the experience of God, whether in prayer, in one's neighbor, in creation or anywhere else is authentic and not a self-projection of one's religious sentiments? The surest guarantee is to see how the experience squares with the sacred scriptures. Being the inspired Word of God, they are unique in the portrait of God which they provide. Better than any other witness they describe the authentic way in which God deals with his people. Since God is always the same, he deals with his people today as he did in biblical times. Openness to the scriptures is basically a contemplative stance. A person must accept the Word as it stands; every effort must be made to avoid manipulation of the texts to suit one's own theories, prejudices or limited vision. God is truly encountered in his Word when the human spirit is free from unhealthy attachments both to material things and even to spiritual props.[33]

---

[32] Chastity and poverty were added to the single vow of obedience by Innocent IV.

[33] Cf. the works of John of the Cross.

The Rule has been called a prolongation of Christ himself, an irradiation of his mind, of his heart, of his perfection. The Rule is not a substitute for but a compendium of the Gospel; a fragment of Jesus Christ who is holiness itself. The Rule provides the quintessence of the words of Christ himself: faith, trust, charity, love of neighbor, worship of God, obedience, poverty, chastity, humility, abnegation, a spirit of sacrifice, the beatitudes. The Rule envisions that the Carmelite will have personal contact with the scriptures: day and night he is to commit himself to ferret out ever deeper meanings. Every day he is to use the Psalms as the ordinary nourishment of his prayer.[34] During meals the religious is to be nourished not only materially by food, but also spiritually by the reading of scripture. This immersion in the Word of God will make it possible for the Word "to dwell abundantly on his lips and in his heart." Carmelite spirituality is characterized by the Rule's strong biblical strain.

The Good News of Jesus Christ integrated all the truth of the Old Testament, completing its definitive message. All is centered on following authentically in the footsteps of Christ Jesus. Even the precept of meditating day and night on the law of the Lord, together with the prescription to watch in prayer, is but an echo of the Psalmist's insight.[35] The heart of the chapter on "spiritual arms" is the commandment to love. The Rule is thoroughly catholic in presenting an integral, theologal life which penetrates even the details of daily living by means of obedience: "He who hears you hears me." The lawgiver is not sparing in his demands for interior self-emptying which is authentically evangelical: not to own anything as one's own, to live in solitude, to avoid even the slightest useless word, to renounce one's own autonomy.

The assimilation of the Word of God is a wholesome experience which was meant to take in the entire person. Often

---

[34] Innocent IV made explicit the duty of choral recitation of the Divine Office, which the hermits were probably already celebrating as a normal part of their community's prayer life.

[35] Ps 1:2.

the Word was read aloud so as to fix it in the ear and in the memory. Meditation proper followed, which was not necessarily prayer; it was what we today would call exegesis, hermeneutics, comparison of texts and arriving at the original meaning. Medieval spiritual writers warned that this stage, which was largely an intellectual appreciation of the biblical texts, should not be confused with prayer itself. True prayer must encompass the whole person—heart and will must come into play. The Word of God is assimilated, not just on a sensual level, nor even on an intellectual level, but also on a deep volitional and affective level; only this is capable of changing the person, of penetrating even to the inmost depths where motivations and convictions and intentions are harbored, reshaping these into Christ-like and Christ-inspired options. Finally, the Word of God is assimilated fully when it is put into practise in the charitable, forgiving, concerned living out of one's life. Authors point out this latter quality as the surest guarantee of prayer's authenticity.

Another essential element of the Carmelite's contemplative rationale according to the Rule is the celebration of the Liturgy. The *daily* Eucharist (something rare in the legislation of 13th Century hermits) should be seen in its normal context of the Divine Office, of which the Eucharist was undertood to be the culmination. Even if the original hermits did not have the obligation of reciting the Divine Office, but only recited the Psalms in the way proposed by their desert forefathers, nonetheless their desire was to serve the Lord Jesus in the first place by liturgical worship. Today we are wary of such juridical prescriptions that obligate religious to choral celebration of the divine praises; the medieval tendency would have been the opposite. Groups of religious people would have been anxious to be commissioned to perform what was considered the normal sign of being a full-fledged ecclesial entity. The group of Latin hermits on Mount Carmel, as attested by the papal bulls they were able to obtain, were anxious to be able to celebrate the liturgy in their chapels. Not only was this considered the moral duty and privilege of religious, but it also provided a regular source of sustenance.

The contemplative dimension of the liturgy has yet to be explored and explicitated. The Order has been challenged on more than one occasion to do just this in these days of greater liturgical awareness. What a grace it would be for the whole church, if this original, contemplative aspect were to become vital and inciseful again! The liturgy is a "given" in the sense that it was left to the church by Christ Jesus to be elaborated by that church. The presence of Christ in liturgical celebrations is his guaranteed presence. The *ex opere operato* aspect of the sacraments does not make them magical, but it means that Christ is true to his word. He is present with his saving power in authentic, liturgical, ecclesial celebrations. This does not eliminate the need for collaboration, but it does mean that the deepest substratum of the liturgy comes from on high and, once again, needs a basic openness and availability if it is to be efficacious as the Lord wills. The present liturgy, with its immersion in the riches of the Word of God, with its space for sacred silence, with its official possibilities for adaptation to the worshipping community, can be more of a meaningful contemplative event than ever.

Carmel's Rule points out the ordinary means and attitudes for the contemplative experience. This is why confreres like Blessed Titus Brandsma insisted so strenuously that mysticism is for everyone. It is truly a gift, but God offers it more often and more abundantly than we realize. The proof of all this is that the road to contemplation is no esoteric path reserved to elite souls, but is a wide avenue on which Catholics of every stripe are invited to travel. The means by which they may do so are the ordinary means available to all followers of Christ. Carmel's Rule aims to provide the right atmosphere that these means might reach their grace-filled and fulfilling goal: the summit of the mount which is Christ Jesus himself

3. Desert Spirituality and the Rule

Another layer of the Rule's spirituality is that of the Desert Fathers. The lay hermits lived elements that pre-dated the classical Rule of St Benedict. The hermit in the Christian tradition is one who must be ready to accept life as a trial and to engage in hand-to-hand combat with the forces of evil. This struggle would have made much sense to the crusading mentality which surrounded Carmel. The soldier of Christ arms himself with the disarming attitude of Christ[36] and is consequently able to work quietly and steadfastly.[37] A separate cell for each hermit[38] made it possible for him to spend day and night pondering the Word of the Lord.[39]

The role of hesychasm in desert spirituality was indispensable: it denoted the quiet and peace that must envelop the person intent on living in the truly "real" or spiritual world and on experiencing "the real thing," with the same kind of awareness that earthly-minded people have for external realities. It meant leaving the world, family, material goods which menace the quiet of the spirit needed to focus on the real, eternal world. The hermit left the company of confreres in his quest for hesychasm. The means used by the hesychast, which are found featured in the Carmelite Rule, were: abstinence, fasting, vigils, sleeping on the ground, manual labor. By means of this ascetical effort the hesychast was able to achieve a purity of vision and heart which escaped so many others; the simplicity and freedom of spirit which became his hallmark was the surest disposition for prayer and contemplation. The combat which he undertook against his unruly passions had as its scope union with Christ.

Chapter 14 of the Rule begins with a reference to "tempta-

---

[36] Chapter 14.

[37] Chapters 15-16.

[38] Chapter 3.

[39] Chapter 7. Cf. also *The Rule of Carmel*, p. 4.

tion," or to the spiritual battle which every monk or hermit must be ready to wage against the powers of evil, both within and outside of himself. Job (and Jesus even more so) was faced with the dark side of human life. Unlike external realities, these powers of evil cannot be easily pointed out; yet they are only too real, both in individuals and in communities. The deep-seated hankering for "having" and possessing, for manipulating and using others, for opting to "go it alone" are the object of the heart's combat. God himself is involved in this battle. The temptations of Jesus in the desert are often found in the lives of the Desert Fathers and in the lives of all those who follow Jesus Christ radically.

St Paul warns that "all who wish to lead a life faithful to Christ will suffer persecution."[40] In this same context St Paul speaks of those perilous times when man's evil inclinations will predominate—egoism, avarice, pride, calumny etc.[41]—although there will be a counterfeit religion in evidence.[42] But these people will be found out.[43] Followers of Christ must persevere and suffer through these temptations. Temptations are just part of being Christian.[44] St Peter evokes the image of "the devil, your adversary, prowling around like a lion, seeking out persons to devour."[45] He is writing to people who, through no fault of their own, must suffer persecution. They should not consider this as extraordinary—suffering goes hand in hand with being a Christian.[46] They must aid one another like members of one flesh.[47] The enemy will thus not be able to make a surprise attack on them like a lion.[48]

---

[40] 2 Tm 3:12.

[41] 2 Tm 3:2-4

[42] 2 Tm 3:5.

[43] 2 Tm 3:6-9.

[44] 2 Tm 3:10-12.

[45] 1 Pt 5:8.

[46] 1 Pt 4:12-14.

[47] 1 Pt 5:1-8.

[48] 1 Pt 5:8-9.

Using imagery that would have made much sense to people in those war-saturated times, St Albert calls on the hermits to put on the "armor of God" because human defenses are not enough when waging war on "princedoms, powers, masters of this world of darkness, evil spirits in the heavens." John Cassian in his *Collationes* (VII, 5) uses 2 Cor 10:4-5 to describe the "arms of our warfare" and "walking in the footsteps of Jesus" as linked when he paints the picture of a soldier putting on the armor of God to fight the battles of the Lord. The medieval "pilgrimage to Jerusalem" was very much tied up with the need to do battle, sometimes physically but always spiritually, in order to reach the promised city which was the symbol of Jesus' patrimony, acquired at the cost of his blood.[49]

The paradox of *God's weaponry* becomes immediately evident as St Albert lists the various pieces of *armor* required to protect a warrior-for-the-Lord's-sake. While even more courage is required for such a warrior than for a military man, still his fight is in an entirely different direction. By means of his spiritual arms he seeks to disarm the forces of evil which beset him from without as well as from within. The attitudes and values which God's "arms" represent are just the opposite of the armor used by the crusaders in their battle to recoup the Holy Land from the Saracens.

"Gird your loins with the *cincture of chastity,"* St Albert begins. The hermit's constant struggle must be the purification of the whole inner man, a control of the concupiscence that is his heritage after Adam's fall. Only too often the lower instincts, in a crass and self-centered form, demand a dominant role. The chastity envisioned here certainly has to do with the correct use of sex and sexual powers according to God's will, but it goes beyond, to a wholesome freedom from subjection to base motives, to momentary, fleeting pleasures, to aberrant affections. Control of one's instincts in no way means to

---

[49] Cf. *The Rule of Carmel*, p. 35.

destroy them, but to channel them so that they contribute to the growing maturity of the whole person. St Albert, good pastor that he was, gives a positive means for achieving this: "Let your breast be protected by holy thoughts, as it is written: 'holy thinking will preserve you.'" Self-control and self-discipline are helped mightily by the positive effort to become vitally involved in good, holy, true things. Rather than allowing the mind to get mired in all the things that besmirch the inner person, St Albert has a far more effective means: fill your minds with good, holy thoughts, ideals and aspirations. The Carmelite practise of the presence of God[50] is a direct outgrowth and application of this injunction of the Rule.

"Don the *breastplate of justice*, so that you love the Lord your God with all your heart and all your soul and with all your strength, and your neighbor as yourself." Paradoxically, the breastplate protects the main portion of one's body, covering the heart and other vital organs; yet in the spiritual armor it is linked with *justice* which has to do with others: giving their due to all of them. This is a profound insight. We can best protect our own deepest integrity by treating others as we should. Personal fulfillment is best served not by a refusal to turn in on oneself, thus tremendously cramping one's possibilities, but rather by a resolute effort to reach out to all others. In another valuable insight, St Albert says that the process of self-fulfillment through attention to others will blossom into love for God and neighbor. How much could be made of the insight that true love and charity must be based on justice (the ramifications of this in the context of social justice are immense). It is also a warning that authentic love is the greatest of the commandments of Jesus. While this fraternal charity and love for God go beyond natural instinct (with a certain amount of passion attached), it is not an abstract, disinterested love. It is a share in God's *agape*, which is a love that is

---

[50] For a good example of this, cf. Kilian Healy's *Walking with God* (New York: McMullen; 1948).

not self-seeking, and so allows a religious to keep giving even when love is not requited—just as the Lord does.

The consecrated person gives of himself to others full-time, but with this difference: he renounces the right to possess anyone or anything, but vows himself to service and to the gifting of himself to others without expecting or asking for a return. The renunciation aspect of this kind of love witnesses to the fact that love in a purely human form is not definitive. Most of the time it does pass through the human, but it cannot be exhausted in it. Christ clearly proclaims that if a person does not love him more than others, he cannot be a disciple; but he teaches just as emphatically that he cannot accept love that is not extended to one's "brothers" as well. The human aspects of love and friendship are subsumed and included in the higher gift of charity.

"In all things take up the *shield of faith,* with which you will be able to extinguish all the flaming darts of the evil one; without faith you cannot be pleasing to God." This image is anything but static. Faith is not a calm, philosophical rumination over the niceties of dogmatic definitions. St Albert sees it as a battle against flaming darts of the *most* evil one. The presence of these evil forces can, at times, almost be touched. Interestingly enough, our day has seen a new, even frightful, interest in the devil. Paradoxically, the Rule calls for a return to faith in order to defend oneself from the devil's cunning. Faith is seen in context of *violence,* of a battle against overwhelming odds, but also of a heart full of confidence in the object of our faith: the faithfulness of God who alone is one hundred percent faithful to his side of the alliance. In his description of the gradual, grace-filled purification of this faith, St John of the Cross is the world master.

Religious profession merely reinforces the pilgrimage of faith begun in baptism, but it also presupposes a dynamic with which our great brothers and sisters in Carmel were never done throughout their lifetimes. Faith means witnessing to the abiding presence of the living God—often in the desert, in the night, in doubt and temptation, when the battle with hedonism, materialism and consumerism rages around us. Pure faith implies the surest defence: letting go of all and allowing our "yes" to God to permeate every fiber of our being. This is what makes us pleasing to God, i.e., the closest we, on the pilgrimage of faith, can come to the image of Christ Jesus with whom all of us have been sealed in the sacrament of faith.

"You must also put on the *helmet of salvation*, so that you hope for salvation solely from our one Savior; it is he who frees his people from their sins." Salvation, in biblical terms, was the breaking out from the cramping limitations of the human condition, marred by imperfection, sin and eventual death, and the introduction to the work of God on our behalf. In Christ Jesus the precariousness of human existence is overcome by the triumph of his resurrection and his gracious sharing of this new condition with those who belong to him. The helmet which protects and saves the head is precisely Christ the Head of his Body. He is Savior insofar as he guarantees for us a share in the Kingdom, in the resurrection of the body and in life everlasting. He continues (notice the present tense of the verb) his combat against sin until the end of time, *now*, through us his followers. This pardon of sins becomes all the more credible insofar as we are in solidarity with *those in need of pardon*, or as St Thérèse put it, we too "sit at the table of sinners." During her lifetime she prayed for those sinners *out there;* at the end of her life, her prayer became "have mercy on *us sinners*." We include ourselves among those who are weak, poor, imperfect and sinful, ever needful of the healing action of Christ in order to hear his call, respond to it and zealously persevere in it until death.

"Finally let the *sword of the Spirit*, which is the Word of God, dwell on your lips and in your heart with all its richness. All that you have to do, do it in the Word of God." The offensive weapon, the sword, is the Word of God, *made powerful* by the Spirit of Jesus. Familiarity with scripture is not a process by which a person becomes learned, but rather wise. Medieval people allowed the Word of God to become part of their own language, and it became their deepest conviction and motivation in order to know how to live in a way that related all of creation to its origin and end, God. Action by the hermit should follow from this immersion in the Word both by his lips and by his heart. In other words, the Word of God assimilated would allow the hermit to forge words and deeds into a life lived from scripture. In this context Col 3:12-17, St Paul describes what this new type of existence entails: "Clothe yourselves with heartfelt mercy, with kindness, humility, meekness and patience. Bear with one another, forgive whatever grievances you have against one another. Forgive as the Lord has forgiven you. Over all these virtues put on love, which binds the rest together and makes them perfect. Christ's peace must reign in your hearts ... Dedicate yourselves to thankfulness." This idyllic description of someone who has "put on the mind of Christ" demands the two-edged sword of God's Word in order to achieve the transformation into Christ which human nature resists, often in subtle, even in pseudo-spiritual ways.

One last "constant" of desert spirituality was *work* which is explicitly dealt with in Chapter 15 of the Rule. As did the Fathers of old, so St Albert recalled the great temptations of contemplative life—apathy and idleness, which often lead to locquaciousness, gossip bearing, restlessness. To counteract this very real danger St Albert proposes work, not as a sporadic means to straighten oneself out, but as a constant component of life in Carmel. He gives the concrete example of St Paul who, although he was called by God to be preacher and teacher of the Gentiles, dedicated himself to manual work—to his trade as tentmaker. Manual work was considered servile, i.e. for the *servi* or lower classes. This would have led the hermits to choose this means in order to identify all the better with the emarginated segments of medieval society. It is interesting to note that in 1271 the great "traditionalist," Nicholas of Gaul, understands this chapter to refer first of all to spiritual activity (reading, meditation and prayer) and only secondarily to manual labor, such as the copying of the codices and farm work. When the mendicant elements came to predominate in the Order, there was an ever growing stress on the apostolate as "work."

Chapter 15 has particular resonance in our society where the poor, who used to beg, now work for a living wage. Religious, who before subsisted largely on the alms of the faithful, today are being challenged to follow the way of the poorer classes and become "workers" themselves. In this context Albert refuses to see a dichotomy between work and contemplation; on the contrary, he sees that work can even be necessary in order to avoid certain pitfalls for the contemplative. Today the distinction between intellectual and manual labor is not stressed as much as in the past. Work, as such, has its own theology. It aims at human promotion both in motivating society to realize one's potentialities and in getting beyond one's present condition. Like all values, work too can become an escape or an idol; but this danger gives us no permission to neglect to make it, too, part of our Carmelite spirituality.

Everyone ... should live a life of allegiance to Jesus Christ and serve him faithfully with a pure heart and a good conscience ...

The Participants
Mount Carmel Spiritual Centre
Niagara Falls, Ontario

7

MARY AND THE CARMELITE IMAGINATION

Noel Dermot O'Donoghue, O.C.D.

As I travelled through London—or beaneath London, for I was being swept along in the tube or Underground—on my way to Victoria Station and Aylesford Priory, I was struck by the contrast between what was all around me and what I was trying to evoke and understood with my head and heart: *the world of those hermits* who long ago, nearly eight centuries ago, on the slopes of Mount Carmel, asked the Patriarch of Jerusalem for a rule of life, a *formula vitae* by which together they might give themselves totally to the life of contemplation and the following of Christ.

1. The Woman of the Mountain

How different this world of glitter and glamor and of urban grime from that of those men of long ago in their rough striped "habits" who had no personal property, and were allowed (as a kind of privilege) the common ownership of a few donkeys and a small hen run. How different those two worlds and the type of consciousness creating those worlds and created by them! What could that ancient way of life possibly have to say to this world around me? If, as Collingwood says, history is the reenactment of past experience, what possible purpose could be served by my attempt at reenacting today this ancient way with its *formula vitae* that aimed at bringing to life an even more ancient simplicity beside that fountain named after Elijah, the fiery prophet of the Lord God of Hosts?

And then it came to me, a voice from far away—or from deep within myself—saying: *they are all one in their loneliness.* And I felt that I had here the key to open the door to the past and let its radiance and its shadows fall across the present, my present and the present of the men and women around me. Moreover, I saw that this common human loneliness, this basic dimension, or in Heidegger's terms, *Existenzial,* provided the ambience for the glory of womanhood that broke in on the meditation of these dedicated men, and made them and all their successors troubadors and jongleurs, and, at times, ecstatically happy slaves of that woman whom they saluted as *Regina Decor Carmeli,* a title not at all adequately translated as "Queen Beauty of Carmel."

I say "broke in on their meditations" for there is not one single word about Mary in the original *formula vitae* called "The Rule of St Albert." Not one word about Mary, nor any of Mary's words! Moreover, the little group of hermits is not in any way named as Marian. They are not yet the "Brothers of St Mary of Carmel," as they later came to be called. They are that very paradoxical mélange, as motley as their habits, a *group* of *hermits!* That is all; a "group of hermits" living beside a fountain on the Holy Mountain of Carmel, sacred to Elijah, and (it would seem) also to Pythagoras; a strange place with strange connections, but not a place named after Mary of Nazareth. Yet they took this Rule away with them, went back to their mountain and fountain, and very soon became as totally woman-oriented as any group of mortal men from the beginning of the world until now.

So it was that when I arived at Aylesford Priory, where that first style of life is honored and in a sense reenacted, I found that a statue of the *Woman* dominated the whole central area, and that there were several other images of the Woman within the monastery, including one in the room put at my disposal by my hospitable brethren. I would reckon that there must be at least a hundred images of the Woman in Aylesford Priory, and in this it closely resembles that other Carmelite center which I had just left, the Discalced Carmelite Priory at Boars Hill, Oxford. The image of the Woman is everywhere in Carmel, and so, too, is the imagination that expresses itself in these images. It is this I want to talk about, this Carmelite imagination in its creative discovery of the Woman who stands behind Christ in the Gospels and yet remains for the most part hidden in the shadows, and is in very deep shadow indeed in the Pauline writings, and in the Epistles generally. In the Carmelite imagination she shines forth in glory, appears, discloses herself steadily and continuously with the same clarity as at special moments in the Gospels and in the Apocalypse.

2. Queen Beauty of Carmel

Let us return to that first group of hermits, God's lonely men, as they faced forward into the profound and terrifying solitude of our common human condition, and took with them a Rule of Life back to their quiet place among the hills.[1] The Rule was and is a short, clear, sensible document, setting down at once the end or purpose of their life and the way to achieve that purpose. It places each of them in his own space to deal with his own solitude by way of prayer and work, and a certain minimum of common life. Later, the communal or coenobitical aspect tended to grow at the expense of the eremitical, so as to call forth the fiery protest of Nicholas the

1 As the basic text for all references to this original Carmelite Rule (ca. 1210) I use *The Rule of Saint Albert*, ed. by Bede Edwards, O.D.C. (Aylesford and Kensington, 1973). For a fuller and more recent edition of and commentary on the Rule, cf. Carlo Cicconetti, O. Carm., *The Rule of Carmel* (Edited and abridged by Paul Hoban, O.Carm., Darien, IL: Carmelite Spiritual Center, 1984).

Frenchman some sixty years later. Yet the aloneness and loneliness of the hermit is still at the heart of Carmel, in a sense, is the pulse that tells of its continuing life across the centuries. We Carmelites are at all times a community of solitude, a colloquium of silence, a congregation of solitaries. We are each of us "consumed with zeal for the Lord God of Hosts," whose mysterious radiance and obscurity has called us from all corners of the earth.

Certainly this pulse of silence and solitude is the heartbeat of that first Carmelite Rule, and our understanding of the place of the Woman can only be valid if it emerges from our understanding of this. Somehow in the solitude of this hermitage each of these men heard clearly or "in effect" the voice of the Lord God of Hosts speaking those ancient words, archetypal and creative: "It is not good for man to be alone." Yet these hermits had left behind all the glory and misery of that basic human relationship of man and woman, so it is doubtful whether they had "ears to hear" these ancient words explicitly spoken.

Yet the words were spoken in another way—powerfully, inescapably. They were spoken from the very center of the *loneliness* of the heart of man—from out of that common longing for one another that is the deepest *glory* and profoundest *misery* of man and woman. The hermit who had come all this way from the Western world of the troubador and courtly love had indeed left all this behind at the factual or "ontic" level, but this could only serve to open up that basic *ontological dimension* that a higher love could fill only if it healed and transformed the broken images attendant on those deepest yearnings of the heart. "The heart's a wonder, surely," said Pegeen Mike when she discovered that she had within forever the image of the *Playboy of the Western World.* Who has not felt the magic of this discovery, and who can claim that the austere service of the Lord God of Hosts can absorb it all without remainder?

However, the primitive Rule knows nothing of all this, has nothing to say about womankind or of the Woman who was to be eventually seen as Queen Beauty of Carmel. All the images that lie along the lines of that eminently sensible and mercifully unrhetorical document are masculine images. Even the *diabolus* going about "like a roaring lion" is set in masculine imagery, as are also those mules and asses who enter the scene in the first revision of the Rule. There are the hens, of course, busily scratching away and, hopefully, laying eggs and celebrating the fact; but you will notice that they are carefully hidden under a neutral, descriptive phrase: *nutrimentum volatilium*. Nothing here like the image of that very motherly hen with her chicks under her wings to which Jesus of Nazaareth had compared himself. Indeed this image of Jesus as the hen—the one creature, said one of the Fathers, whose motherhood reveals itself independently of the presence of offspring—has not only no place at all in the Rule but is quite alien to it. Christ is seen as the leader to be served, whose law is to be appropriated in constant meditation. A figure very far from the mother-Christ of Julian of Norwich or indeed of St Augustine! Of course, once Christ is brought in at all—and he is central here—he brings all this manifold glory and graciousness along with him, including his overflowing tenderness; but I am talking here about images, about the way in which that first Rule or *formula vitae* (by which essentially we still live our Carmelite calling) touched or failed to touch the human imagination of those who received it.

However, there is one brief prescription in that first Rule given by St Albert which changes everything, or at least became the occasion for changing everything in this matter of images and imagination: *oratorium construatur in medio cellarum,* "let an oratory be constructed in the midst of the cells." An *oratorium,* a place of prayer, a place of prayer *in medio,* centering everything. *Not* the prior's cell is to center this hermit community, but the oratory. Indeed, the prior is banished to the circumference of the group—on the rather curious ground that he is to act as a kind of *doorkeeper to the community.* The oratory stands at the center, *in medio,* and we know that the oratory came to be, or perhaps *already was,* dedicated to

Mary—as of course were many oratories, churches and cathedrals at that time. There was nothing extraordinary about this dedication in this place. What was extraordinary was that these men were undertaking the task of giving their whole lives day and night to a concentration on prayer in accordance with a strictly masculine image of life, at the center of which appeared this totally feminine image of the Woman, seen as sister and queen and mother and, indeed, as companion and consort.

What kind of lightning will flash forth from this sky in which a little cloud appears that grows into the source of an immense inundation? What kind of lightning can break forth from Carmel today when the *eternal feminine* has found its voice so marvellousely and disconcertingly among the daughters of Eve? In order to try to say something about this I want, in the first place, to bring up and look directly at the power and possibilities of religion and *mystical imagination*.

3. Mystical Imagination

Imagination is not usually given a large place in theories of knowledge, whether at the scientific, historical, philosophical or theological level. Poetry and art—yes: these are the realms of imagination. Rhetoric, too, whether as employed by the politician, the advocate or the preacher, is an occupation where imagination has an accepted place. Rhetoric is a decorative faculty, not serviceable in the discovery of truth—best excluded from the clear and careful expression of what is already grasped as true, however modally conditioned by "possibly," "perhaps," or "certainly."

Imagination is the tailor or dressmaker of truth, never its begetter or discoverer. It has, at best, a secondary or ancillary role. It is dispensable. An optional extra in the world of discourse. Give imagination a primary role and it leads us away into extravagance and eccentricity—especially in religious matters where, most of all, mortal man needs to balance earth and heaven in sober harmony.

All this seems the best of good sense, this putting of imagination in its place well *below the salt* at the feast of knowledge. But such placement has been challenged from time to time. It was challenged by Erasmus in his *Praise of Folly,* lightheartedly, indeed, but with an underlying seriousness. For that dogmatism and fanaticism which Erasmus saw all around him was connected (as it still must be) with a profound *failure of imagination.* That failure was challenged in quite another idiom by Pascal, for the "the reasons of the heart" can only come to speech *by way of imagination.* It was challenged in Germany by Novalis, who had quite a following in his day—though not among philosophers and theologians. Finally it was challenged by a Scottish Congregational minister, who owed something to Novalis but who must stand in his own right, and by his own peculiar genius, as *the prophet of imagination* in modern times. I refer to George MacDonald, hardly known at all nowadays except as the author of a few children's stories, or what he himself called stories for children of all ages: *The Princess and the Goblin, The Princess and Curdie, The Golden Key* and *At the Back of the North Wind.* He wrote novels as well; and he wrote a remarkable essay in defence of imagination, seeing it not only as central to poetry and art, but as the true agent of discovery in all the domains of human knowledge: science, history, philosophy, theology. The essay is called "The Imagination: Its Functions and Its Culture;" it was given as a talk in 1867 and first published in *A Dish of Orts* in 1904. [2]

---

2 It was the discovery of MacDonald that set G. K. Chesterton on his way as an imaginative writer on philosophical and religious topics (see his *Introduction to George MacDonald and His Wife* by Greville MacDonald [London, 1924]. MacDonald also deeply influenced C.S. Lewis and J. R. Tolkein (see H. Carpenter, *The Inklings, Index).* For the past ten years Professsor John McIntyre of the Faculty of Divinity of the University of Edinburgh has been offering a course on "Theology and Human Imagination" partly inspired by MacDonald's essay. To mark Professor McIntyre's retirement a book of theological essays entitled *Religious Imagination,* ed. by J. P. Mackey (Edinburgh: University Press, 1986). has been published. It includes an essay entitled "Mystical Imagination" by the present writer, and this provides the background for what is said here more summarily.

The central insight of MacDonald's essay is that "the imagination of man is made in the image of the imagination of God." All creation is seen as a work of *Divine imagination;* human imagination is a reflection or image or participation in this divine power. McDonald is not questioning the traditional thesis held by Augustine and Aquinas (after Plato) that all things proceed ultimately from the Ideas in the mind of God, but he is saying that these Ideas or 'thoughts' need to be given form and shape as they are *bodied forth* in the material creation, and that *this* is the special work of imagination.

"Imagination," says McDonald, "is the faculty that gives form to thought in the way that the senses can lay hold of." Just as the human intellect mirrors the Ideas, so too the human imagination mirrors that operation by which these Ideas are bodied forth in nature and history, in the great narrative of life and change. Already perhaps we have a point of connection here with our theme, as we think of how a Rule or *regula vitae* may be realized in the everyday, in the ongoing narrative of religious life and experience, both individual and communal. God is present, not only in the Carmelite Idea, but also in the *imaginative translation* of that Idea into the world of human action and human feeling.

In itself imagination is free, unbound and unbounded. Perception is bound. Thought is bound. There the object rules, and I must see things as they are, if I am to see aright. I must think things as they are, if I am to think aright. In imagination these bonds—this bondage—is unloosed. In man, as in God, imagination is totally free. Yet this is but half the story, for I am a being of perception and thought as well as imagination. I am free, but I am also bound (as indeed God is too), and it is precisely in using my freedom, my imagination, within the boundaries set by thought and observation, that I can enter ever more fully into the celebration of truth and the fulness of life.[3]

---

[3] Cf. my "Mystical Imagination" in *Religious Imagination*, note 2 *supra*.

Now the man or woman who seeks the living God, as those first Carmelites did, is held by that quest and by the words and deeds in which the living God has revealed himself. The more fully they follow this way, and the more truly they seek that goal towards which the Rule directs their vision, the more they are called and held by the Source. The goal of this long, hard endeavor is that "Source-experience" which is a kind of marriage of the divine with the human. Yet the Source is veiled in mystery, hiding itself as it shows itself in the darkened mirror of scripture and tradition.

It is by way of imagination that this journey towards the Source is made. This is the world of meditation, and of forays in the dark. This is not an easy way. Yet the Source-experience can issue in that great inundation called *mystical* or "supernatural" knowledge, which brings with it a freedom and spontaneity in which a whole new world of imagination is released.

Imagination leads the way towards the Source by way of what is called "discursive meditation," but it is especially when expressing and communicating the *mystical* that imagination is at its most active and powerful. This can involve visions and other "mystical phenomena." These phenomena are only as valid as the Source-experience itself, along with the love and service that such an experience generates. It is in this context that I want to look at the presence of Mary in the Carmelite origins and the continuing Carmelite tradition.

4. Marian Presence

There are two canons or regulations in the Rule of St Albert, each repeated without change in the revision of Pope Innocent 1V of 1247, which are of central importance from the point of view of tracing the road of the Carmelite imagination towards that fulness of Marian presence which was to become the chief distinction of Carmelite spirituality. These canons are numbered 8 and 11 in Fr Edwards' edition of the Rule: number 8 reads: "Each of you is to stay in his own cell or nearby, pondering the Lord's law day and night and keeping watch at his prayers unless attending to some other duty." This is Fr Edwards' translation, and it will serve my purpose, which is to reflect on the activity called "pondering" or in some translations "meditating"—*meditantes* in the original. This activity, traditional in monastic communities, is given a very moralistic and practical gloss as it appears here: a law to be followed, a careful vigilance to be observed, a set of *occasiones,* or duties, among other *occasiones.* The whole life-style of the hermit is pegged to the ascetical and the practical. His imagination is held severely in check, and it does not look as if he will ever allow himself to sail forth into the dangerous deeps of the mystical ocean, carried along by the wind of the Spirit. He will easily slip into a routine of common life, or listen for *other voices* calling him to preaching or pilgrimage. If he does remain eremitical, he may well become *hermetic* in the sense of being *sealed against* that wicked world that starts at the threshold of his hermitage.

Now let us look at that other canon a few lines further on: "An oratory is to be built as conveniently as possible among the cells where, if it can be done without difficulty, you are to gather each morning to hear Mass." An oratory among the cells, *in medio cellarum,* more accurately perhaps "in the midst of the cells." Already here the individual hermit is pushed out of his *personal space* to create and share and endure a *common* space. This common space is filled by the Mass, which is itself a *shared* space. It allows for a kind of personal space within it, yet the sharing and all it means—attraction and repulsion—cannot be denied. It is a totally masculine space in a way that no corresponding sisterhood could have a totally feminine space, for the priest is a man, and the whole liturgy is masculine in its discourse and music.

Yet into this space, dramatically, Mary comes. The Woman comes. And she changes everything by her quiet and continuously insistent presence. We do not quite know how this little oratory in the midst of these habitations of solitary men came to be dedicated to the Woman who rose out of the earth of nearby Nazareth, who rose out of the shadows of the earth without being touched by these shadows, and who opened as simply as a wild flower to the "overshadowing" of the Most High God. These men knew, as perhaps we do not know in our guilt-laden consciousness, that the shadows are *not* part of the earth, but rather alien to it. They knew that this Woman, in whom the shadows had no place, was by this same token most truly a being-of-earth: most truly and perfectly and vulnerably *woman* in soul and body—spiritually, psychologically, physically. If the shadow was alien to the earth, so, too, were the shadows alien to the physical images of womanhood, however much these shadows in man's possessive and self-indulgent heart might have tainted these images. The great drama that was being worked out in the lives of these men was that of the recovery of the truth of womanhood—and of manhood—through the presence of this Woman at the center of their meditative existence.

So it is that when this meditative style emerges into history, into historical disclosure: we find it to be what can only be called *meditation in the Marian mode,* in which Mary is at once the Vision of Beauty, *Regina Decor Carmeli,* and also the sister companion. If the whole Rule is centered on the service of Christ, *obsequium Jesu Christi,* it is lived in the ambience of Mary, in the home of Mary, in the home *that is* Mary. When many centuries later a voice from Rome spoke the words *totus Carmelus est marianus* it sounded like a definition of the Carmelite way, the Carmelite style, the Carmelite presence in the heart of the church. The church is always looking into its own mind. Not very frequently does it look into its own heart, but when it does it sees Mary; when it does it sees Carmel.[4]

All this process involves doctrine, and the development of doctrine, and the Carmelite contribution to what came to be called Mariology. The more studious and inkstained among

---

4 The statement *"totus Carmelus est marianus"* is attributed to Leo XIII. It may be translated: "The Carmelite spirit is Marian through and through."

the brethren produced in due course little tomes—and even large tomes—in this area of doctrine that was so close to their hearts. It must be admitted that the heart tended to take over from the head at times—so much so that the more hardheaded among the Dominicans and Jesuits saw us as a rather soft-headed lot. I am not concerned with this matter here—it has been dealt with very sensitively by Fr Otilio—but I am concerned with that stream of *imagination in the Marian mode* which flows across the centuries, and which refuses to be contained within the banks and breakwaters of doctrinal formulation: a *Mariophantasia* that cannot be translated without remainder into a *Mariologia.* A poetics that can accept the company of dogmatics only on its own terms. It is with *this* that I am concerned in the next section of this talk.

5. Mariophantasia

The presence (or presences) of Mary in and from the origin of the Carmelite Order must be seen in the general setting of its life of prayer. I am not directly concerned in this talk with the question of the relative importance of the vocal or semi-vocal recitation of the Psalms and the *Pater Noster* in the life of these first hermits. I put this question aside—as well as the question of the balance or misbalance of eremitical and coenobitic monastic styles in the first period or in later periods. What is clear is that there was a place for meditation, at least in the sense of the silent pondering on the law of the Lord. This last phrase has a moralistic ring and ever seems to clang down like an iron barrier against all advance towards the mystical uplands. It seems to turn off that fountain of feeling which in every human being has its roots in the emotional and in the mysterious fountain of *eros,* or, to use the image of St John of the Cross, "in the deep caverns of sense." To "meditate on the law" as such is to keep this force severely in check, to lock up in a stable that spirited steed which Plato in the *Phaedrus* called the Sensual Eros. For Plato, the Sensual

Eros had to be taught to stay in harness with the Intellectual Eros; not stabled or hobbled, but chastened, trained, harnessed into harmony.

Meditation on the law of the Lord could indeed deepen into this acceptance of balance and harmony. In the West, another Albert, to be called Albertus Magnus, was beginning to accept with enthusiasm this Platonic harmony in its Aristotelian form, while St Thomas Aquinas was to bring this fusion of Greek and Christian horizons to fulfilment about the same time that the Carmelites began to settle in the West. Later, at Salamanca and elsewhere, these same Carmelites were to become leaders in this fusion of humanism and Christianity.

Nevertheless I doubt whether this meditation on "the law of the Lord," as originally conceived and practiced, went much beyond the ascetical, the negative, the containment of *eros* in the name of an ethical and sacrificial *agape.* Of course the *obsequium Christi* meant the compassionate entry into the Passion and Death of Christ, as well as a sharing in the joy of the Resurrection and Pentecost. One could perhaps say that, for those who truly entered into it, the Christian liturgy provided and still provides a release and transformation of all the emotions, and thus gave its proper expression to the power of *eros.* Even the manifold repetition of the Lord's Prayer can become a kind of *mantra* that eventually releases inner springs of life and love. It must be remembered that the Liturgy, and indeed the Lord's Prayer itself, is full of images that can nourish the religious imagination.

All this is very well, and it may be said to describe or define a *style* of religious life that is legitimate and acceptable. The way of adherence and of regular observance, in which the emotions are generalised and ritualised, is a way of sacrifice, certainly, but not an inhuman way. This kind of life-style can easily become *militarized,* especially at the level of preaching and of intellectual jousting. A military style code of training or 'exercises' may evolve. All these ways, including the liturgical way, are indeed variously adumbrated in that original Carmelite Rule. They are all variously expressive of the precepts and counsels of the Christian Gospel. But none of them is the Carmelite way *as it came to develop itself* and as it can be developed today.

These hermits almost immediately found themselves in the company of a woman who was one woman and several women, and this woman and these women were all at prayer. They were drawn with them into that cloud which is the *mystery of prayer.* Their meditation was brought powerfully into this *mystery,* turned towards contemplation—in a sense, turned away from action, from the ethical and the ascetical, brought into the strange companionship of Mary of Bethany and Mary Magdalen and above all of Mary of Nazareth. Very soon Mary was with them. She visited them. It was not a long journey from Nazareth to Carmel. They were already there in the time of her girlhood and womanhood—her "brethren" in the Great Mystery, and she their "sister" in the simple glory of unsophisticated grace and beauty. She who was their "sister" would become also their Queen—bringing that glory of childhood and girlhood into full womanhood—Queen Beauty of Carmel.

This flowering of imagination had its roots in history, and drew its sustenance from scripture, not only in the simple and profound Lucan narrative of the infancy of Jesus, and in the theophany of the Woman in the Johannine writings, but also in the Woman of Genesis and in the great Wisdom passages in the Sapiential literature. They were making the discovery that many Carmelites were to make after them: that Mary stands beside Jesus at the center of the Mystery of Salvation, in the inner sanctuary of the mystery of prayer.

This "brotherhood of Mary" gave the Carmelite *obsequium Christi* a special character from the beginning. They saw Jesus through the eyes of Mary, not only with their physical eyes but also with the inner eyes of the heart. They felt the presence of Jesus, not only in the touch of the hand, but in the services of motherhood and in the stirring of the child within the womb. This image, these images, may be seen as the first, basic presence of Mary in the Carmelite imagination. This presence has had several important consequences for the quality and depth of the *Carmelite consciousness,* as I shall go on to show. But first it is necessary to look again at the religious and mystical functions of imagination.

Imagination, as the free use of images, may be merely decorative. In this use it is sometimes called "fancy" or "phantasy." To this decorative function of imagination belong the stories of Mary's visits to the Carmelite hermits of her day, as well as her supposed promises and preferences for the Order. Of course these fancies may be the sober truth for all we know, but in the *order of imagination* they belong to the sphere of the decorative, or what Richard Kroner terms the *imaginary.*[5] It is for the historian to look at the question of their historical truth, but the two *approaches* must not be confused. Whatever basis they have in history, they have their proper place as decorative or imaginary *expressions* of a certain kind of piety—a piety in itself as valid as its groundedness in Christian *agape.*

Quite other is the use of imagination that gives a human habitation to *divine mystery.* Mystery comes through faith. Faith itself involves a leap of imagination, rising beyond the everyday towards the Unseen and Inapprehensible, which calls us—touches us. Elizabeth, commending the faith of Mary, is clearly commending the *imagination* of Mary, *by which* she could open to the dimensions of God-with-us in the flesh, God-with-us in her own womb. Notice how this imagination is balanced by total humility; otherwise it becomes possessive and arrogant.

Imagination opens the space into which the mystery descends in its infinity and freedom; humility extends this space to that infinity in which alone the mystery can dwell. Now this primary imagination of faith, rooted in the humility of love, is

---

[5] S. Kroner, *The Religious Function of Imagination* (New Haven:Yale University Press, 1941), p. 36. For a vigorous defence of the 'Imaginary' see J. R. Tolkein's *Tree and Leaf* (Unwin Paperbacks, 1975 [1967]).

not passive but active. It is always seeking deeper understanding, deeper insight, more ample draughts of intellectual day. Above all, it is seeking a more complete and constant linking of *the mystery* with the every-day, with humanity in its moods and vicissitudes, in its bodily necessities and limitations, as well as in the most intimate aspirations of the heart and the most wide-ranging speculations of the mind. "Most interesting it is to consider," says Coleridge, one of the poet-philosophers of the imagination, "the effect when the feelings are wrought above the natural pitch by the belief of something mysterious while all the images are purely natural." And he adds: "It is here that religion and poetry strike deepest."[6] This is what Kroner calls the *imaginative* use of imagination.[7] Imagination is the handmaid of faith both as leading to the apprehension and acceptance of, and assent to, divine mystery, and as filling the human world and human experience at all levels with the radiance of the mystery thus darkly grasped and accepted.

To return to what I have called the first basic presence of Mary in the Carmelite imagination: Mary and the New Testament sisterhood as sister and companion in the *obsequium Christi* by way of prayer and contemplation. This presence showed itself from early days in three special ways, in three special devotions: devotion to the Childhood of Jesus, devotion to St Joseph, and devotion to the physical detail of the Passion and Death of Christ reaching forward to the Resurrection and Ascension. Obviously this very feminine meditation style found its greatest flowering through the emergence of the Carmelite sisterhoods in later times, but it has remained deeply and continuously present among the Carmelite brotherhoods down to the present day.

To share Mary's love of the child Jesus is to give free rein to the imaginary, but it is also a profoundly imaginative explora-

---

6 S. T. Coleridge, *Poetical Works* (Oxford: University Press, 1969), p. 360.

7 S. Kroner, *op.cit.*

tion of the central mystery of the childhood of God and man and of the man who was God. At the center of the teaching of Jesus is the mystical call to become as little children, which has been disastrously translated into moralistic terms as no more than a call to humility and simplicity. But this is secondary: to be a child is primarily to be open to the full dimensions of the fatherhood and motherhood of God. The mother-God and the mother of God is present whenever the call to childhood is sounded by Jesus. He is himself from first to last the child, the child preaching, the child rejoicing, the child suffering. Above all Jesus is the child praying, in Gethsemane and Calvary, in the Abba-prayer which is his stamp and signature. So it is that the whole of Christian perfection consists of being fully open to the Abba-prayer as a child, as Jesus was all through his life.

It is above all through the presence of Mary, imaginatively realized in the watches of prayer, that this understanding of Christ is gained and brought home to us in our own experience. Here Joseph has his place, a place deeply realized in the Carmelite imagination as giving a masculine balance to the domestic scene of the mother and the child. This was of the greatest importance to St Teresa of Avila, a totally feminine woman totally open to the masculine. Her first foundation was named after Joseph, and one feels that this first Teresian convent was full of Joseph's presence imaginatively realized by women dedicated to living the Christian mystery in full and continuous meditation, as Mary, first among women, lived that mystery guarding it in her heart.

In this imaginative identification with Mary in Bethlehem and Nazareth, Jesus-Emmanuel becomes vividly realized in his individual human beauty and vulnerability. But Mary follows Jesus all the way to Calvary and beyond in deep and deepening understanding, love, compassion and communion. So it is that in this first imaginative presence of Mary the Carmelite follows along the same road. There is no event or emotion, no new illumination of heart and mind, that cannot be material for this meditation. Whatever images and practices suggest themselves—and at this level the Franciscan imagination has been more active than the Carmelite—the deeper imaginative appropriation of the mystery of salvation in the Marian and feminine mode continues, and draws more and more on the hidden springs of the Divine Heart and the divine imagination. Here it is well to recall George MacDonald's statement that the "imagination of man is made in the image of the imagination of God." In MacDonald's language, and in the language of his day, the word man stands for man and woman, yet with a certain priority in favor of the masculine. Today we are learning rather painfully and confusedly to put this priority "under erasure."[8] In fact the first chapter of scripture tells us that it is man and woman *together* who are made in the image of Yahweh-Elohim, and so if we are to accept MacDonald's daring statement, we must see the divine imagination reflected *equally* in man *and* woman. We may say then that the imaginative appropriation of the life-and-death of Jesus *in the Marian mode* is itself a revelation of the feminine face of God. It is a face of grief and tears, of the sorrowing virgin and the sorrowing mother, a face reflected in the heart of every Carmelite; but it is also a face of joy and glory and the New Creation.

This imaginative identification with Mary in the living and lived appropriation of the mystery of Jesus-Emmanuel is of course part of universal Christian experience: in a sense all that the Carmelite way provides is a special instance of this meditation. Yet the Carmelite way has about it a certain domestic and everyday quality which is best identified in the ancient title of the Order as that of the Brothers of Mary. It is, I

---

[8] Here we follow the suggestion of the philosopher Jacques Derrida who employs this phrase for areas which need to have new terms of description, but for which the terms have not yet evolved. Currently we employ the pronoun "he" to refer to God. While being aware of the need to be more respectful of women, and yet wishing to avoid the neologistic "he/she" terminology, one is forced to occasionally resort to the pronoun "he" while using it "under erasure," or "*sous nature.*" Cf. Jacques Derrida *Of Grammatology* (Baltimore: John Hopkins University Press, 1974); especially the "Introduction," pp. xiv ff.

think, a special and precious heritage which in due course has been enriched by the various Carmelite sisterhoods living in everyday closeness to Mary of Nazareth.

6. The Woman of the Place

Mary is sister: the feminine presence that illumines that first ascetical, and very masculine, spiritual enterprise in a bare and desert place; a presence imaginatively known, loved and lived in an ever deeper appropriation of the mystery of Jesus-Emmanuel. Mary is also queen, mother and bride. All four "imaginations" interweave and form a pattern; yet the various strands of this pattern can be distinguished. Perhaps it is possible to press the metaphor a little further and say that each Carmelite creates his own pattern from these primary elements variously emphasized and blended. It can also be said that in any particular case one aspect of Mary's presence will be dominant, and it is possible also that one or more may be left in shadow. But I think all four must be taken into account in trying to understand the presence of Mary in the Carmelite imagination.

A queen may rule a kingdom, or she may be the consort of a king who rules a kingdom. In the Carmelite and Catholic imagination Mary is queen in both senses—quite firmly so. She rules supreme, in her own right or by divine right. No less clearly she is the consort of the King. This came to be delicately developed as a minor theme in certain ancient and medieval writers: *Maria sponsa Christi.* But the consort as *sponsa* is not strictly an equal partner, for the king is the unique and supreme lord and master. The queen gives him glory and reflects his glory, and without this full and constant reflection of the glory of the king she cannot shine forth. The king needs the queen, as in St Paul's doxology of the sexes man needs woman, for woman is "the glory of man" (1 Cor 11:7). But distinct from this spousal partnership of inequality, and distinct also from the queenship that rules the kingdom—or queendom!—there is the queenship of equal partnership, that which came in time to be daringly stated iconically all over the Catholic world, in a certain kind of Catholic piety, in the representation of the Heart of Jesus and the Heart of Mary side by side. This can be seen as a development of the Woman-theology of the Johannine writings: the Woman of the Great Sign of the Apocalypse, the Woman of the beginning of signs at Cana, the Woman standing by the cross of Jesus to whom the beloved disciple is entrusted—not in the words, "*Mother*, behold thy son," as, incredibly, the first edition of the New English Bible translated it, but in the words "*Woman*, behold thy son." Here, as partner and equal, the queen glorifies the king, is glorified in turn, as ultimately man is glorified by woman and woman is equally glorified by man, thus completing the Pauline doxology of the sexes. So it is that the glorification of Mary is a central concern for the Carmelite, and indeed the Order of Carmel is seen as founded for this purpose: the words of Isaiah *decor Carmeli data est ei*, "the beauty of Carmel is given to her,"[9] are accommodated to express this glorification of Mary.

We are here in the world of mystical and devotional imagination, an imagination grounded in history and doctrine, but taking flight in its own way. It is predoctrinal, an imaginative exploration of the Christian mystery that still awaits doctrinal and dogmatic formulations. For this we need the emergence of a theology of glory far different from that *theologia gloriae* that Luther rejected. This theology has not yet come, though perhaps von Balthasar's "theology of beauty" may well be a first sketch of it. I can only herald its possibility here.

In the meantime it must be said that the Carmelite glorification of Mary as the Queen of Carmel sees Mary as in total relationship with Jesus-Emmanuel, who is Christ the

---

[9] Is 35:2, speaking of the wilderness in the renewed Zion.

Lord, and is an expression on earth of the glory of the Father-Mother God in the heavens, εν τοις ουρανοις, that is to say as surrounded by the eternal hierarchies, *Dominus Deus Sabaoth.* This earthed glory is first and last a light shining in the dark, and not only in the dark but into the darkness, transforming it painfully in the ambiguities and vicissitudes of everyday existence. This is the place of the sword that pierces the heart of the Woman, which is perhaps the source of salvation, a new stream of pure water, the immaculate heart of the "new earth," the waters of Lourdes and of all the holy wells of Ireland. All in all, a world of mystical imagination that awaits a theology of glory.

I mention the holy wells of Ireland, not I hope chauvinistically, but because in the Celtic world especially there is a lived and felt continuity between fore-Christianity (often dismissed as paganism or heathenism) and Christianity, and there is a strong feeling of this continuity in the cult of Mary among the first Carmelites, not only in terms of Elijah and the "little cloud"[10] seen as a foreshadowing or forelighting of Mary of Nazareth, but also in the seeing of Mary as the *domina loci,* a feminine divine presence inhabiting a certain place as Pallas Athena dwelt in Athens or Diana dwelt at Ephesus. We know how strongly Catholic devotional imagination has attached itself over the centuries to the *localization of Mary,* so that Our Lady of Guadalupe is distinguished (though not separated) from Our Lady of Lourdes or Our Lady of Fatima. So strong is the force of imagination in this matter that votaries of one localization of Mary may resent an emphasis on other localizations, or at best treat them with indifference. I do not want to examine this strange variety-in-unity any further here, but only to note that the localization of Mary as the *domina loci* of the first Carmelite hermitage belongs to what may be called a structure *a priori* of the religious imagination that goes back beyond Christianity and has lost nothing of its peculiar power

---

10 Cf. 1 Kgs 18:44, in which the small cloud presages the rain to come.

in the Christian imagination. One could say that in such cases the natural provides a place for the coming of the supernatural or revelational, but this would be to miss the point that there is unity and continuity in the development of the religious imagination. I cannot help thinking that if St Paul had listened more carefully as the Ephesians glorified Diana he might have learned something about the message he himself was preaching, that it was a message about a woman as well as a message about a man, so that Diana had to be recognised in her "eternal truth" and not totally rejected. But perhaps this kind of recognition of the truth-behind-the-imperfect-appearances was not yet possible and had to bide its time. It came later, like a new sunrise, and by the 13th century it had reached high noon; and so these hermits in their mountain solitude could let this "ancient and ever new" feminine presence in the oratory and in the fountains fill their imagination to overflowing. There was a sense in which the whole life of these hermits was a glorification of the Woman, and this sense of being totally the glory of Mary has never departed from the Order in any of its branches! It is now, as always, the sign of our unity, the expression of our family resemblance. We are the guardians of an ancient mystery—a mystery that, as David Jones saw, reaches back to the Willendorf Stone, the mystery of the Woman clothed in that Light that was born with her at the beginning.[11]

7. Bridal Motherhood

Mary is *sister* to her Carmelite brothers, Mary is *queen* to her devoted subjects: two imaginative involvements with the Great Mystery, two doors to a meditation renewed every day, two contemplative approaches to mystical union. Mary is also *mother* and *bride,* in these same ways, and equally deeply, ap-

---

[11] David Jones, *Anathemata* (London: Faber and Faber, 1972 [1952]), p. 60.

prehended by the Carmelite imagination. We know that in the years immediately preceding Vatican II there was a lively debate among Mariologists as to the relative priority of Mary's *motherhood* and Mary's *bridal* relationship to the Father and to Jesus Christ her Son, a debate reaching back to the great theologian Matthias Scheeben for whom the *bridal motherhood* of Mary was a central theological insight.[12] It was from out of this debate that the concept of Mary as the type and exemplar of the church came to be given a central place in the chapter on Mary in the Dogmatic Constitution on the church, *Lumen Gentium,* the culminating chapter in the central and centering document of Vatican II.

It has been said that the motherhood of Mary as ecclesial and universal did not establish itself immediately among the first Carmelites,[13] though of course she was for them always the Mother of Jesus, and as such the Mother of God. Nevertheless it seems that her presence from the beginning was a mothering presence in that she was the very air and atmosphere of Carmel; one recalls Hopkins' marvellous image of Mary as "the world-mothering air." But there is no doubt but that it was the bridal aspect of Mary's presence that most of all filled the hearts and minds of the first Carmelites and that has

---

[12] See Noel Dermot O'Donoghue, "Our Lady and the Church" in *Mother of the Redeemer*, (Ed. by K. McNamara, New York: Sheed and Ward, 1960), pp. 230 ff.

[13] For the historical framework in which Carmelite devotion to Mary arose see René Laurentin, *Traité de theologie Mariale,* translated as *Queen of Heaven* (Dublin: Clanmore and Reynolds, 1961): "Till the end of the eleventh century no one had ever considered any rôle of Mary except that which was hers at the beginning of salvation, namely in the Incarnation; from now on what is envisaged very explicitly is her part in the accomplishment of the Redemption. She was considered before as the Mother of Christ, not so far as his permanent associate ... What was now more and more considered was her heavenly life and her daily rôle: her watchful motherhood of all Christians. The Virgin no longer appeared as just the type and exemplar of the Church; she became its Queen, mother and mediatrix: *Collum ecclesiae,* to use the expression that made its appearance with Hermann of Tournay (d. 1137)," cf. p. 58. Clearly, perhaps providentially, the ground was prepared for the emergence of a totally Marian Order and Marian consciousness within the church.

shone forth at all times at the center of Carmelite consciousness. Mary's purity, Mary's virginity, Mary's emergence as the new immaculate creation: this glory of bridal beauty has dominated the Carmelite imagination at all times, has done so with such clarity and power that sometimes Carmelites have pushed their dogmatic affirmations far too absolutely and dogmatically. All these epithets: "purity," "virginity," "immaculate conception" fall heavy on our ears today; and if we are to enter imaginatively into that original and continuing imagination we need to look carefully at their original, illuminative significance for mind and heart.

Virginity, purity and immaculate conception all have to do with "the New" and with the mystery of "the New" that is also a "New Mystery." "The New" is eternal, immortal, original; it comes straight from the creative source; otherwise it has been contaminated by "the Old." It is that which has been "hidden" from the foundation of the cosmos, as if it had been foreseen that a dark power could overshadow the cosmos, as if it had been foreseen that the streams of human generation would become corrupted, poisoned, polluted. It was at the very place of generation itself, in the inner sanctuary of life-creating *eros* that the powers of evil were most destructively present. So it is that "the New" must be a recovery or reaffirmation of the *primal innocence* of the love between man and woman. Yet here we encounter a major difficulty! We do not have the words, the language, the discourse to speak of this love, to open up the horizons of this mystery that has been hidden from the foundation of the world. So it is that the Marian mystery in its imaginative beauty and holiness is expressed in a kind of "yes" and "no" language that is also an abstract language, hanging in the air as it were. Mary is a virgin who "knows not man", yet she is not only a mother but a wife as well, so that the marriage of Mary and Joseph is the model of all good marriages. No more can be said, not because of the lack of warmth and tenderness in this man-woman relationship, but because our language has been too deeply contaminated to be available. The rest is silence.

But this silence is the silence of "mystery." It is the silence that fills the Carmelite cloister with meaning and glory. Within this silence of ordinary predication the world of Carmelite contemplation speaks its own language, a language of prayer and psalmody, of litanies telling of the manifold glory of Mary ever Virgin, a language that at its most venturesome echoes the imagery of the Song of Songs. In these and other ways the New is being affectively and imaginatively apprehended and appropriated into the "deep heart's core" of the Carmelite brotherhood and sisterhood. Here the symbols speak, indeed they dance and sing: in the *Salve Regina,* in the Litany of Loreto (so-called), in the Rosary seen as the Crown of Roses placed on the head of Mary. This imaginative apprehension of Mary is of course common to many traditions and many families within the Christian fold, but it has a particular atmosphere of human proximity in Carmel, which has a powerful symbolism in the habit or dress worn by Carmelites. Not only the scapular, but the whole habit is Marian; as if a mother lovingly dressed her child in garments she herself has woven with love; as if a woman were to weave and fashion a robe for the man she loves. Symbolic images can be turned round to catch the light variously, and so the Carmelite sister can make this mystery her own in her mystical apprehension of Jesus-Emmanuel, for the bridal motherhood of Mary is there not only for the giving but also for the sharing in that giving.

This mystery of love in the mode of "the New," in the atmosphere of the Immaculate Conception is mediated in a thousand ways in the relationship of the men and women of Carmel among themselves. In our century this holy mystery of "the New" has had its radiant fulness made manifest in the lives of two Carmelites who, as it were, stepped forward into the light of history: Thérèse of Lisieux and Titus Brandsma. In each of them the Carmelite imagination reached into the deepest recesses of the world's darkness to provide light and hope for all future ages. In each of them the light shone into the deepest darkness of our age. We touch here on the mystery of glory, the glory of man and woman in the image of Elohim, the glory of Mary and Jesus-Emmanuel, the ancient beauty that is always new.

I want to go on, in my last sally of Celtic imagination, to try to say something about this glory and the possibility of discovery or rediscovery of a theology of glory.

8. The Glory of Mary

The medieval schoolmen who, rightly it seems to me, loved identifying ideas as well as using them, defined glory *(gloria)* as *clara cum laude notitia,*[14] literally "clear knowledge with praise." In this definition glory is a kind of "knowledge" or "knowing." It belongs to that mysterious inexhaustible human dimension which reflects itself in being itself: "To know," says Aristotle, "is to know that I know." So it is that the depth and clarity of my "knowing" is always measured by the depth and clarity of my sense of my own deepest intimacy as myself. This deep, clear self-apprehension is the opposite to what is ordinarily called "self-consciousness." So it is that the more deeply and clearly I speak to you from out of my self the more light I have to share with you; but if I begin to think self-consciously of what I am doing and how you see me, the more that light becomes dimmed. To enter the Lost Paradise of totally deep and clear "knowing" I must divest myself of all that I wear, to present myself and walk in the nakedness of total innocence. I speak of course in what may be called "psychological" terms, yet since we live in the body, the physical image is not far away—nor should it be entirely excluded.

Now glory is not only deep and clear knowledge, *clara notitia,* it is this knowledge accompanied by praise, *cum laude.*

---

[14] Cf. St Thomas Aquinas, *Summa Theologiae Ia-IIae,* 9.2, a.3. St Thomas and the tradition to which he belonged and which, more or less untouched by the Reformation, reaches down to the present day, preferred happiness *(beatitudo)* to glory as the fulfillment of human destiny, thus preferring quiescence to radiance as the highest good of men and women. Perhaps the time has come to question this order of priority.

It is a deep and clear knowledge of an object that is affirmed as "shining forth" in one facet of its being or in some or many or all facets of being. The object reflects or radiates the highest or transcendental illuminations of unity, goodness, truth, being and beauty: that is to say, it appears thus when that object is given praise *in all its fulness*. This is *real;* this is *what-it-is;* this is *good;* this is *true;* this is *beautiful.* Above all, this realization reaches inwards to the depths of my own being as self and as person-revealing-itself-as-self-and-person. We are in the world of what Martin Buber, in the wake of Gabriel Marcel, calls the I-Thou relationship and way of communication.

When I praise another self, another person, a T*hou* that says T*hou t*o me, I lay some of the ground-of-my-being open to the sun of the other. I let the light of the other illuminate, more or less deeply, some area of my being, and in this communication I am revealed as who-I-am. This is glory and the light of glory, and this light begins to transform the world, my world, that U*mwelt* or *surround-of-consciousness* of which Husserl and the phenomenologists speak.

Now praise, as the r*evelation o*r *unveiling* of the ground-of-my-being may be said to have three dimensions analogous to breadth and depth and height: b*readth* in relation to the many ranges of concerns and aspirations; d*epth* in relation to the various levels of meditative entry into and exploration of the furthest reaches of heart and mind, of memory, thought and imagination; h*eight* in relation to my power to look towards large horizons and possibilities.

In all these dimensions praise tends towards its own fulness in the basic activity of adoration. Adoration is the opening up of all the dimensions of my being towards a being that illuminates and fulfills all these dimensions. This is total transparency; this is the way back to the primal innocence of paradise; this is glory in its essence and fulness. It is the promise of this glory, never fully realised, that illuminates the world briefly or steadily when two people fall in love, or discover a really deep soul-friendship along the pathway of their common pilgrimage. But it is most of all in *mystical love* in its various levels and in manifestations, and mediations, that glory illuminates and transforms the human world.

It is in meditation, in the sense of the discursive step by step use of *imagination,* that the Carmelite reaches upwards towards mystical contemplation. Here the *imaginative entry* into the Marian mystery opens the way to the mystical apprehension of this mystery; and this apprehension comes *from above* (ανωθεν)[15] through an inflowing of the Holy Spirit in, with and through the Virgin Mary. This experience brings with it a deep almost painful desire to glorify Mary—that is to say, to open ourselves to the light of Mary's presence in all the dimensions of our being. This is not simply the glorification of Mary; it is also, profoundly, a participation in the "glory" of Mary. Thus for these first hermits the words of St Paul were entirely fulfilled, that woman is the glory of man, fulfilled and also completed in that these men were *the glory of the Woman.*[16]

Both the meditative and the mystical operations of imagination explore the mystery of Mary which is a way of approach to the mystery of Jesus-Emmanuel, and of the Face of the Father-Mother God seen in the living atmosphere of the Holy Spirit. This is exploration, which has its steadying and enclosing poles in everyday sense experience and in the intelligible world of the lamps of the mind: *viz.* unity, truth, being, goodness and beauty. But imagination is also a power of dis-

---

[15] Jn 3:3.

[16] Cf. 1 Cor 11:7-8. "A man has no need to cover his head, because man is the image of God and the mirror of his glory, whereas woman reflects the glory of man." There are various interpretations of these statements. I see the heart of the matter in the fact that for St Paul, as for the Christ whom Paul reflects (v. 1), Christian fulness consists in *the recovery of childhood* in that maturity by which men and women become fully open to each other. So it is that a man finds his *childhood* in woman, as reflected in woman-love, just as God establishes his own *childhood* in man as the image of the Son. So, too, finally woman finds her *childhood* in man and glories in this and in "submission" to it. Man's "submission" to woman is no less deep as he enters through total and terrifying loneliness into his own nothingness. It seems to me that here, as elsewhere, St Paul is glancing at a mystical horizon, and that to take his words moralistically or dogmatically is to falsify them. A *theology of glory* can live and grow only in the world of mystical imagination.

covery, a kind of deep inner perception that opens to its own proper world of objects. It sees what the Sufi mystical tradition calls the imaginal world, the celestial earth, the angelic universe of which our astronomy, our physics, our botany, etc., provide but sketches and skeletons, in comparison with which the fields of summer are but desert, and in the light of which the desert flowers in a thousand blossoms. This imaginal world stands unrecognised at the center of Catholic devotion, for it is the world of the Sacred Heart of Jesus-Emmanuel and the Immaculate Heart of Mary: queen, mother, sister and bride. For to the mystical devotee these symbols are more than symbols; they are an inner radiance: super-physical, but not simply spiritual; not merely symbolical. The celestial earth is not bounded by the laws of the physical earth, yet it is the truth and meaning of the physical earth. It is the truth and meaning of the land of Carmel, of the hills and the fountain, of the flowers and the seasons. This is glory, the glory of the New, of the Resurrection, the Glory that was from the beginning.

Perhaps I could bind this little sheaf of thoughts together by recalling again my journey through the London Underground on my way from the Carmelite house at Boars Hill, Oxford, to the restored Carmelite Friary of Aylesford. The sense of glitter and glamor I felt is surely a kind of dim and darkened *hope of glory.* I said that what united these men and women around me with the first hermits on Carmel was and is their *loneliness,* a loneliness that is but the empty vessel of glory; a vessel that the glitter and glamor will never fill. Not indeed but that some of them may have discovered the ancient springs; I am talking only of a general atmosphere and a general impression. Yet, when I look again at the end of my meditation on Mary and the Carmelite imagination, when I look again in the light of that inner vision of a celestial earth, I have glimpses of a pilgrimage behind all their many journeyings. I have glimpses of a *light* deeply hidden behind the glamor. I look around me with a mother's heart that has been bathed a little in the original fountain. And I know that these hermits and the great procession of men and women that follow them are engaged in bringing the whole world under the mantle of Mary and into the childhood of God in Jesus-Emmanuel.

Our task as Carmelites is to restore its *lost childhood* to a world come of age. For that we need something of the spirit and power of Elijah; but most of all, we need the all-mothering love and humility of Mary and, with this, that *imagination* by which Mary could walk through the darkness into the light of the Resurrection.

FOR FURTHER READING

Paul Chandler, O. Carm.

The Rule in English Translation

EDWARDS, BEDE, O.C.D. *The Rule of St. Albert. (Vinea Carmeli,1).* Aylesford and Kensington, 1973.

A translation of the Rule with a lengthy introduction emphasizing its eremetical nature. A list of significant dates in Carmelite history is included along with a useful bibliography. The enumeration used here treats the Prologue as chapter 1 and the Epilogue as chapter 20, as opposed to the more usual enumeration of 18 chapters with a Prologue and Epilogue.

STEGGINK, OTGER, O. CARM., JO TIGCHELER, O. CARM., KEES WAAIJMAN, O. CARM. *The Carmelite Rule.* Almelo: n.p., 1979. Translated by Theodulf Vrakking, O. Carm., and Joachim Smet, O. Carm.

An interpretative translation based on a study project of the Rule done in the Dutch Carmelite province. It offers a wealth of annotations, especially valuable for placing the vocabulary of the Rule into its thirteenth century context.

Studies of the Rule:

POSSANZINI, STEPHANO, O. CARM., *La Regola dei Carmelitani: Storia e spiritualità.* Firenze: 1979.

This work addresses itself particularly to the spirituality of the Rule.

CICCONETTI, CARLO, O. CARM., *The Rule of Carmel.* Darien, Illinois; 1984. Translated by G. Pausback, O. Carm., edited and abridged by P. Hoban, O. Carm.

An abridgement of *La Regola del Carmelo: origine, natura, significato* (Rome: Institutum Carmelitanum, 1973). This was the author's doctoral thesis in Canon Law, and an important study of the Rule in its historical context. This work occasioned a debate between Bede Edwards, O.C.D., and Adrian Staring, O.Carm., about the significance of the revisions of 1247. Edwards stressed the continued eremitical nature of the Rule: cf. *Ephemerides carmeliticae* 24 (1973), 428-432. Staring supported Cicconetti's conclusion that the revisions marked a definite transition to mendicant status: cf. "Four Bulls of Innocent IV: A Critical Edition," *Carmelus* 27 (1980), 273-285.

SECONDIN, BRUNO, O. CARM., *La Regola del Carmelo. Per una nuova interpretazione.* Rome: Edizioni Institutum Carmelitanum, 1982.

__________.*La Regola del Carmelo oggi.* (Atti del Congresso Carmelitano, Roma/Sassone, 11-14 ottobre 1982). Roma: Edizioni Institutum Carmelitanum, 1983.

These two works summarize a project of study on the Rule from numerous perspectives by Italian Carmelites. Secondin proposes a new reading of the symbolic structure of the Rule based especially on the image of the first Christian community in Jerusalem (*Acts* 2:42-46).

General Reading on the Carmelites

Dizionario degli Istituti de Perfezione. Rome, 1973- .

This dictionary contains the best and most up-to-date short articles on the Carmelites, with valuable bibliographies. See particularly the articles: "Carmelitani," II:460-521: Storia (L. Saggi); Spiritualità (O. Steggink *et al*); Secondo e Terz'Ordine (C. Catena). See also "Carmelitani scalzi" II:523-602 (V. Macca); "Regola del Carmelo" VII:1455-1464 (C. Cicconetti); etc.

FRIEDMAN, ELIAS, O.C.D., *The Latin Hermits of Mount Carmel.* Rome: Teresianum, 1979.

This is a study of the archaeological evidence for the settlement on Mount Carmel, as well as the testimonies of pilgrims to the Holy Land.

ROEFS, V. "The Earliest Evidence Concerning the Carmelite Order," in *The Sword* 19 (1956), 224-245. Translated by Sean O'Leary, O.Carm.

Still valuable today.

SMET, JOACHIM, O. CARM., *The Carmelites: A History of the Brothers of Our Lady of Mount Carmel.* Darien, IL: Carmelite Spiritual Center, 1975-85. 4 volumes in 5.

An indispensible guide to the history of the Order.

__________.*Cloistered Carmel: A Brief History of the Carmelite Nuns.* Rome: Institutum Carmelitanum, 1986.

The only history of the Ancient Observance nuns in English. There are some very valuable bibliographies at the end of this book on specific Carmels and on individual nuns.

General Background Reading

LEYSER, H. *Hermits and the New Monasticism: A Study of Religious Communities in Western Europe, 1000-1150.* London, 1984.

A brief survey of the rebirth and insitutionalization of eremitical life in the 11th and 12th centuries.

LITTLE, L.K. *Religious Poverty and the Profit Economy in Medieval Europe.* Ithica, NY, 1978.

This study links hermits, mendicants, the poverty movement and the development of a new urban spirituality against a backgound of social and economic change. An important and stimulating work.

MAYER, H.E. *The Crusades.* Oxford: University Press, 1972.

A reliable, brief history.

PARTICIPANTS

Sr: Anthony Joseph, O. Carm.	Rhinegeck; New York
Sr. Lynn Barfknecht, O. Carm.	Hudson, Wisconsin
Fr. Gregory Battafarano, O. Carm.	Niagara Falls, Ontario
Bro. Eric Bell, O. Carm.	Houston, Texas
Fr. Lucien Belzner, O. Carm.	Troy, New York
Fr. Eugene Bettinger, O. Carm.	New Baltimore, Pennsylvania
Mother Tessa Bielicki	Crestone, Colorado
Sr. Claudette Blais, O.C.D.	Concord, New Hampshire
Bro. David Blanchard, O. Carm.	Washington, D.C.
Fr. Hein Blommestijn, O. Carm.	Nijmegen, The Netherlands
Fr. Raymond Bonin, O. Carm.	Joliet, Illinois
Fr. Roger Bonneau, O. Carm.	Tucson, Arizona
Fr. Henry Bordeaux, O.C.D.	San Antonio, Texas
Sr. Patricia Boyd, O.C.D.	Elysburg, Pennsylvania
Fr. Leonard Broughan, O. Carm.	Mahwah, New Jersey
Fr. Michael Buckley, O.C.D.	Alhambra, California
Fr. Emeric Carmody, O. Carm.	Nyack, New York
Sr. Ruth Carr, O.C.D.	Little Rock, Arkansas
Fr. Augustine Carter, O. Carm.	Los Angeles, California
Fr. Paul Chandler, O. Carm.	Toronto, Ontario
Fr. Carlo Cicconetti, O. Carm.	Rome, Italy
Sr. Michael Ann Cladek, O.C.D.	Beacon, New York
Sr. Genevieve Clements, O.C.D.	Beacon, New York
Fr. Raymond Clennon, O. Carm.	Mundelein, Illinois
Fr. Robert Colaresi, O. Carm.	Joliet, Illinois
Fr. Adrian Cooney, O.C.D.	Little Rock, Arkansas
Fr. Romaeus Cooney, O. Carm.	Williamstown, Massachusetts
Fr. Charles Countie, O. Carm.	Englewood, New Jersey
Fr. Christopher Crowley, O. Carm.	Dublin, Ireland

Fr. Kevin Culligan, O. Carm.	Hubertus, Wisconsin
Sr. Mary Davin, O.C.D.	Boston, Massachusetts
Fr. Matthias DesLauriers, O. Carm.	Purchase, New York
Sr. Sharon Doyle	Kemptville, Nova Scotia
Fr. Michael Driscoll, O. Carm.	Tarrytown, New York
Fr. Marcel Dube, O. Carm.	Harper Woods, Michigan
Sr. Therese Dugre, O.C.D.	Elysburg, Pennsylvania
Sr. Constance FitzGerald,O.C.D.	Baltimore, Maryland
Sr. Mary Gillson	Chester, New Jersey
Fr. Eltin Griffin, O. Carm.	Dublin, Ireland
Fr. Ashley Harrington, O. Carm.	Englewood, New Jersey
Bro. Brian Henden, O. Carm.	Williamstown, Massachusetts
Fr. John Horan, O. Carm.	New York, New York
Sr. Agnes Horth, O.C.D.	Concord, New Hampshire
Bro. Gregory Houck, O. Carm.	Williamstown, Massachusetts
Mother Immaculata St. Anthony	Amery, Wisconsin
Sr. Joseph Catherine, O. Carm.	Bayside, New York
Sr. Mary Kekiak, O.C.D.	Cleveland Heights, Ohio
Fr. Michael Kenny, O. Carm.	Mutare, Zimbabwe
Sr. Rosemary Kiuepfel, O.C.D.	Saranac Lake, New York
Sr. Josephine Koeppel, O.C.D.	Elysburg, Pennsylvania
Fr. Alphons Kroese, O.C.D.	Hazerswoude-Rijndijk, The Netherlands
Fr. Charles Kurgan, O. Carm.	North Hollywood, California
Fr. Michael Kwiecien, O. Carm.	Houston, Texas
Fr. Fergus Lickteig, O. Carm.	Mahwah, New Jersey
Fr. Mario Lopez, O. Carm.	Fairfield, California
Fr. Daniel Lynch, O. Carm.	Scarborough, New York
Sr. Magdalen Joseph, O. Carm.	Bronx, New York
Fr. Stanley Makacinas, O. Carm.	Mississauga, Ontario
Fr. John Malley, O. Carm.	Rome, Italy
Fr. Ivan Cormac Marsh, O. Carm.	Williamstown, Massachusetts

Fr. Stephen Marsh, O. Carm.	Aylesford, England
Sr. Mary Collette, O. Carm.	Bronx, New York
Sr. Mary Cornelius, O. Carm.	Germantown, New York
Sr. Mary Damian, O. Carm.	Bronx, New York
Sr. Mary Elizabeth, O. Carm.	Bronx, New York
Sr. Mary Joachim, O. Carm.	Bronx, New York
Sr. Mary Lois, O. Carm.	Germantown, New York
Sr. Mary Lourdes, O. Carm.	Bronx, New York
Sr. Mary Patrick, O. Carm.	Germantown, New York
Sr. Mary Rosemary, O. Carm.	Germantown, New York
Sr. Mary Vincent, O. Carm.	Germantown, New York
Fr. Vincent McDonald, O. Carm.	Middletown, New York
Fr. Patrick McMahon, O. Carm.	Closter, New Jersey
Fr. William McNamara, O.C.D.	Kemptville, Nova Scotia
Sr. Laura Melancon, O. Carm.	New Orleans, Louisiana
Sr. Philomena Moolasseril, O. Carm.	Downsview, Ontario
Fr. Finian Monahan, O.C.D.	Dublin, Ireland
Fr. Anthony Morello, O.C.D.	Rome, Italy
Fr. Michael Mulhall, O. Carm.	Niagara Falls, Ontario
Fr. Gary O'Brien, O. Carm.	Washington, D.C.
Sr. Patricia O'Brien, O.C.D.	Cleveland Heights, Ohio
Fr. Noel Dermot O'Donoghue, O.C.D.	Edinburgh, Scotland
Sr. Carolyn O'Hara, O.C.D.	Beacon, New York
Fr. Míceál O'Neil, O. Carm.	Rome, Italy
Bro. Bernard O'Neill, O.C.D.	Little Rock, Arkansas
Sr. Mary O'Neill, O. Carm.	Hudson, Wisconsin
Sr. Daniela Orazzo, O. Carm.	Downsview, Ontario
Fr. Riccardo Palazzi, O. Carm.	Rome, Italy
Sr. Paul Francis, O. Carm.	Bayside, New York
Sr. Mary Teresa Perez, O.C.D.	South Dartmouth, Massachusetts
Sr. Annie Peta, O. Carm.	Downview, Ontario
Bro. Brad Peterson, O. Carm.	Williamstown, Massachusetts
Fr. Kenneth Peterson, O. Carm.	Port Melbourne, Australia

Fr. Murray Phelan, O. Carm.	Barrington, Illinois
Fr. Djanar Poespowardojo, O. Carm.	Rome, Italy
Sr. Rosemary Quinn, H.M.C.	Amery, Wisconsin
Fr. John Radigan, O. Carm.	New York, New York
Sr. Regina Carmel, O. Carm.	Bayside, New York
Fr. Ralph Reyes, O.C.D.	Dallas, Texas
Sr. Rita Immaculate, O. Carm.	Bayside, New York
Sr. Jean Ryan, O.C.D.	Little Rock, Arkansas
Sr. Salete, O. Carm.	Downview, Ontario
Fr. Lukas Schmidt, O. Carm.	Newport News, Virginia
Fr. Bruno Secondin, O.Carm.	Rome, Italy
Sr. Vilma Seelaus, O.C.D.	Barrington, Rhode Island
Fr. Kevin Shanley, O. Carm.	Joliet, Illinois
Bro.. James Sidoti, O. Carm.	Williamstown, Massachusetts
Fr. Aloysius Sieracki, O. Carm.	Darien, Illinois
Fr. David Simpson, O. Carm.	Scipio, Kansas
Fr. Malachy Smith, O. Carm.	Niagara Falls, Ontario
Fr. Aquinas Stack, O. Carm.	Tarrytown, New York
Fr. Wayne Stanhope, O. Carm.	Port Melbourne, Australia
Sr. Mary Elizabeth Stanton, O.C.D.	Barrington, Rhode Island
Sr. Marian Steffens, O.C.D.	Barrington, Rhode Island
Sr. Robin Stratton, O.C.D.	Baltimore, Maryland
Fr. Gerald Taylor, O.C.D.	Brookline, Massachusetts
Fr. Robert Traudt, O. Carm.	Leonia, New Jersey
Fr. Redemptus Velabek, O. Carm.	Rome, Italy
Fr. Kees Waaijman, O. Carm.	Nijmegen, The Netherlands
Fr. Piet Wijngaard, O. Carm.	Aylesford, England
Sr. Anita Wasserman, O.C.D.	Cleveland Heights, Ohio
Fr. John Weber, O. Carm.	Houston, Texas
Fr. John Welch, O. Carm.	Washington, D.C.
Fr. Jerry Williams, O. Carm.	Chicago, Illinois